*Out of Care: The Community Support of
Juvenile Offenders*

Out of Care: The Community Support of Juvenile Offenders

D. H. THORPE
D. SMITH
C. J. GREEN
J. H. PALEY
University of Lancaster

London   Boston   Sydney
GEORGE ALLEN & UNWIN
for the Centre of Youth, Crime and Community, University of Lancaster

First published in 1980

GEORGE ALLEN & UNWIN LTD
40 Museum Street, London WC1A 1LU

British Library Cataloguing in Publication Data

Out of care.
  1. Juvenile corrections − England
  I. Thorpe, D H
  364.6   HV9146.A5   80−40739

ISBN 0−04−364018−4
ISBN 0−04−364019−2 Pbk

Set in 10 on 11 point Times by Computacomp (UK) Ltd,
Fort Willam, Scotland
and printed in Great Britain
by Biddles Ltd, Guildford, Surrey.

Contents

Foreword

How are we to cope with the problem of juvenile delinquency? This has been a perennial question posed by policy makers, practitioners and the public for the past twenty years and one suspects, for much longer: indeed ever since society decided that juvenile behaviour was a separate and distinct problem which required its own resolution. However, the last twenty years have proved crucial, since in spite of changes in the law and the arrival of a number of apparent 'cures' the numbers of young people apprehended for, admitting to, or being found guilty of delinquent behaviour has continued to rise. Although the rise in juvenile crime has been no greater than the rise in adult offending and even though juvenile crime tends to be petty theft or damage, it has become the focus of much public concern. Indeed, it is probably the petty nature of the offences, which often have a high nuisance value, which leads to the public concern. It is the 'man in the street' who is inconvenienced by vandalism to telephone boxes, or damage and disruption on public transport, outraged by graffiti or threatened by rowdyism in the street. It is significant that this public concern has been made manifest by demands for more law and order and control and not directed, as it could justifiably have been, into concern about the fact that proportionately the number of young offenders incarcerated has increased substantially compared with adult offenders. Whereas the proportion of adults who offend and go to prison has been steadily in decline, the reverse is true for juveniles.

The Children and Young Persons Act 1969 embodied much of the thinking articulated in a series of White Papers throughout the decade of the 1960s, and attempted to make three major shifts in policy: (1) juvenile offenders were to be offered help by social services rather than punishment, (2) services for juvenile offenders were to be a matter determined at local rather than national level, (3) juvenile offenders were to be helped in the community rather than by dispatch to isolated institutions. Events in the decade since the passing of the Act clearly illustrate a failure to achieve this shift in policy. Inevitably one must ask why.

Part of the reason for the failure must lie squarely at the door of the social work profession. Social services managements have failed to provide clear policies on juvenile delinquency for their departments; very few departments have undertaken systematic studies of juvenile crime within their area and gone on to develop policies to cope with the problem. Social work academics have failed to address themselves to the research required to enable them to develop theoretical models for social work with juvenile offenders. They have failed to get to grips with the crucial issues of what social work has to offer the juvenile offender in order to reduce the likelihood of his reoffending or, even more importantly, how one can train social workers to control offenders in the community if that is now what is expected of them. Social work practitioners have failed to accept the results of what little research has been done and to modify their practice accordingly. They have failed to grasp that national trends are merely aggregates of individual decisions by practitioners and that consequently the number of young people being incarcerated is linked with the recommendations they make in their social enquiry reports to the juvenile courts and the practitioners' willingness or otherwise to develop alternative community-based methods for helping young offenders.

This book, written by four people who have been both practitioners and researchers in the field of juvenile delinquency over the past decade, attempts to redress the balance. The authors link empirical research with theory and practice. Stan Cohen, one of the founders of the new deviancy school of sociology, recently acknowledged that the new theories had not really helped the development of policy or practice and indeed often, in misinterpreted form, had hindered, hamstrung and handicapped developments. This book is founded on research – but not of the kind that focuses on the deviant almost to the point of idealisation. Instead it focuses on the services. The research asks quite simply what is happening in this sytem of services. Are children being diverted from crime or projected into it? On the basis of a full and comprehensive picture of what is happening at the local level, the book examines theories which may explain these phenomena, but more importantly it outlines policies which can be employed to reverse or redirect them. It sounds too simple to say that the way to keep children out of institutions is to have a policy of keeping children out of institutions. Yet this is the message that comes through all too clearly from the research: that a firm commitment to a policy of decarceration can and does work. The authors are not content to stop at inventing policy slogans, they move on to outlining the range and type of services required to achieve the policy ends and point out that the control of juvenile delinquency is not the prerogative of any one agency. Social services and probation must learn to work closely with the courts, education services, the police and industry to prevent juvenile crime. Social services must also provide a range of highly specific services aimed at helping the juvenile offender in the community, at the same time maintaining the community's faith in these approaches.

This book reaffirms that social work and social workers are serious about both controlling and helping juvenile offenders in the community. It also illustrates the involvement of academics in both training practitioners and influencing policy at local levels. Inevitably change at local levels and the demonstration of clean models of good practice will eventually have a profound influence on national policy. The following chapters will ensure that a wider audience are made aware of local advances.

NORMAN TUTT
*Professor of Applied Social Studies
and Director of the Centre of Youth,
Crime and Community,
Department of Social Administration,
University of Lancaster*

Acknowledgements

Our thanks are due to the staff of the various agencies which gave us access to their records; to Geoff Woodhead and Malcolm Briscoe of New Planet City and to the New Planet Trust; to the social workers and probation officers who made possible the project described in Chapter 7; to the M.Sc. students at Cranfield whose work is used in Chapters 5 and 6; to Norman Tutt for his advice and encouragement; and to all the students who attended the short course on intermediate treatment at Lancaster in 1978 and 1979, for their creative work and stimulating criticism. Also to Chris, Judy and Linda for their support; to Mandy Green, Bobbie Nunn and Gilly Rowell for typing successive drafts; and to Ben, Arthur, Paggie and Ribby for leaving their marks on the book.

1

The 1969 CYPA and Its Aftermath

During the late 1950s and early 1960s, social policy analysts in Britain took stock of the welfare state. Over ten years had passed since the great reforming legislation of the immediate postwar era when the foundations of a variety of new state services were laid. The affluence of that period did little to mask the shortcomings of many of these relatively new services. The Butler Act of 1944 permitted the establishment of a new, tripartite system of secondary education – yet, fifteen years later, it was becoming clear that those children who most needed to benefit from education, by virtue of the poverty of their circumstances, were the least likely to get a place at a grammar school and the resulting passport to success. While the 1948 National Health Service Act had provided free health services, it had not materially affected the lot of the mentally ill and handicapped, the majority of whom remained incarcerated in large, impersonal asylums. For the poor generally, the 1948 National Assistance Act did, theoretically at least, provide a basic level of income below which it was not possible to fall – yet the National Assistance Board itself was an administratively weak institution which responded inadequately to the demands of consumers. The new local-authority-based child care services provided by the 1948 Children's Act had proved to be fairly successful in terms of their impact on deprived children in need of care, but they did nothing to ameliorate the circumstances of the families whose children were likely to come into care or for delinquent children who were still basically catered for within a junior version of the penal system.

Clearly, the new system of public welfare represented a great improvement on what had preceded it but the affluence of the period which followed the establishment of the new services served to highlight their inadequacies. Moreover, the administrators had learnt much from their experiences and were able to articulate their visions of improved and more effective welfare provision, casting their eyes on new and potential consumer groups not included originally in the 1944–8 legislation. One result of this was a veritable proliferation of academic research and government White Papers during the 1960s, which covered the whole range of social, health, education and local government services. This activity promised to improve on existing state welfare, especially by extending the reach of service providers beyond institutions and into the community itself. The concept of community care received its first concrete expression in the 1959 Mental Health Act, and changes envisaged in other areas of service were similarly intended to shift the focus of intervention into the very fabric of society itself. Firm powers were given to the Secretary of State for Education to enforce reorganisation in secondary education, while simultaneously providing extra resources for those very poor districts defined as Educational Priority Areas. The Department of Health and Social Security was deliberately created as a new and powerful organisation which could, theoretically at least, hold its own with other government departments – and this new organisation was to provide the impetus for reform in health, income-maintenance and child care fields, as well as developing services for the elderly and disabled.

To the 1960s generation of social reformers, the 1970s must have appeared as a nightmare. In contrast to the preceding twenty-five years, this decade has seen growing waiting lists for health services, public alarm at the prospect of children leaving school unable to read and write, mounting demands from an exploding population of elderly and infirm people and apparently startling increases in child abuse and juvenile crime. Indeed, the very viability of state welfare itself has been questioned in a way which has not been possible since before the Second World War. A number of reasons have been suggested to account for these apparent failures. These include the raising of service expectations by the public to unrealistic levels; the reorganisation of services as a result of new legislation, leading to disruption in service delivery; and perhaps most importantly, lack of finance to provide the services. The last factor is generally believed to be a result of Britain's relative economic decline. In fact British society has become so obsessed with its economic health that the 1979 Conservative government has gone so far as to suggest that the country's economic decline is, at least partly, a direct result of expenditure on welfare at the expense of investment in industry in the preceding twenty-five years. This reasoning has been used, inevitably, to justify the latest round of cuts in public services, so as to permit the relocation of finance into private industry, thereby hopefully revitalising the economy.

If the 1969 Children and Young Persons Act (CYPA) is but one example of the several stillborn and controversial pieces of legislation passed during the 1960s, then its failure should prove an interesting case study for future students of social administration, for virtually every reason advanced for its ineffectiveness by politicians, the police, the judiciary, the service providers and the media fails to stand up to scrutiny. These misconceptions stem basically from two vital factors – first, a total misunderstanding and misreading of the true policy objectives of the Act and secondly, a very basic ignorance of the operational complexities and decision-making processes of the whole juvenile criminal justice system. This book aims to deal with both these issues, not merely from an academic and theoretical point of view, but from the perspective of the practitioner within the juvenile criminal justice system, for it was the decision-makers – policemen, social workers, probation officers, magistrates and social service administrators – who effectively abandoned whatever potential for reform the 1969 CYPA contained. Quite simply, cumulatively, these disparate bodies of professionals made the wrong decisions about the wrong children at the wrong time.

To begin with, at the highest levels of government, the 1969 CYPA was highly controversial. In its final form, it was the fruit of several years of discussion, discord and compromise, which began very quietly with the Ingleby Committee in 1956.[1] Part of the committee's remit was to inquire into the working of the law on juvenile courts, while the other part was to consider the position of deprived children. When the committee finally reported in 1960, it gave a clear recommendation that the age of criminal responsibility be raised from the 8th to the 12th birthday and eventually to the 14th. The committee suggested that below these ages, criminal prosecution should be replaced by some form of civil proceedings similar to the Fit Person Proceedings of the 1933 Children's Act which required proof that a child was so deprived by his home circumstances that it was necessary to commit him to the care of the local authority. Although that committee was set up by a Conservative government and reported to one, there was a marked reluctance to move on these particular proposals – which, by raising the age of criminal responsibility, implied a large measure of decriminalisation. Within the Conservative Party itself, there had been moves to reintroduce corporal punishment as a juvenile court sentence, which the government had only just avoided.[2] In the 1960s, the only major moral crusade against disorderly youth had been that against the teddy boys. It cannot be surprising that, ten years later, after mods and rockers, long-haired drug addicts, skinheads and football hooligans, the Conservative government was even less willing to sanction decriminalising legislation in the 1969 CYPA. In 1963, the government proposed a new Bill which was intended to incorporate some of the Ingleby Committee's proposals, but which, as a consequence of party pressure, did not mention the possibility of raising the age of criminal responsibility from 8 years. In the event, however, the House of Lords debate on the Bill produced a majority of one in favour of an opposition amendment to raise that age to 12 years. As a consequence, the government was forced to compromise and raised it to 10. This became law in the 1963 CYPA. Several years before the publication of Becker's *Outsiders*[3] and a decade before his theories began to have any impact on British criminology, the Ingleby Committee had grasped the essentials of the fact that criminal prosecution was not only irrelevant to controlling juvenile delinquency, but was also likely to have consequences which could generate even more delinquency. Miss Alice Bacon, leading for the Opposition in the debate on the Bill in the same year as *Outsiders* was published, said: 'It is not just the nature of the charge made in court, it is the appearance in court which can do so much damage to a young child'.[4] If at the time, the liberal reformers of the juvenile criminal justice system saw this 'damage' as meaning psychological trauma heaped on an already deprived and traumatised child, then they were wrong. If, however, they interpreted 'damage' as implying the reconstruction of social reality by a range of officials – policemen, teachers and probation officers – then they were right. The chances are that child care experts took the former view rather than the latter; they were right on the issue of decriminalisation but for the wrong reasons. The Ingleby Committee had considered the position of deprived children in general, as well as delinquent children. Much of the report was devoted to advocating the creation of 'preventive' child care services, devoted generally to supporting poor families whose children were 'at risk' of becoming delinquent or being received into care as a result of family breakdown. Mundane as this may seem twenty years on, the concepts 'at risk' and 'prevention', while conceivably bringing benefits to some families, were to widen the target population for social work intervention to such an extent as to constitute a major influence in the failure to develop services for actual delinquents themselves.

In Ingleby, the major thrust of policy was directed at decriminalisation and the provision of services in the community to delinquent and pre-delinquent children in the context of their families. These two issues have remained behind much of the debate at political and professional levels since that time. Ironically, these issues have themselves become lost, particularly in the 1970s. For the moment, however, it is sufficient perhaps to record that while Ingleby raised the issues for debate, they are still with us today.

The Labour Party responded to the 1963 CYPA by forming a private committee, chaired by Lord Longford. This committee recommended the abolition of the juvenile courts and advised the development of family services which would deal informally with children in trouble. Shortly after Labour came to power in 1965, a new White Paper, *The Child, the Family and the Young Offender*[5], was published. This White Paper closely followed the decriminalising and service-providing policies of the Longford proposals. Bottoms comments that

In retrospect, it is difficult to recall the heat of the battles in those days, though a reading of, for example, the special issue of the *British Journal of Criminology* (April 1966) shows the bitterness of the struggle seeping out behind the intellectual debating points ... The main opposition came from lawyers, magistrates, and probation officers. The last group is of particular interest, as they shared much of the psychoanalytic ideology of other social workers; but they also had a long tradition of independence of local authorities and of services to the courts and it was from this standpoint that their critique was made. On the other side of the debate the main supporters of the proposals were other social workers, particularly members of the child care service, and many of these talked openly of their gaining through the proposals much more professional prestige and recognition for their service which was still less than 20 years old.[6]

The maturing local authority child care service undoubtedly represented the latest generation of 'child savers'. Their view was that delinquency was a symptom of emotional disturbance, created by a troubled family background and that, crudely speaking, criminal prosecution and punishment merely hid these causal factors, as well as failing to provide the necessary services to deal with them. This, of course, constituted a massive threat to the police, magistrates, lawyers and probation officers, for these professional bodies had hitherto possessed a virtual monopoly of the processes of defining delinquent acts, publicly judging them, determining the form of punishment and then passing sentence. These processes were essentially mediated through the juvenile courts. The police controlled the appearance of delinquents; the magistrates symbolised the state and community in the judicial process; the lawyers negotiated with them on issues of fact as well as character; and the probation officers advised on sentencing and sometimes themselves carried through the sentence, as in the case of probation orders or after-care supervision. These groups may be termed the significant definers within the juvenile criminal justice system as it existed prior to the 1969 CYPA. Abolition of the juvenile courts would have meant a major relocation of significant definers within the system and the implications of this appeared to be very far-reaching indeed. An example of one argument against allowing the child care service to become the new body which could define guilt and pass sentence was given by the National Association of Probation Officers which said: 'No action should be taken to interfere with the liberty of an individual on grounds of his conduct, or with the rights of parents on allegations of their failings, except as a result of a judicial assessment.'[7] As we shall see, the child care services eventually joined the ranks of the significant definers and became one more element in the already complex juvenile criminal justice system and, as will be shown in later chapters, became in practice more punitive than the probation service – not necessarily because they were punitive on principle, but primarily because they had a licence to collect information about families even before their children were in trouble. By the mid-1970s they had developed and were in control of very large numbers of institutions to which delinquents could be sent.

The Child, the Family and the Young Offender was dropped. As explanations Bottoms mentions[8] the very small majority in Parliament of the Labour government, the appointment of a new Home Secretary in 1965 (Mr Roy Jenkins), and lack of enthusiasm from Home Office civil servants who were apparently not represented on Longford's group. Three years later, a new White Paper, *Children in Trouble*, was published as replacement for *The Child, the Family and the Young Offender*. Unlike its predecessor, this new White Paper was very rapidly framed into statutes and a year later became the Children and Young Persons Act 1969. Again, the twin themes of decriminalisation and service provision reappeared, but while this time the decriminalisation proposals were less radical (the juvenile courts were to remain, but with greatly restricted powers), the service provision proposals were far more radical. The concept of 'intermediate treatment' was introduced as a supplement to normal supervision (the supervision order replacing the probation order) and as an alternative to a custodial sentence. These proposals were expressed thus:

> Existing forms of treatment available to juvenile courts distinguish sharply between those which involve complete removal from home and those which do not. The juvenile courts have very difficult decisions to make in judging whether circumstances require the drastic step of taking a child away from his parents and home. The view has often been expressed that some form or forms of intermediate treatment should be available to the courts, allowing the child to remain in his own home but bringing him into contact with a different environment.[9]

This paragraph implied that many children who committed offences would no longer need to receive custodial sentences if new services were developed. *Children in Trouble* contained the elements of what came to be called a policy of 'decarceration', non-custodial services to juvenile delinquents who would otherwise have gone to institutions.

Unlike the 1965 White Paper, *Children in Trouble* betrayed a massive child care influence in its formulations and represented a major victory for the social work profession. Virtually every stage of the proposed new juvenile criminal justice system either depended on participation by a social worker in making a decision, or left the social worker free to exercise his discretion without judicial sanction. The hour of the 'child savers' had finally arrived — and we shall see in subsequent chapters of this book how this body proceeded to spend the money which was made available to it, what kinds of decisions it made as a result of its new status within the system and whom it blamed for failure. The civil service favoured the 1968 White Paper. Bottoms[10] comments that *Children in Trouble* was in fact largely the product of a small group of people at the Home Office with professional social work backgrounds who were able to transform the earlier, more radical proposals into ones which were both politically and professionally acceptable, by retaining the juvenile court and giving more discretion to child care professionals. Perhaps it was, in the end, this civil service support which resulted in the proposals becoming law. The Conservative Opposition attempted to prevent the passing of the Bill by amending as many clauses as it could. By and large, the Opposition failed, but the minutes of the House of Commons Committee on the Bill make very revealing reading.[11] The Conservatives appeared intent on preserving the traditional powers of the magistrates and police as the significant definers of juvenile crime. Section 1 of the Act, which deals with care proceedings for both deprived and delinquent children, was attacked over the so-called 'care or control' test, the Conservatives justifiably claiming that this test was biased against the working class. However, Mr Mark Carlisle, leading for the Opposition, betrayed the real reason for his party's unhappiness with Section 1 when he referred to the penalties built into that section in the event of a delinquent child being found to be in need of care or control: none of them constituted what he called a 'punishment' – they were either pure welfare measures or what amounted to deferred fines.[12] Three important areas of change in decision-making were suggested by the draft Bill. These were concerned with shifting authority and discretion from the police and magistrates to social workers, specifically in connection with attempts to divert juvenile offenders from prosecution by means of care proceedings or local action with teachers, parents or other bodies (Section 5), with diversion from custody by means of intermediate treatment – but at the discretion of the supervisors (Section 12), not the court; and with giving virtually complete control over custodial placements, in the event of the making of a care order, to the local authority (Section 7[7]). Much of the committee's discussion was purely at an anecdotal level and hardly any attention was paid to the actual extent and nature of juvenile crime, nor to specific details of how the juvenile criminal justice system was working. To any student of social policy, these omissions are very striking. One is given the impression of heated debate in a complete informational vacuum, rather like a discussion on the relative merits and demerits of two different cars with absolutely no reference to the facts of size, weight, engine size, performance and fuel consumption. By the same token, the government was unable to produce a convincing rationale for decriminalisation other than very vague references to the 'damaging effects' of prosecution and the greater vulnerability of working-class children compared with middle-class children to police activity.

To be fair, everyone argued on the grounds of principle, but no one seems to have been able to relate their principles either to existing or proposed practice. The principles were, of course, fairly clearly derived from opposing views on who should be allowed to define delinquency and who should be allowed to decide what happened to delinquents. The Labour government wished to enlarge the ranks of the decision-makers and introduce fresh perspectives into both definitional and disposal processes. The Conservative Opposition wished to retain the *status quo*. Neither had a clear view of either the major policy issues or of the complexities of the system which had to carry through these objectives.[13]

Despite a last-minute attempt by the Opposition to move an amendment on the Bill suggesting that it could be 'unjust as between different children in like case', the Act passed through both Houses of Parliament and was set to be implemented in stages from 1 January 1971. The tragedy that has occurred since can be best described as a situation in which the worst of all possible worlds came into existence – people have been persistently led to believe that the juvenile criminal justice system has become softer and softer, while the reality has been that it has become harder and harder.

Even before the Act was due to come into operation, the Labour government which championed it fell from power. The incoming Conservative government of 1970 almost immediately declared that it would not implement the vital decriminalising Sections 4 and 5, which were intended to raise the age of criminal responsibility and to provide diversionary services through local authority social work intervention. Other key sections were, however, allowed to proceed and it was left to the discretion of the police, magistrates, probation and social services departments to find means of altering the patterns of sentencing as well as of liaising to develop a process for deciding whether or not to prosecute. The outcomes were that the police created juvenile bureaux, magistrates simply became angry at the withdrawal of their right to send younger delinquents directly to establishments, the probation service half-heartedly prepared to withdraw from juvenile courts and the local authorities, guided by the Department of Health and Social Security, set about (at enormous expense) reorganising, modernising and expanding the custodial sector over which they had achieved control.

Within a very short period of time, the magisterial revolt led the Employment and Social Services Sub-Committee of the House of Commons Expenditure Committee to examine the working of the Act in December 1973, only two years after its implementation. Since the Act had been very heavily influenced by the civil service, which had virtually written the 1968 White Paper, it is interesting to see how civil servants accounted, at that very early stage, for the 'failure' of the legislation.

The sub-committee began by hearing evidence from the civil service in February 1974 and ended just over a year later by receiving evidence from the same group. Of the twenty-three pages of written evidence submitted by the DHSS, twenty-two were entirely devoted to the administration and financing of the new community homes system which had replaced the old

approved schools.[14] Similarly, the verbal evidence given by the same group
was largely concerned with answering questions about the provision of
custodial facilities. Very early on, it was revealed that over the next four to
five years, it was intended that £57 million would be spent on building
residential accommodation for juvenile offenders by local authorities.[15]
Juvenile delinquents had not previously been the primary concern of the
group of civil servants involved, as the main responsibility of the Children's
Department of the Home Office had been for deprived children.

This may, at least in part, account for their obsession with custodial
facilities. Some of the questions from sub-committee members and the
replies from DHSS staff are very revealing:

Mrs Renee Short MP (Chairman):	'What are the provisions of the Act which have not been implemented, apart from the building programme?'
Mr J. W. Stacpoole (DHSS):	'I have a note of these provisions. They are not of concern to the Department of Health and Social Security and they are Section 4, Section 5(1) to (7), Section 7(1) to (3), Section 8 and Section 29(4).'
Mrs Renee Short MP:	'They are not your responsibility?'
Mr J. W. Stacpoole:	'No.'
Mrs Renee Short MP:	'I am asking about your responsibility?'
Mr J. W. Stacpoole:	'There are no sections which are our responsibility which have not been brought into operation.'
Mrs Renee Short MP:	'It is really a matter of degree, is it? You are concerned about the setting-up of homes. You have a considerable building programme and you have an assessment of the future needs as regards places, but you say that is on the way to being implemented?'
Mr J. W. Stacpoole:	'Yes, indeed.'

The magistrates, on this evidence, had nothing to fear. Not only was a lot of
money being spent on custody, but the DHSS and the sub-committee clearly
demonstrated that their main concern was with the provision of custodial
facilities. This was very much in contrast with the Home Office's views on
the use of custodial facilities for delinquents. Mrs P. D. White of the Home
Office was the last person from that government department to give verbal
evidence in July 1974, and she told the sub-committee that not only did the
pre-1969 CYPA juvenile criminal justice system work badly, but that the
much-treasured approved schools of the past, and therefore by implication
the spanking new community homes replacing them, were unlikely to be of
much use:

Before the Act, it was not as if we had a system which was not working well and gradually improving. The magistrates may well feel aggrieved at losing their freedom to commit to approved schools. Unhappily, they were not succeeding; there was about a 65 per cent reconviction rate in three years. Such research and evidence as we have suggested, as the Advisory Council pointed out in their conclusions, that the results of treating offenders as far as possible in their home community, in their own family, and not isolated in places of custody, are at least as good as, possibly better than, the old methods.[16]

The DHSS civil servants devoted their time and energy to providing places in institutions; the Home Office civil servants concluded by declaring them ineffective. But it was the building programme which counted in the end, for at least that could be accepted as a tangible and literally concrete expression of progress. Mr J. W. Stacpoole of the DHSS was the last witness to address the sub-committee before it wrote its report. He was asked: 'Is it your overall impression that the Act is working well, reasonably well, not well or badly? That, in the end, is what we have got to try to decide. What is your impression?'

Mr J. W. Stacpoole:

'I certainly could not put a tick in the box, but I think that we ought at least to be clear that the Act now six years after its enactment is still presenting very serious problems. If I may be as general in my reply as you were in your question, I think that when one is considering how well the Act is working it is necessary, if we are confronted, as we are, with these very serious problems, to ask, would they have been there had there not been an Act? How far could the Act have solved these problems? It can scarcely be in the mind of Parliament simply to tear this very substantial Act up. It covers a very wide range of matters. One would look, I think, for things that are working well and less well. I do not think that I can really go further than that.[17]

Had Mr Stacpoole examined the sentencing trends in juvenile courts from the mid-1960s, he could have answered his questions very easily. 'These very serious problems' were nothing to do with the 1969 CYPA, for the sentences being meted out in juvenile courts, as he spoke, were merely exaggerations of trends which had been developing over the previous ten years. Added to that, however, were the aggravations caused by the discomfort of the police and magistrates in having to take account of a new group of significant definers (local authority social workers) and administrators, armed with their child-saving ideology and prepared to use institutions at the drop of a hat and to spend as much money on building them as they could. In doing this, they were very greatly encouraged by the DHSS Child Care Development Group, which concentrated virtually all its efforts on changing the regimes inside the old approved schools from traditional training and education routines to a more treatment-centred approach which used therapeutic community techniques. The newly created children's regional planning committees had similarly devoted most of their energies to the role of institutions in delinquency management. In all, very little effort had been expended on the development of services in the community. Having heard all the evidence given to the House of Commons sub-committee and having looked at trends in juvenile court disposals, Thorpe commented:

In a time of economic restraint, it might have appeared sensible to radically re-examine the distribution of resources in the delinquency field, yet it seems that local authorities have chosen the most expensive and yet least effective alternative. As at April 1st, 1973, approval has been given for a further 7,666 places in community homes at a cost of £29,500,000 at 1972 prices. If the 1972–73 rates of increase of care orders are maintained for delinquents, these places will be filled within ten years. Little wonder that the committee reported that secure accommodation should be found for highly delinquent children in existing homes.

There seems to be only one alternative to ending this depressing downward spiral of more committals to institutions and more late-adolescent recidivism, and that is to stop the community home building programme now and plough the money into intermediate treatment. Decisions such as this rest within the social services departments; they could recommend more supervision and less care. It would be a courageous but sensible director of social services who could look at his local declining ratio of supervision orders to care orders on delinquents and resolve to re-allocate available funds. But if the present depressing trends are to be reversed, then these issues must be examined and the savings calculated. The financial and social costs of our current delinquency policies are rapidly becoming too great.[18]

An examination of the sentencing practices of juvenile courts before, during and after the 1969 CYPA's implementation serves to illustrate the point. The most striking feature of Tables 1.1 and 1.2 is the marked decline of the use of community-based services for 10–13-year-old males found guilty of indictable offences in England and Wales between 1965 and 1977. This decline was, however, already well established before the 1969 CYPA was even debated in Parliament, but while it had only amounted to 4·9 per cent in the six years leading up to the Act, in the seven years following the Act it accelerated by a further 7·3 per cent. In view of the fact that after 1971,

Table 1·1. *Juvenile courts in England and Wales, disposals as a percentage of those found guilty of indictable offences. 10–13-year-old males.*

	Fit Person Order/ Approved School	Probation	Fine	Conditional Discharge	Attendance Centre
1965	8·5	33·0	17·8	26·4	9·8
1966	8·9	32·0	19·5	24·7	10·6
1967	8·8	30·4	18·7	28·0	10·6
1968	9·0	29·3	17·7	28·5	11·7
1969	9·4	31·4	18·2	27·2	11·6
1970	10·1	28·1	18·6	27·3	12·7
	Care Order	*Supervision*	*Fine*	*Conditional*	*Attendance*
1971	12·6	28·4	19·3	25·1	12·2
1972	11·6	25·7	20·6	26·9	12·7
1973	11·8	25·1	22·2	26·4	12·3
1974	12·0	23·9	21·8	28·5	12·0
1975	11·7	22·7	21·0	30·1	12·5
1976	10·9	21·4	21·4	31·0	13·9
1977	9·4	21·1	22·2	32·5	13·2

Source: Derived from Home Office, *Criminal Statistics, England and Wales, 1965–77* (London: HMSO, 1978).

Table 1·2. *Juvenile courts in England and Wales, variation in disposals as a percentage of those found guilty of indictable offences. 10–13-year-old males*

	1965–77			
Fit Person Order/ Approved School Order and Care Order	Probation/ Supervision	Fine	Conditional Discharge	Attendance Centre
+1·4	−11·9	+4·4	+6·1	+3·4

Source: Home Office, *Criminal Statistics, England and Wales, 1965–77* (London: HMSO, 1978)

boys of this age were passed from the probation service to local authority social workers, these figures already give some indication of the extent to which the new body of service providers were very unwilling to deliver their services to boys who lived at home. While a third of those who were found guilty of indictable offences in 1965 were placed on probation, by 1977 just over a fifth were placed on supervision. The use of custodial measures had in contrast increased most markedly after the implementation of the Act, but had fallen into a decline afterwards. The rapid rise between the late 1960s and early 1970s probably caused an immediate shortage of places, so that a substantial number of 10–13-year-old boys who received

Table 1·3. *Decisions in the juvenile courts, 1965–77 as a percentage of all those found guilty of an indictable offence. 14–17-year-old males*

	Fit Person and Approved School	Probation	Fine	Conditional Discharge	Attendance Centre	Detention Centre	Borstal
1965	8·3	28·5	31·1	18·1	7·1	2·4	1·5
1966	8·6	27·3	33·3	16·6	7·5	2·3	1·8
1967	8·0	26·6	33·3	18·6	6·9	2·4	1·8
1968	7·6	25·6	31·8	19·9	7·6	3·1	1·9
1969	7·2	23·6	36·4	18·3	6·8	3·3	2·0
1970	8·0	21·8	37·9	17·1	7·3	3·5	2·4
	Care Orders	Supervision	Fine	Conditional Discharge	Attendance Centre	Detention Centre	Borstal
1971	7·9	19·4	39·8	17·0	7·5	3·3	3·1
1972	6·7	17·0	42·4	17·2	7·6	3·8	3·3
1973	6·8	17·3	40·9	17·3	7·9	4·6	3·4
1974	6·1	17·2	40·3	18·0	8·7	5·0	3·1
1975	5·9	16·0	39·4	18·5	8·9	6·1	3·8
1976	4·8	15·3	38·1	19·4	9·6	7·3	3·9
1977	4·2	15·0	39·1	19·8	10·2	7·3	3·3

Source: Home Office, *Criminal Statistics, England and Wales, 1965–77.*

care orders between 1971 and 1975 had to remain at home simply because places could not be found for them in institutions.

Table 1.3 indicates that for boys in the 14–17 age group also, the 1969 CYPA has achieved nothing, except perhaps to accelerate trends that were already identifiable before 1971, when it came into effect. A system that was intended to produce a shift towards the use of community homes and supervision in the community has in fact produced a dramatic increase in custodial sentences. The loss of the approved schools has very nearly been compensated for: in 1965, 11·4 per cent of the boys in this age group received an approved school order, a detention centre order, or a recommendation for borstal training; in 1977, 10·6 per cent went to a detention centre or were referred to the crown court. In absolute terms, this has meant a staggering rise – almost 4,000 – in custodial sentences between 1971 and 1977. Meanwhile, supervision has continued the trend established by the probation order between 1965 and 1970: a dramatic decline. It is, of course, true that many more boys in this age group are coming before the courts and being found guilty; but the extra numbers are being dealt with by referrals to crown court, detention centre orders, attendance centre orders, fines and conditional discharges – and especially the first two – rather than by the 'soft' welfare options represented by supervision and (with reservations) the care order.

It was the practice, by local authority social services departments, of sending children home when magistrates had made Section 7(7) care orders on them, which provided at least some tangible evidence to the right-wing critics of the 1969 CYPA. Before the Act, magistrates had been able to send such children directly into custody by means of the approved school order. Unfortunately, however, no clear statistics were available to give any idea of how widespread this new practice was, nor whether or not juvenile offenders sent 'home on trial' immediately after the making of a care order committed more offences than those who were admitted to custody. Senior local authority social services managers, like the DHSS child care advisers, were also obsessed with places in custodial establishments. The Association of Directors of Social Services listed five reasons for the failure of the Act in their evidence to the House of Commons Employment and Social Services Sub-Committee. Brief mention was given of lack of finance, the reorganisation of local authority departments in 1970 and 1974, and the shortage of custodial resources. On this, they commented:

> The existing level of provision within the Community Home system for both assessment places and long term treatment places is a major problem. The two categories of provision are, of course, complementary. An adequate level of assessment places is essential for the development of effective placement machinery, but an adequate number and variety of treatment places is equally important to prevent long delays in finding suitable placements and a consequent blockage at the assessment stage. The system is currently suffering from inadequate provision on both counts and the resultant problems are exacerbated by the uneven distribution throughout the country of the places which are now available.
>
> The plans prepared by the Regional Planning Committees in 1971–72 estimated that in order to provide for the number of children who would need to be accommodated in Community Homes on 31st March, 1975, 448 new homes would need to be constructed, providing a total of 7,666 additional places. For reasons already mentioned this target will clearly not be reached.[19]

Of the eight pages of evidence submitted by the Association of Directors of Social Services, seven and a half were entirely devoted to discussing the shortage of places in community homes with education (CHEs) and observation and assessment centres, the quality of residential care staff and the progress of the building programme.

One is given the impression from both the DHSS advisers and the local authority policy implementers, that the debate about the 1969 CYPA was one which focused almost exclusively around custody and nothing else. In the process both bodies appear to have completely lost sight of the original twin-policy objectives of decriminalisation and decarceration – indeed their obsession with increasing the numbers of available places in custodial establishments shows that they regarded services to be provided for delinquents as being primarily of a custodial nature. In that sense, they were the inheritors of a tradition of 'child saving' which went back into history for over 150 years.

This tradition first emerged at the beginning of the nineteenth century, at a time when imprisonment as a punishment for criminals was rapidly replacing the stocks, the whipping-post, transportation ships and the gallows. In early-nineteenth-century Britain, children, as a particularly vulnerable and easily exploited section of society, were regarded by and large as miniature adults who would gradually grow older and stronger and thus more able to perform harder manual tasks. Since the amount of work a person could do in an agricultural society was determined by his or her physical strength and size and since while children took a long time to become capable of hard manual labour, they nevertheless always did some work, it did not seem inappropriate that they should also work in the new factories and coal mines of the industrial society. Child labour was taken for granted by parents and industrialists alike. Those who opposed the factory legislation of 1833 and 1844-7 could not understand why, as they were paid for their work, children particularly required protection. Their defence of the employment of children of any age under virtually any conditions echoed the defence of slavery, which cited the subhuman nature of black people and their happiness and contentment with whatever an employer or slave-master wished to provide. Unsurprisingly, those who wished to abolish slavery were the ones who also wished to end the overt and often cruel exploitation of child labour in factories. Numerous accounts of apprenticed children in mines, factories and as chimney sweeps graphically illustrated a situation in which the weak and immature were constantly exposed to serious physical danger, disease, neglect and violence from masters. Children, unlike slaves, did not even possess the physical capacity to revolt. The Philanthropic Society, founded in 1788, which campaigned actively for restrictions on child employment, factory inspection and measures to protect orphaned children, was also concerned with the lot of the child criminal. While in practice the rudimentary judicial systems of all pre-industrial societies accepted the notion of diminished responsibility by virtue of age, the philanthropic movement linked together both age and deprivation as factors which argued against the full use of available penal sanctions for child offenders. Justice had very firmly encountered welfare.

The welfare measures initially consisted of placement in training ships or in very small family cottages.[20] However, after reorganisation in 1800, the Philanthropic Society began to establish institutions for orphaned, destitute and delinquent children. The switch from community placement to institutional placement was no doubt necessary on the grounds of both economy and scale. Significantly, in the same period industry switched from a cottage to a factory base, the penal system from the stocks to newly built prisons, and help for the poor from outdoor relief to the workhouse. The age of the total institution had dawned − not on the grounds of humanity, but primarily on the grounds of efficiency. Just as it was more efficient and profitable to gather together workers from scattered looms and cottages under one factory roof where bigger machines could be employed, separate tasks allocated to the workforce and supervisors and managers placed in a position to make easier assessments of supply and demand factors, so it was more efficient to gather together the mentally ill and handicapped, the unemployed, debtors, criminals and orphaned or abandoned children into institutions where they could be more efficiently controlled. That the Philanthropic Society moved from community care to institutional care for deprived and delinquent children was more a sign of the times than a deliberate strategy. But the legacy of that change is still with us in the form of borstals, detention centres and CHEs. In 1838, the Parkhurst Act created the first state institution exclusively for juvenile offenders at what became Parkhurst Prison. The objectives of that establishment were clearly rehabilitatory: 'It is a great public advantage that a Prison be provided in which young offenders may be detained and corrected and receive such Instruction and be subject to such Discipline as shall appear most conducive to their Reformation and to the Repression of Crime'(Preamble to the Parkhurst Act, quoted in Boss, P., *Social Policy and the Young Delinquent* (London: Routledge & Kegan Paul, 1967) p. 23). By 1884, however, this establishment had closed, largely because of the development of a new range of custodial establishments pioneered by the Philanthropic Society. These institutions were called reformatory and industrial schools and were introduced primarily to save child offenders from imprisonment. It is not without significance that the first laws relating to the use of such institutions, in 1854 (and in Scotland only) made such provision available to vagrant, mendicant or homeless children and not to juvenile offenders alone. By means of this Act, the Scottish courts could send any child under the age of 14 years to reform school, who was deemed to be 'at risk'. For the first time, official focus was off delinquency and on attitudes and life-styles. The logical development of such thinking was to lead inevitably 150 years later to the Section 7(7) care order (a custodial sentence based almost entirely on welfare and not delinquent considerations) and the use of voluntary intermediate treatment for children perceived to be 'at risk' of committing offences. In the former case, it has permitted the institutionalisation of large numbers of children who, as we shall see in later chapters, are only very marginally delinquent, and in the latter case the 'guiding' into correctional programmes of large numbers of children who have not even committed offences but merely come from disorderly families. Rather than becoming an instrument with which to reform the juvenile criminal justice system, preventive intermediate treatment, by ignoring the labelled delinquent, has effectively allowed correctional agents to penetrate even further into the lives of 'deviant' adolescents.

Further legislation in 1854 and then in 1857 and 1866 effectively ensured that the state took over responsibility for financing the building and running of reformatory and industrial schools from the voluntary bodies which had initially set them up. The pioneer of reform schools, Mary Carpenter, and her followers had succeeded in creating virtually an entirely separate system of custody for young offenders who henceforth were not to be contaminated by adult offenders and, wherever possible, not placed in prisons. While in many important respects this was undoubtedly a major reforming achievement, the introduction of welfare considerations into the sentencing of juvenile offenders was to have a number of repercussions a century and a half later. The links between deprivation and delinquency were firmly established, but the emphasis has increasingly been on deprivation and the search for more effective methods of discovering it, measuring it and compensating for it – in institutions.

The 1908 Children Act institutionalised the increasing separation of juvenile from adult offenders by creating the juvenile court, with more relaxed trial procedures and the abolition of imprisonment for children under 16 except in certain defined cases. In effect, the 1908 Act created the basic structure of what we now understand as the juvenile criminal justice system. Since that time further efforts to reform this system have pulled in two superficially similar but essentially contradictory directions. On the one hand, there have been further moves to increase knowledge about, and treatment programmes for, delinquents. On the other, there have been moves to take delinquent behaviour away from criminal prosecution and to develop programmes for dealing with infractious adolescents which focus on the delinquent act itself in the locality where it took place. Superficially these developments both appear to run in a similar direction since they imply a belief that delinquency is caused by a number of socio-emotional factors. However, the 'diagnosis and treatment', or pure welfare response, de-emphasises the delinquent act and focuses instead on the attitudes, relationships and family of the delinquent; it permits intervention in any situation where attitudes, relationships and families exist which are considered to be 'criminogenic', regardless of whether or not a delinquent act has actually occurred. In contradiction to this, those who focus on decriminalisation and decarceration as the areas for reform would claim that both criminal prosecution and the use of custody are not only irrelevant and ineffective as measures for dealing with delinquent acts, but that they are likely to exaggerate the effects of such acts by creating a delinquent career; and further that intervention in the lives of non-delinquents, identified as a result of their attitudes and relationships as 'at risk', is potentially dangerous to them as individuals as well as taking scarce non-custodial resources away from those who need them most – those actually in custody.

While the 1933 Children and Young Persons' Act did little else but rename the reformatory and industrial schools 'approved schools', the White Paper which preceded it in 1927 represented a further milestone in developing the links between justice and welfare. It declared that delinquent and deprived children in care were virtually indistinguishable from each other. By 1969, essentially the same measure, the care order, had been produced to deal with both delinquent and deprived children alike and the treatment/welfare orientation was enshrined in legislation.

As we have seen, opposition to the 1969 CYPA centred around the issue of attempts to restrict the circle of significant definers to the juvenile courts and those professional bodies which serviced the courts at that time. Ironically, the child care lobby, which did so much to produce the Act and supported its implementation, in the end proved to be an even more conservative force than its opponents. As the evidence given to the House of Commons sub-committee in 1974 and 1975 has shown, the child care experts, in attempting to broaden the type of information used to judge a delinquent by including deprivational indicators as much as infractional indicators, and by providing custodial facilities to compensate for the deprivations, have succeeded in creating a juvenile criminal justice system which deals with delinquents in a way which is even further removed from the actual situation and events surrounding the original infraction. Moreover, it opened the floodgates of preventive work. As Morris and McIsaac comment:

a social welfare approach provides justification for early and extensive intervention in the lives of children and their families: if delinquency reflects a maladjustment which can be treated then it is wrong to restrict the availability of treatment or to deprive the child of it. The net of control is cast wider since it is thought that something constructive can be done for delinquent children.[21]

If, by taking into account personal background factors thought to be associated with delinquent behaviour, the Philanthropic Society had originally intended to temper the savagery of nineteenth-century justice for juveniles, the eventual outcome of broadening the basis for decision-making and the measures adopted for rehabilitation is a system which provides custodial programmes for deprived children who commit offences and non-custodial programmes for children who come from backgrounds which are considered to be likely to create delinquents.

Chapter 4 of this book contains information on juvenile offenders in care and shows that most of them have only committed a very small number of relatively trivial offences. The warning issued by the Ingleby Report in 1960 has become a reality. Welfare considerations, the report maintained, could result for example in a child being charged with a petty theft or other wrongful act for which most people would say that no great penalty should be imposed and the case apparently ending in a disproportionate sentence. For when the court causes enquiries to be made the court may determine that the welfare of the child requires some very substantial interference which may amount to taking the child away from his home for a prolonged period. It is common to come across bitter complaints that a child has been sent away from home because he has committed some particular offence which in itself was not at all serious.[22]

Not surprisingly, when the House of Commons sub-committee reported in July 1975, its recommendations took two entirely different directions. A total of forty recommendations were made, fifteen of which were concerned with improving and expanding custodial facilities. Ten were concerned with the development of non-custodial facilities (intermediate treatment), eight with strengthening the powers of juvenile courts, and seven with strengthening and broadening the possibilities for discussion between the police, social workers and local communities in order to prevent the need for prosecution and to encourage the development of local crime-prevention programmes. It can be seen from this that the recommendations relating to custodial facilities and the powers of the juvenile courts were primarily concerned with prosecution and custody as one strategy for managing delinquents, while those relating to the development of intermediate treatment and very localised liaison procedures between the police and social services implied a strategy of decarceration and decriminalisation. These contradictory recommendations were then taken up by the government which published a White Paper in response to the House of Commons sub-committee report in May 1976. The White Paper suggested, however, that money would be made available for the construction of 'secure' facilities in CHEs so as to stop the remanding of juvenile offenders in adult prisons.

The Government share the Committee's concern that certificates of unruliness, authorising committal to a prison service establishment, should not be issued unless they are necessary, particularly in view of the fact that only about half the young persons remanded in this way receive custodial sentences. They have even considered the possibility of requiring local authorities to pay for juveniles remanded to prison service establishments: but this would be a cumbersome process and would require legislation. They would prefer, therefore, to rely on the process taken in the Children Act 1975 to prescribe in regulations, criteria which are to be met before any certificate is given.[23]

The building of 'secure' accommodation, then, was the answer to the demand by magistrates for power to enforce a care order by ensuring that they could send a child directly to an institution. The government's reply was that this would be rendered unnecessary by the provision of secure accommodation. Leaning in the opposite direction were the suggestions about the development of intermediate treatment and community-based alternatives to residential care.

Even if there were an unrestricted supply of additional resources for the implementation of the Act, would the Government think it right that it should be devoted to a massive programme of residential provision – though there are particular gaps in provision, detailed below [those of secure accommodation], the filling of which deserves a high priority? On the contrary, the Government share the Committee's view (paragraph 167) that there should be, within the framework of the Act, a major shift of emphasis towards non-residential care including supervision, intermediate treatment and fostering.[24]

The White Paper then continued by emphasising the need for 'greater mutual understanding, consultation and co-operation among all those who share responsibility for helping children in trouble and protecting and reassuring the community'[25] – a message which could be interpreted as one which encouraged the management of juvenile delinquency outside institutions and outside juvenile courts. The White Paper demonstrated the government's unwillingness to continue spending vast sums of money on custodial facilities, but admitted a need for secure accommodation, primarily to halt remands in prison establishments. In order to bring this about clear criteria were suggested for the granting of certificates of unruliness, so that delinquents would be accommodated in local authority rather than prison department facilities. It also clearly indicated a preference for community-based as opposed to residential control, and called for local machinery which would contain delinquency where it occurred rather than permitting prosecution.

In many respects, therefore, this White Paper represented a significant step forward, in three ways:

(1)   It recommended a shift to non-custodial control.
(2)   It recommended that delinquent behaviour be dealt with locally.
(3)   It suggested criteria to be applied to certain delinquents before they could be remanded in prisons.

The last point appears to mark the first time that, in cases of criminal prosecution, juvenile courts could only take certain measures if they were satisfied that other possibilities were not available. In this case the White Paper was specifically concerned about unruly certificates which juvenile courts could issue at the request of the police in order to detain juvenile offenders in prisons. The government was clearly aware that even with the availability of secure accommodation in local authority establishments, it was likely that this could be filled by children who would not necessarily be in need of the type of security offered in a prison. Accordingly, it was decided to insert a 'gate' by suggesting, *inter alia*, that before juvenile courts could issue such certificates, the local authority would have to supply a written statement to the effect that it did not have any suitable alternative accommodation to a prison. This gate became the Certificate of Unruly Character (Conditions) Order 1977. It amended some sections of the 1969 CYPA which were concerned with such certificates by stipulating that a juvenile offender could only be remanded in prison if he had committed a very serious offence (punishable, in the case of an adult with fourteen years or more imprisonment) or an offence or previous offence of violence; and if a written report was obtained from the local authority saying that there was no suitable accommodation available in a CHE, or that the young person in question had persistently absconded or disrupted the running of a house.[26] This order came into effect on 1 August 1977. At the time, Boylan[27] was undertaking research into the making of unruly certificates. He claims that the new order had an immediate and dramatic impact, particularly on 14-year-old male juvenile offenders. Unwittingly, therefore, by inserting specific criteria, the government had created a 'gate' which restricted access to a particular form of custody. The significance of this cannot be overestimated; for the 1969 CYPA in its original form also contains a number of 'gates' – which restrict, for example, both the possibility of prosecution and the range of permissible sentences – notably in the unimplemented Sections 4, 5(1) to (7), Sections 7(1) and (3), and Section 8. These particular sections, which will be dealt with later, lay out the basic framework for decriminalisation and clearly specify the conditions under which criminal prosecution can occur. Although they have never been implemented, the 1976 White Paper's reference to 'greater mutual understanding, consultation and co-operation' might well have been meant as a signal to explore the possibilities of informal local arrangements between the police, social services and juvenile courts which would have the effect of producing strict gate-keeping criteria relevant to a particular locality. These criteria could be used to restrict prosecution and, in the event of prosecution, the resulting sentence. They also assume the development of informal measures to provide services for delinquents in the community.

The importance of developing strict criteria for prosecution and the delivery of services becomes clearer when one considers that the policy trends towards decriminalisation and decarceration require that both delinquent acts and delinquent youngsters be looked at in isolation from each other and then responded to by the provision of appropriate services. Very clearly, this has not been happening. Although the police, for example, have criteria which they apply to juvenile offenders in respect of decisions about cautioning and prosecution, generally speaking other professions in the juvenile criminal justice system are unaware of them. Similarly, local authorities do not tend to have clear criteria for juvenile offenders in terms of the services they provide. The widespread practice of using intermediate treatment for non-delinquents not only demonstrates a lack of firm policy guidelines, but may also account for the fact that while intermediate treatment has been developing, it has had absolutely no impact whatsoever on sentencing trends in juvenile courts.[28] Clearly, the reason why the social work professions define services in terms of 'soft' information about the attitudes, family background and general behaviour of children labelled 'at risk' is that they tend to see a delinquent act or career (created by decisions made about delinquent acts within the juvenile criminal justice system) as less relevant than the supposed causes of the act. Moreover, the services they provide were designed almost entirely to deal with the 'causes' and not the acts themselves.

There can be no doubt that the 1969 CYPA was abolitionist in intent. It anticipated the end of a penal/custodial system for juveniles and its replacement by something completely new: 'care and treatment'. The age of criminal responsibility and the lower age limit for borstal were to be raised. Attendance centres and detention centres were to be phased out and replaced by intermediate treatment. Approved schools were to be assimilated into a community homes system. But what really did happen? If one compares the sections of the Act that were implemented with those that were not, the answer is simple and obvious: a new system came in but the old one did not go out. Intermediate treatment arrived, but detention centres and attendance centres remained; the community homes system was created, but the approved schools retained their character and borstals were still available for 15-year-olds. Care proceedings made their début, but as long as it was still possible to take criminal proceedings with children under 14 there was never any reason to make use of them.

What happens when a system that is intended as a replacement is simply grafted on to its predecessor and run in parallel with it? The 1969 CYPA makes a wonderful case study. Considered abstractly there are two possibilities, of which the first is intense conflict and abrasion. While there has indeed been a great deal of conflict at the ideological level (i.e. on the part of those whose duty it is to make as much official noise as possible), this simply has not happened in practice. The other possibility is that the two systems come to some form of accommodation, an implicit set of demarcation agreements and neutral zones, and that the sector served by the old system simply expands in order to make room for the newcomer. It is in this direction that all the available evidence points in the case of the 1969 CYPA. The two systems have, in effect, become vertically integrated, and an additional population of customer-clients has been identified in order to ensure that they both have plenty of work to do. There is no doubt, of course, that the two systems are, in the final analysis, opposed to each other. But the present situation is one of more or less peaceful coexistence. Very roughly (and with certain qualifications) the new system has been deployed with the younger age groups and has adopted a 'preventive' policy. The concept of children 'at risk' is invoked in the identification of a new population for whom social work intervention is appropriate prior to confrontation with the courts. Once such children begin to appear in court, however, they are fairly rapidly phased into the penal system (a high proportion of care orders are made on a first or second court appearance). It is tempting to argue, in cases like this, that if field social work has already 'failed' (as it must have if the child is now before the court), more social work is not likely to succeed and it is therefore time to try something new and different. Hence there is a form of collusion: the agreement between magistrate and social worker that it is now necessary to remove the child from home and place him, initially at any rate, in care. Hence, too, the emergence of concepts like 'need for structure' associated with recommendations for care, detention centres and even borstal. It is precisely this kind of extension in the social work vocabulary that enables integration between the two systems to take place.

We have described this as 'vertical integration'. Seen from a vantage point in the old system, the new system extends its scope, its range of intervention and surveillance, down through the age groups, and acts as a feeder mechanism for the courts and custodial institutions. One unfortunate, but apparently inevitable, consequence of this arrangement is that children now coming under the jurisdiction of the old system will tend to be younger (and may tend to have fewer 'problems') than formerly. As a result, pressure is exerted on the 'upper reaches' of the system as delinquents progress to the later stages of their careers more swiftly. (Note the falling average age of borstal intake, for example, and the fact that detention centres and borstals between them have already taken up the slack created by the 'loss' of the approved schools.) Given the restricted number of places available, it follows that the older and more 'difficult' children will become progressively harder to place (and as a consequence of this, once can expect demands for even more places). Alternatively, seen from a vantage point in the new system, the old system represents a convenient way of disposing of the older children, while at the same time it provides a context and rationale for preventive work (there must, after all, be something that you are trying to prevent). An unfortunate consequence of this arrangement is that when children do come to court, they may be more vulnerable than they might otherwise have been since more is known about them and social work intervention has already been tried (and seen to fail). On the other hand, each child who does not come to court (or who does not come to court again) can be counted as a success. As we have noted, the social work vocabulary does need to be stretched a little to justify handing over delinquents to the penal system, but the evidence suggests that neither this nor social workers' professional antipathy to 'punitive' methods functions as an irremovable obstacle to integration.

The supervision order can be thought of as, in effect, a demilitarised zone. Although its use has declined relatively owing to the greater numbers of children coming before the courts, the number of children subject to supervision orders at any one time has remained stable and roughly equivalent to the numbers subject to probation orders prior to 1971. One might have expected the supervision order to become a battleground when the 1969 CYPA was only partially implemented. But the practical philosophy of peaceful coexistence means that the additional population of clients and customers has been absorbed in the respective spheres of influence on either side of the demarcation line. Intermediate treatment has, of course, been routinely practised in the supervision zone. But it has functioned as an optional extra for children already on supervision, and for this reason has presented no kind of a threat to the older, established system.

If the supervision order is a demilitarised zone (continuing and possibly overextending this metaphor), the care order is a no-man's-land in which skirmishes are still occasionally fought, and in which the exchange of prisoners takes place. The old system has more or less resigned itself to the loss of the approved schools (while increasing its use of detention centres and borstals to compensate) and, with many reservations about the effectiveness of the care order, has ceded the community homes to social work. However, the prestige of the residential sector is not high, and many social workers regard CHEs as custodial institutions not significantly different from detention centres and borstals. For both sides, therefore, the granting of a care order serves to convey the child into a kind of limbo. On the one side, it represents a moment of transition, the point at which the field social worker gives up and the new system abdicates in favour of the old. On the other side, although it does not yet represent a point at which the penal system automatically claims jurisdiction, it does define one set of conditions under which it reserves the right to do so. When the workings of the Act were investigated by the House of Commons sub-committee, the civil service and directors of social services showed themselves to be almost exclusively concerned with the provision of custody; the police objected to the decriminalising sections of the Act (which had not even been implemented!) and wanted more custodial facilities; and the magistrates focused almost exclusively on a very small minority of juvenile offenders and used them to make a general case for the introduction of new powers. None of the representatives of these professions showed any grasp of the principles of the Act (indeed, the police appeared to be opposed to broadening the circle of 'significant definers' by opposing Sections 4 and 5).

Even more significantly, they all presented evidence which, with the clear exception of the 'number of places in CHEs' issue, was entirely impressionistic. Whatever was really going on within the juvenile criminal justice system was obviously not a matter for discussion. In 1976, the government White Paper which responded to the sub-committee's report generally rejected the 'custodial solution', except for the provision of a small number of secure places, and advocated the use of non-custodial facilities as well as a policy of dealing with delinquency in a locality as opposed to a juvenile court. It may be that the police at the time saw the juvenile court as an institution which legitimated their behaviour, that the magistrates saw it as one way of maintaining the privileges of a powerful minority in a highly symbolic way, and that the central and local government officials who provided services saw these, for historical reasons, as being primarily of a custodial nature. In practice, what seems to have happened is that each group pursued its own interests and misguidedly reacted to what was supposedly the behaviour of other groups — and none of them was in a position to know, as there was no information.

The service providers at least should have known better since they saw themselves as the legitimate heirs of over 150 years of reform. Moreover, they were the ones who stood to gain most from the 1969 CYPA since it gave them new responsibilities in creating local services for diversion from prosecution or, failing that, diversion from custody. Instead, they created more places in institutions.

Faced with this enthusiasm on the part of the policy makers for institutional care, what can the individual social worker do? We shall argue that, paradoxically, he is in a unique position to bring about changes in policy and produce appropriate services. As far as policy change is concerned, the social worker should be able systematically to collect information on the local workings of the juvenile criminal justice system which can be used to develop appropriate policies by the police, magistrates and social services managers. It is this information which represents reality — the numbers of children who commit delinquent acts, the nature of those acts and where they occurred, the decisions made by police to caution or prosecute, the response to police referrals by the local authority, the recommendations contained in both probation and social services social enquiry reports to juvenile courts, and the magistrates' response to those recommendations, followed eventually by the correctional effectiveness of any particular sentence or services. It is these interconnected processes which constitute a juvenile criminal justice system. To plan services in an informational vacuum is tantamount to repeating the errors which appear to have been made at fairly senior levels of local and national government. The debate on juvenile delinquency needs to be based less on emotional impressions about delinquency and emotional responses to it and more on what actually happens at a very local level — for that is the level at which the services must be provided. First, however, we must provide a theoretical justification for our advocacy of a switch of resources from institutional care to community support for juvenile offenders.

REFERENCES: CHAPTER 1

1   *Report of the Committee on Children and Young Persons*, Cmnd 1191 (London: HMSO, 1960).
2   Advisory Council on the Treatment of Offenders, *Corporal Punishment* (London: HMSO, 1960).
3   Becker, H. S., *Outsiders: Studies in the Sociology of Deviance* (New York: Free Press, 1963).
4   *Parliamentary Debates (Hansard)*, House of Commons, Vol. 672, Col. 1,288.
5   Home Office, *The Child, the Family and the Young Offender*, Cmnd 2742 (London: HMSO, 1965).
6   Bottoms, A. E., 'On the decriminalisation of English juvenile courts', in Hood, R. (ed.), *Crime, Criminology and Public Policy: Essays in Honour of Sir Leon Radzinowicz* (Heinemann: London, 1974), pp. 329–30.
7   'The child, the family and the young offender: observations by NAPO', *Probation*, no. 11 (1965), p. 184.
8   Bottoms, op. cit., pp. 330–1.
9   Home Office, *Children in Trouble*, Cmnd 3601 (London: HMSO, 1969), p. 9.
10 Bottoms, op. cit., pp. 332–3.
11 *Parliamentary Debates (Hansard)*, House of Commons, Vol. 672, Col. 1,288.
12 See 1969 CYPA, Sect. 1.
13 See House of Commons Debate on the 1969 CYP Bill.
14 See *Eleventh Report from the Expenditure Committee Session 1974–5. The Children and Young Persons' Act 1969, Vol. II, Minutes of Evidence and Appendices* (London: HMSO, 1975), pp. 1–23.
15 ibid., p. 60.
16 ibid., p. 97.
17 ibid., p. 405.
18 Thorpe, D. H., 'A half-hearted act of treatment', *Community Care*, no. 95 (28 January 1976), p. 19.
19 *Eleventh Report from the Expenditure Committee*, cit. no. 14, p. 103.
20 See, for example, Heywood, J., *Children in Care* (London: Routledge & Kegan Paul, 1959).
21 Morris, A. and McIsaac, M., *Juvenile Justice?* (London: Heinemann, 1978), p. 51.
22 *Report of the Committe on Children and Young Persons*, para. 66.
23 Home Office, Welsh Office, DHSS and DES, *Children and Young Persons' Act 1969: Observations on the Eleventh Report from the Expenditure Committee*, Cmnd 6494 (London: HMSO, 1976), para. 19, p. 7.
24 ibid., p. 4, para. 10.
25 ibid., p. 4., para. 11.
26 Certificate of Unruly Character (Conditions) Order 1977, no. 1027.
27 Boylan, F., Unpublished paper on unruly certificates (1979).
28 See, for example, Thorpe, D., 'I.T. – A Service for the Kids or for the Courts?' Unpublished paper given to 4th NITF Conference, December 1978.

2

Decarceration, Welfare and Law

In this book we argue for a policy of 'decarceration': the removal of the majority of juvenile offenders from residential care, or custody, and the development of a range of facilities which will enable them to be supported in the community. In later chapters we shall provide evidence of how large the majority is which could be decarcerated and describe the research strategies and negotiating tactics which are needed to implement the policy. But, first, our advocacy of decarceration has to be explained and justified. This is the principal aim of this chapter. The explanation will inevitably entail an analysis of the nature and scope of welfare, of the criminal law, particularly as it affects juveniles, and of the penal institutions associated with it.

It would be possible to urge a policy of decarceration simply on the grounds that the institutions in which juvenile offenders are presently incarcerated have been shown not to work. On might couple this with the argument that community-based alternatives, while not necessarily more effective, are at any rate likely to be cheaper. These are, of course, familiar and time-honoured arguments, as Foucault[1] has clearly shown they have been around ever since custodial institutions first explicitly set out to reform, rehabilitate, train, treat or by whatever means correct offenders. Yet it is still, it seems, necessary to restate the case because despite what by now amounts to overwhelming evidence of the failure of such institutions, they not only survive but flourish and proliferate, as has been shown in the preceding chapter.

Indeed, it is especially urgent to re-emphasise the evidence in the present political context. The Conservative government's enthusiasm for cutting public expenditure seems to cool remarkably when its gaze falls on juvenile offenders. It is still toying with the idea of reverting, in effect, to the pre-1969 approved school order in the new shape of a residential care order, with the possible additional refinement of a secure care order; these measures, if implemented, would explicitly be designed to increase the numbers of children in custody. It has decided that the short sharp shock of detention centres is no longer sharp enough, and from its predecessor it has inherited a commitment to increase tenfold the provision of secure accommodation for juveniles (by no means all of them offenders) compared with the 1964 level.[2] It would certainly be a mistake to suppose that this kind of penal crusade can be effectively fought by mere facts and figures; but the story they tell is so clear, their implications for policy so apparently unmistakable that they are worth rehearsing.

Cornish and Clarke, reporting the results of their comparative study of two different kinds of regime in Kingswood Training School, concluded that 'institutional' intervention had provided more than a temporary interruption of their delinquent behaviour for only about 20 per cent of the boys admitted.[3] Seventy-five per cent of all boys discharged during the period of the study were known to have been reconvicted within two years of discharge. There was no difference in reconviction rates between boys discharged from a 'therapeutic community' regime and those from a traditional regime. The failure rate reported by Cornish and Clarke is rather higher than that claimed in official statistics — 65 to 70 per cent reconvicted in a three-year period after discharge.[4] As they point out, the official figures were based on incomplete information and, in any case, the official failure rate can only be put forward as evidence of the schools' success if one makes 'the improbable assumption that *all* boys admitted to approved schools would have remained, or become more, delinquent had they been left at home'.[5] For one thing, not all the children admitted to these schools were (officially) delinquent in the first place; offending after the approved school experience would have to be regarded as something worse than failure. Secondly, the well-established phenomenon of growing up means that a substantial proportion of approved school inmates could be expected not to reoffend anyway, no matter what institutional or other experience they had undergone, if any. In fact the official figures look even worse when it is remembered that they cover only the period of statutory supervision on licence; longer-term reconviction rates are still less encouraging. Certainly there are variations in reconviction rates between schools which cannot entirely be accounted for by differences in their initial intake,[6] but these variations imply only that some schools failed less spectacularly than others.

Approved schools and their younger cousins, community homes with education on the premises (CHEs), were intended to provide 'care and treatment in a planned environment'.[7] Their success, however, has not been noticeably greater than that of the institutions for juveniles which are more or less frankly prisons. Junior detention centres and borstals are managed by the Home Office and staffed by a prison service which has increasingly abandoned any pretensions to rehabilitative prowess. Indeed, considering that only 12 per cent of boys in detention centres, and about 3 per cent of borstal inmates, are first offenders,[8] unlike many of the children who are

sent to CHEs, the staff of these institutions need not feel threatened by
comparisons with supposedly more progressive or enlightened
establishments. The figures are nevertheless depressing enough. Seventy-
three per cent of boys released from junior detention centres in 1974 were
reconvicted within two years; for borstal trainees discharged in the same
year the figure is 81 per cent.[9] Again, these figures are rather worse than
they look because at the time in question there were periods of compulsory
after-care supervision of twelve months in the case of detention centres and
two years for borstals. The figures naturally deteriorate further if the
follow-up period is extended beyond two years.

This gloomy record should be considered alongside another set of figures
which suggest that the implications for sentencing which have been drawn
from the reconviction statistics are somewhat paradoxical. Admittedly there
is no evidence that the number of children in CHEs has increased in the past
ten years. Tutt[10] gives figures, for the years 1972–6 only, which suggest that
while there is a good deal of variation from year to year, the CHE
population has remained relatively steady over a longer period – about
6,800 in both 1972 and 1976. The picture in the explicitly penal institutions
is very different. Between 1969 and 1977 the number of juveniles sent to
detention centres went up by 158 per cent, from 2,228 to 5,757. In the same
period borstal sentences on juveniles rose by 136 per cent, from 818 to
1,935.[11] Parallel with this increased use of custody has been a decline in the
use of supervision in the community, a trend already discernible before the
1969 CYPA. There were 3,500 fewer supervision orders in 1977 than
probation orders on juveniles in 1969.[12] The popular idea, assiduously
maintained by some politicians and sections of the press, is that the 1969
CYPA ushered in an era of excessive mildness in the correction of juvenile
offenders. These figures show that this is a myth. They also provide perhaps
the hardest available evidence that the Conservative victory in the 1970
election was a real watershed in the recent history of the relationship
between authority and deviance, the state and its disorderly subjects.
According to Stuart Hall and his co-authors

the state has won the right, and indeed inherited the duty, to move
swiftly, to stamp fast and hard, to listen in, discreetly survey, saturate and
swamp, charge or hold without charge, act on suspicion, hustle and
shoulder, to keep society on the straight and narrow. Liberalism, that last
back-stop against arbitrary power, is in retreat. It is suspended. The times
are exceptional. The crisis is real. We are inside the 'law-and-order'
state.[13]

The nature of the economic crisis which lies behind this shift in official
attitudes is not our concern here. But the harsh fate of juvenile offenders in
the 1970s is one sign of the new authoritarianism which has informed

much government policy in the last decade. In retrospect the 1970 election appears to mark a crucial point: when the reformist optimism, liberalism and toleration of 'permissiveness' and dissent which had characterised the late 1960s finally gave way before the demands of 'Selsdon Man' for a reassertion of the values of discipline, order and respect for authority. In retrospect, too, it is symbolically apt that one of the first acts of the newly elected Heath government was to announce that crucial sections of the 1969 CYPA would not be implemented.[14] There was little talk of reviving them when Labour returned to power in 1974.

The question remains: Why should a government, elected, like its forerunner in 1970, on a platform in which law and order was a very substantial plank, not only tolerate but actively promote institutions whose contribution to the maintenance of legality is, on the evidence, of a negative kind? To answer it we must look at their ideological function – often described as hidden, but in the present context increasingly apparent. Not that it has ever been much of a secret. Anyone who has observed how the walls of Victorian prisons brood darkly over areas of working-class housing (or where the houses used to be) can scarcely doubt that they were meant to serve an important symbolic function – as very present and substantial reminders of the ultimate power of the state. More elaborately, it may be, as Foucault has argued,[15] that we should stop supposing that the aim of correctional institutions is in fact to eliminate or even reduce criminal behaviour. Perhaps, on the contrary, the real purpose of the criminal law and the institutions at its disposal is to isolate and organise, and thus survey and control, one particular kind of illegal behaviour, in the process diverting attention from others. At least in Foucault's version, this argument is applied not only to custodial institutions but to agencies dealing with offenders in the community as well. It is a form of what Jock Young has called 'left idealism'.[16] The characteristics of this stance are 'a coercive conception of order' and a functionalist, sometimes conspiratorial, view of all existing social institutions which are supposed to operate, in a uniform, straightforward and homogeneous way, in the interests of the ruling class (which is itself seen as internally cohesive and in no doubt about what its interests are). 'In its most extreme form', Young writes, 'left idealism is unable to distinguish the factory from the prison, education from brainwashing ... fascism from democracy.' Or, one might add, supervision orders from CHEs, intermediate treatment from detention centres, social workers from policemen. Other versions of this drastically simplified and schematic Marxism will be encountered later in this chapter. Quite apart from its intrinsic implausibility, which will be argued later, a major problem with this position is that it leaves its adherents with few openings or opportunities actually to do anything, except perhaps hasten the revolution or add to the already considerable volume of denunciations of the welfare state in general and social work in particular. For social work practitioners, the only attitude it appears to lead to is a bleak, passive fatalism: since it is all about social control anyway, why bother to try to do anything well, why worry if children are incarcerated for offending rather than allowed to remain in their communities? It has recently been noted[17] that Foucault's own work constitutes a major argument against such fatalism and for our present purpose it does draw attention to an important fact: that custodial institutions are relatively immune to charges of correctional inefficiency. Indeed, their longevity is a powerful argument against another kind of Marxist oversimplification − the crude economic determinism which supposes that all the policies of capitalist governments are solely dictated by the basest of financial considerations.

Our principal argument against the large-scale use of custody for juvenile offenders is not, therefore, that it has proved an expensive failure. This does not, of course, rule out the possibility of using cost-effectiveness arguments as a tactic in the overall process of trying to change the policy of particular agencies towards juvenile delinquency. But our opposition to large-scale incarceration is ultimately based on an ethical and political choice, about whose side, in Becker's formulation, we are on. This book presents evidence that the majority of children in custodial institutions for committing offences have been sent there unfairly, not just unnecessarily and damagingly. The unfairness can be judged not only in relation to some abstract principle of natural justice (which nevertheless remains an important concept) but very concretely and directly: by reference to the sentencing practices of adult courts. Section 7(7) of the 1969 CYPA empowers courts to make a child subject to a care order as a direct response to a criminal offence; that is, to impose a semi-indeterminate sentence which can, at the discretion of the executive rather than the judicial authorities, be spent partly or wholly in some form of custody. Very frequently, as we shall show, this sentence is passed on juveniles for offences which could not conceivably be dealt with by even a short prison sentence in the adult courts. With this in mind we shall argue not for a 'return to justice', or to a strict sentencing tariff, but for the restoration of a basic sense of proportion in juvenile court sentencing. We do not deny that there is a proportion of juvenile offenders who ought to be removed from home − we shall suggest later that this means something under 20 per cent of those incarcerated at present. Nor do we deny that there is a much smaller number who, because of the nature of their offences, have to be kept in secure conditions. But overwhelmingly the offences committed by juveniles constitute a nuisance, not a menace, to society. This book is intended, then, to put a spoke in the wheels of the law-and-order bandwagon; and to be of some service to the children now senselessly and unfairly incarcerated. Our experience both in practice and research has convinced us that we should be on their side.

It is not self-evident, however, that this moral and political commitment inevitably implies a policy of decarceration. It cannot simply be assumed that this would be 'better' for the children – more humane, more constructive, less damaging. The point needs to be argued. We had better say at the outset that we accept that there is bound to be an element of social control in the community-based alternatives to custody which we advocate. But, contrary to the 'left idealists', this does not mean that they can therefore be dismissed without further discussion as yet another example of the ruling class's ingenuity in masking its repressive designs. It is not simply that social control takes many forms and that some are more damaging than others. The very concept of social control is highly problematic and, especially in arguments about the ideological function of social work, frequently so abstract as to lose all human intelligibility. Jordan has remarked that 'we are all potential agents of social control ... Most of life consists of attempting to influence the behaviour of others and to evade others' influence in about equal parts'.[18] But one does not get rid of a dilemma merely by showing that it is universal. A major premise of this book is that the labelling, stigmatising and controlling activities of official agencies, including those which employ social workers, are qualitatively different from those of everyday life and make a large contribution to our present mismanagement of delinquency. It is true that a decarceration policy in itself provides no absolute guarantee that juvenile offenders will be subjected to fewer or less harmful forms of social control; as Stan Cohen pointed out in a discussion of the potential of a decriminalisation strategy, 'someone still has to man the control machine'.[19] But there is more than one machine. It does matter what form social control takes; above all, it matters to those on the receiving end of the controlling enterprise. Incarceration in a CHE, detention centre or borstal is, in most cases, actually experienced as worse than being worked with and supported in an open, honest and comprehensible way in the community in which one has a stake and which is the source of one's most valued and positive experiences as well, perhaps, as of one's problems. This may be the place to add that we do not feel unduly apologetic about advocating a policy that admittedly contains an element of control or, at any rate, of regulation. It is impossible to imagine any developed society without a fairly elaborate apparatus of social control; and in the specific case of crime, it is important to remember, as some radical criminologists have belatedly recognised, that it is working-class people who are the main victims of working-class offending.

The best-known and most extended critique of the decarceration strategy is Scull's.[20] We have no argument with parts of his account. He is right to say that the rehabilitative efficacy of decarceration is at best unproved, at worst an illusion; it does not herald 'the advent of the therapeutic millenium'. He is right also to suggest (particularly in the case of mentally ill people discharged into the community) that decarceration often, in effect, means abandonment: ex-patients are expected to survive somehow in run-

down lodging houses, poor hostels and slum bed-sitters, in twilight ghettoes
deprived of normal social amenities, 'amidst neighbourhoods crowded with
prostitutes, ex-felons, addicts, alcoholics, and the other human rejects now
repressively tolerated by our society'.[21] One would like, perhaps, to have
that 'repressively tolerated' expanded somewhat, but no matter; Scull has
convincingly described the shortcomings of 'community care' for the
mentally ill, and his analysis applies to Britain as much as to the USA.
Unfortunately the same cannot be said of his analysis of the decarceration
of the criminal and delinquent; on this, indeed, he presents no convincing
British evidence at all, and admits as much.[22] He quotes figures from Florida
and California which demonstrate a great increase in the use of probation in
the late 1960s and early 1970s, but the figures for England and Wales,
which he does not quote, in fact show a significant decrease between 1971
and 1976, exactly the period in which, according to Scull, the decarceration
policy was being most enthusiastically implemented.[23] He is reduced to
saying that the population of prisons and borstals did not rise by as much,
proportionately, as the numbers potentially 'eligible' for imprisonment
between 1951 and 1972; but fining people rather than imprisoning them in
already overcrowded institutions can be counted as decarceration only by a
drastic extension of the meaning of the word. Scull predicts that 'the still
nascent English tendencies towards community corrections will be greatly
strengthened in years to come';[24] but, as we have noted, a diametrically
opposite trend is clear, at least in relation to juvenile offenders. Scull's
analysis of the decarceration of offenders is questionable on two points.
First, he can see nothing in 'decarceration, deinstitutionalisation, diversion
– under whichever name the process currently masquerades',[25] except a
new mode of 'domestic pacification and control'.[26] Even if one disregards
the exaggerated vocabulary, which invites the reader to equate the
regulation of ex-inmates of psychiatric hospitals with the 'pacification' of
insurgent Vietnamese villagers, this position is at the very least an
oversimplification. Scull, however, is not only a 'left idealist' but a vulgar
Marxist as well. For him, the real and sole motive behind the
implementation of decarceration schemes is financial:

> It reflects the structural pressures to curtail sharply the costly system of
> segregative control once welfare payments ... make available a viable
> alternative to management in an institution. Such structural pressures are
> greatly intensified by the fiscal crisis encountered in varying degrees at
> different levels of the state apparatus.[27]

Scull does recognise that 'noninstitutional approaches are less
immediately palatable when, instead of "sick" people, their object is
criminals and delinquents'. But he surely underemphasises the ideological
function of incarceration and of the criminal law as a whole. He offers no

explanation of the fact that while the 'fiscal crisis' has been more serious and prolonged in Britain than in the USA, decarceration has, on his own account, developed much more slowly in this country.[28] Obviously short-term economies can contribute, here and there, to certain kinds of 'decarceration': old people's homes can be, and are at present being, closed down without great political difficulty, and to a lesser extent the same applies to the closure of psychiatric hospitals. In the case of offenders, it is likely that there is some scope for decarceration on simple economic grounds in the USA where state welfare services are less developed and resistance to taxation apparently more organised. The truth is, however, that it is only by taking a God's eye-view of economic interests that one can account on these grounds for the militant carceral enthusiasm which is such a central feature of the public face of the present British government.

Scull, as quoted above, evidently thinks that decarceration and diversion are interchangeable terms. They are not used in this way in this book. The argument in this chapter has so far been quite explicitly about decarceration – which means what it says. Diversion refers to a different question: not how to get children out of institutions, but how to stop them being put into them in the first place. When we come to analyse the actual workings of the 1969 CYPA it will be clear that they have not only led to the incarceration of more and more children; they have also produced an increase in the far greater number of children officially labelled criminal. It is to this much larger group that diversion refers. We shall be suggesting methods of intervention which we believe could effectively divert juveniles from the officially constructed delinquent career which ends in custodial institutions. These methods are quite specific. In a necessarily more schematic way, we shall also outline a more radical form of the strategy of diversion, in which juveniles would be 'diverted' not just from custodial institutions but from the criminal justice system itself. (This was, of course, the sort of model envisaged in the 1965 White Paper.) In effect, this is a proposal for decriminalisation to be achieved less by freeing certain acts from legal sanctions than by substituting a different kind of sanction – one more akin to the customary processes of civil law than to those of the criminal code. But, as Cohen was perhaps hinting in his remark quoted above, this strategy raises the problem of social control in an acute form. It is time that we made clear where we stand in what is often referred to as the 'justice versus welfare' debate. We shall approach this question by an analysis of the nature of welfare institutions and of the criminal law, in which the ambiguous and contradictory elements of both will be emphasised. We shall then argue that our proposals for the development of community-based programmes for juvenile offenders, while necessarily containing some of the ambiguities of both welfare and law, nevertheless avoid their most stigmatising and punitive characteristics.

We shall look first at the area of welfare ideology and policy formation which is most relevant to this book, what has been called 'the child-saving movement'. A more general analysis of the nature of welfare agencies and institutions will follow. It might be as well to declare in advance that we shall be putting forward a qualified defence of some aspects of the 'welfare model'. In the past few years this has not been an intellectually respectable position; at any rate, it has been well outside any of the most fashionable sociological milieux. The whole concept of welfare and the institutions which are supposed to administer it have been enthusiastically assailed by advocates of the labelling perspective, radical deviancy theorists and their influential Marxist successors. The last, perhaps inevitably, eventually lost sight of the original object of their critique through straining after an all-embracing 'critical consciousness'.[29] More oddly, social workers themselves have internalised this sustained denunciation and gone in publicly for prolonged penitential self-flagellation, in *Case Con* particularly, but also in more recent texts such as Mike Simpkin's *Trapped within Welfare* (London: Macmillan, 1979). Our objection is not just that this position is paralysing and ultimately undermining for social workers; it is also that it seriously oversimplifies the nature of the historical contribution and present potential of the welfare model. Some characteristic oversimplifications appear in Anthony Platt's *The Child Savers*, an influential work whose title has become a convenient shorthand, knowing and dismissive, for a wide range of child care theorists and practitioners. We use the term in this book because it so neatly encapsulates a long tradition of endeavour. But is saving children necessarily a repressive and therefore undesirable activity?

Platt declares: 'The child-saving movement was not a humanistic enterprise on behalf of the working class against the established order.'[30] But who ever said it was? It was clearly not a revolutionary movement (which seems to be Platt's complaint); perhaps it was not even a socialist one – though it certainly gained the adherence of socialists. But it may still have been a 'humanistic enterprise' of some sort. The fact that social work has not produced a social revolution does not make it, as Platt and his co-believers suppose, a tool, witting or otherwise, of a ruling-class conspiracy. Platt himself identifies a number of themes characteristic of his late-nineteenth-century 'child savers' which do not self-evidently belong with the political right. Their anti-urbanism, their Arcadian yearnings, their sense of the corrupting power of industrial society, their romantic nostalgia for an image of childhood innocence – these are not ideologies which obviously serve the needs of a developing capitalist society. They suggest William Morris rather than any ruthless, hard-nosed industrialist. Platt himself notes sometimes the implicit or explicit radicalism of the 'child savers'. Thus 'Jane Addams wrote perceptively of the numerous ways in which children were being objectified by modern industrialism' but (without Platt's benefit of hindsight) 'resisted the logical consequences of her arguments which pointed to an indictment of capitalism'.[31] On the next page but one, we are told that 'one of the significant consequences of the child-saving movement was the successful reification of youth'. No doubt Platt knows what distinction he intends between 'objectifying' and 'reification' — the one the work of industrialism, opposed by the child savers, the other one of their significant achievements — but he does not explain it, and the distinction is not exactly transparent. Elsewhere he quotes Governor Altgeld of Illinois, whose endorsement of the child savers' reforms was part of a radical social critique: 'No government was ever overthrown by the poor, and we have nothing to fear from that source. It is the greedy and powerful that pull down the pillars of the state ... It is the criminal rich and their hangers-on who are the real anarchists of our time.'[32]

To be fair, Platt does comment explicitly on Altgeld's radicalism and his awareness of the shortcomings of the criminal law but he does not explain how a man with these views 'enthusiastically welcomed' the child savers' proposals, when it is so evident to Platt that these were 'new forms of social control' devised by 'the middle and upper classes ... to protect their power and privilege'.[33] Nor does he comment at all on this advocacy of the juvenile court by one of his chief villains, Frederick Wines:

> We make criminals out of children who are not criminals by treating them as if they were criminals ... We ought to have a 'children's court' in Chicago and we ought to have a 'children's judge' ... We want some place of detention for those children other than a prison ... No child ought to be tried unless he has a friend in court to look after his best interests.[34]

This sounds remarkably like an argument for a separate court (though Wines explicitly argued against a separate jurisdiction) for juveniles, on the ground that it would be more *just*. But justice, according to Platt, did not interest the child savers; they were supposedly interested only in treatment and the 'rehabilitative ideal'.

This account is of course one-sided. It is intended merely to show that the child-saving movement was not, as Platt argues (and, with the chance of an enlarged second edition, argues more vigorously), an enterprise conceived and promoted by a ruling class anxious to extend its control and domination. It is also clear that some child savers at least were more conscious of the fundamental inequities of the criminal law than some 'back-to-justice' enthusiasts today. Platt does acknowledge that 'the child savers were responsible for minor reforms in jails and reformatories'. Lest this seem excessively indulgent, he immediately adds that where they were most active and successful was 'in extending governmental control over a whole range of youthful activities which had been previously ignored or dealt with informally'.[35] While this was by no means the achievement of the child savers alone (as Platt recognises in the introduction to the second edition) it undoubtedly happened. One may wonder whether it was necessarily worse for the children concerned than the informal control or neglect they had encountered before, but it is nevertheless recognisably a phenomenon which is still with us, in the increasing numbers of children sucked into the ambit of official control since the 1969 CYPA. A large part of Platt's case is of course proved. Frederick Wines after all got it wrong: the juvenile court has in very obvious ways failed to produce justice for children. (What has not necessarily been disproved is the idea that something recognisable as justice is compatible with a policy of individualised sentencing.) However, Platt touches on a theme central to this book when he writes: ' "Delinquents" were increasingly committed to institutions on the grounds that their reformation was more likely if they were removed from "immoral" parents and a "vicious" environment.' It is again not self-evident that this is wrong. If one said 'vicious parents and an immoral environment' it would be quite easy to argue that this represented an enlightened and genuinely humanitarian policy. The present authors are not experts on late-nineteenth-century Chicago, but it seems possible that it was exactly that. But Platt is writing specifically of the juvenile court and of identified offenders and his example is a very clear case of the disastrous consequences of making 'reformation' the aim of a criminal justice system. Our present quandaries over juvenile justice represent one of the worst legacies of the positivist tradition in criminological and penal thought, of which, albeit in an idiosyncratic way, Platt's 'child savers' were pioneers. It is also clear that one of their most durable achievements has been the reliance on residential institutions as a means of reforming disorderly children.

The fuzziness of the dividing line between residential care and punitive custody was recognised early in the life of juvenile courts. 'There is often a very real deprivation of liberty', wrote Edward Lindsey, an early critic, quoted by Platt, of the juvenile court from the standpoint of a legal constitutionalist, 'nor is that fact changed by refusing to call it punishment or because the good of the child is stated to be the object'.[36] Residential institutions with a reformative or character-building intention were not, however, specifically the product of the child savers' efforts in the way that the juvenile court was. In one form or another, they had existed since the early nineteenth century, particularly as public schools for the (temporarily) disorderly younger sons of the wealthy. Evelyn Waugh said that prison could hold no terrors for anyone who had survived a public school education and, as Frank Musgrove has demonstrated, the early years of highly respectable public schools were marred by riots and disorder of an intensity now more readily associated with particularly heavy borstals.[37] In fact as Musgrove makes clear, the problem of controlling young people had been a concern of educationalists and social reformers for much longer than

Platt recognises – ever since steam power began to replace child power in manufacturing processes and more and more children fell outside the control of either the school or the workplace. It was not seen as a problem which was exclusive to the children of the dangerous classes: Arnold of Rugby was as concerned to generate a wholesome environment conducive to the repression of original sin in his proposals for reforming the public schools, as Mary Carpenter, the English pioneer of 'reformatory schools', ever was when she argued that the principles informing the regimes of institutions for delinquents should be those of good parenting.[38] The resemblances between our present reformatory schools, whose name changes more often than their nature, and our present public schools are more than fanciful. They have in common their architecture, their generally Arcadian location, their preoccupation with discipline and regularity, even their division into mutually competitive houses. Waugh's suggestion may indeed point to a necessarily hidden reason for the continued popularity in some circles of the institutions which are the direct descendants of Mary Carpenter's schools. If someone has personally experienced the drawn-out, dehumanising misery of a public school education (as described in innumerable autobiographies) and has with maturity come to realise that his school days were the happiest of his life – why should he not then suppose that a similar period of incarceration in a CHE (admittedly with shorter holidays) should prove equally beneficial to the unhappy miscreant in the dock?

All this at least suggests that there was some consistency in Victorian attitudes to deviance. Nineteenth-century penal reformers were prepared, with appropriate modifications, to apply the same exacting standards to themselves, or at least to their children, as they were to the children of the poor. In the late eighteenth century John Howard, the prison reformer, had in a similar manner subjected himself to the same stern regime as he desired for his ideal prisons.[39] But this consistency is more than a chance by-product of the engagement of the puritan conscience in social reform. It also indicates what was authentically radical in the child-saving movement. The early reformers of the juvenile justice system actually believed that every child, however deprived and powerless, was worth worrying about. In this sense, the movement *was* a 'humanistic enterprise', though not of course 'on behalf of the working class'. (Still it is a little unfair to blame the child savers for failing to anticipate Lenin's strategy for revolutionary change.) This radicalism, often only implicit but none the less real, is a neglected part of the 'welfare model' and it is possible to recognise it without compromising a position central to this book: that the aims of a criminal justice system should never be confused with those of therapy or reform. This tension is important in the argument which follows in which we shall attempt a summary of the issues in the present debates about the nature of welfare, with particular emphasis on social work.

Social work has come in for a good deal of punishment in the last few years. Some of this has no doubt been deserved. Much of the deserved criticism is a product of the tendency of social workers, and particularly social services departments in the immediate post-Seebohm period, to try to take on everything, with the inevitable result that they take on nothing effectively. One of the ways in which this book is meant to be helpful to social workers is in suggesting that in order to achieve change they must work towards a clearly defined target and very rigorously maintain a narrow, specific focus in their work. Otherwise, for example, there is nothing to prevent intermediate treatment programmes which start off with persistent juvenile offenders as their target group from gradually becoming more and more diffuse until they are merely one more part of the blanket of prevention spread in a stigmatising and suffocating way over the supposedly dangerous or at least irresponsible people in society. Much of the criticism of vague preventive work, which has been mounted by Bill Jordan in particular,[40] is in accord with the basic themes of this book. Indeed work directed at specific individuals and groups with the aims of preventing offending where none has yet occurred can be seen both as a threat to civil liberties and as likely to result in damaging and punitive outcomes. If the unlucky recipients of this pre-emptive supervision (un-authorised by any court and unspecified by any law) eventually do offend, in spite (or because) of all the efforts made on their behalf, they run the risk of being stigmatised almost as effectively in the social inquiry report of a disappointed social worker as they would be by a substantial record of previous convictions. There is good research evidence that the prevention of crime can best be achieved by the reduction of opportunities for its commission.[41] Social workers might therefore be better employed in encouraging shopkeepers to display their goods a little less temptingly, conducting campaigns for the use of steering column locks on cars, and working out effective methods of supervision with the police than in, so to speak, getting their retaliation in first with groups of allegedly pre-delinquent children. At most they might, as community workers, try to engage local residents in attempts to claim their social rights effectively with a view to bringing about some recognisable improvements in a neighbourhood's quality of life.

These strictures do not, however, necessarily imply a wholesale denunciation of social work or its practitioners. Preventive work of this vague and frequently prolonged kind is a clear instance of the abuse, or malpractice, of a set of ideals which are not in themselves by any means indefensible. Crudely, they are connected with a belief that the processes of the juvenile criminal justice system can be humanised, softened and even made more just by the intervention of social workers guided by values and assumptions which are in some ways at odds with those of the criminal law. But this belief may not be true. Bean, for example, has from the point of view of the 'justice' lobby launched a vigorous attack on the involvement of probation officers in the work of the courts. He quotes American studies which suggest that probation officers may be 'more punitive than judges' and suggests (on rather more tenuous evidence) that the same applies to Britain.[42] Bean's argument is weakened by exaggeration and unsupported statements, for example that 'probation officers invariably suggest to the courts who should, or who should not, be placed on probation and the courts invariably agree'.[43] Rather few practising probation officers would corroborate this claim and it is undoubtedly a wild overstatement. Nevertheless his basic argument that a concern with the rehabilitation of offenders is very far from being the same thing as a concern for leniency is important, as is his wider theme that offenders should not be sentenced to receive treatment or, in other terms, that rehabilitation should not become the aim of a criminal justice system. The evidence on whether social work does in practice moderate the harshness of the penal tariff is in fact somewhat contradictory. Hardiker, for instance, found that 'probation officers *are* crucial implementers of the reverse tariff, where individualistic recognition of the person is affirmed' and that 'treatment ideologies may be liberating'.[44] The 'reverse tariff' refers to probation officers' assessment of an offender's level of deprivation and hence of 'need'. In fact there is some evidence presented in a later chapter of this book that Bean, who is inclined to salute social workers as possible secret carriers of 'subterranean values', as opposed to his conformist and conservative probation officers, identified the wrong group as his main object of attack. Social workers appear to be somewhat more likely than probation officers to recommend custodial sentences for juveniles, a finding which may well damage the self-concept of both groups as well as the image the Conservative Party has traditionally had of the probation service as an altogether more tough-minded outfit than social services departments. This peculiarity to one side, the further finding that social workers are, for instance, less inclined to recommend supervision orders and more inclined to recommend care orders than magistrates are to make them is one which ought seriously to disturb social workers in any agency and calls for a clear and positive response. The truth is that in juvenile courts, at least, there is no evidence that the presence of social workers shifts sentencing practice towards humanitarianism or leniency. Most social workers would instinctively deny this, but more than a passionate denial is necessary. One is therefore reduced to saying that social workers *could* influence sentencing in a humanitarian direction. This can be more than a pious hope. In later chapters an attempt is made to outline a specific strategy which can enable social workers to become effective 'gate-keepers' within the juvenile justice system and to begin to divert children from custodial institutions and their often disastrous consequences.

Social workers who attend juvenile courts regularly often speak as if their main experience is of seeing injustice done without generally feeling able to intervene in the process. Its apparent inexorability, its massive calm, its smooth self-assurance, its arcane and complex rules, hallowed by a vague but ancient and powerful tradition – all these are features of the public face of the criminal law which so often seem to awe social workers into deferential anxiety. It is time now to consider the most obvious and most developed alternative to the 'welfare' model in juvenile justice – the idea that many of the problems and injustices which are evident at present could be removed by a return to the principles of classical justice, to the eighteenth century, to a strict sentencing tariff, to a recognition of the individual's right to punishment, or what you will. Stan Cohen has crisply summarised the recent history of the relationship between radical criminologists, psychiatrists and lawyers and given one view of just what it is the justice lobby is suggesting we should return to:

> Once upon a time it was 'radical' to attack law; then it became 'radical' to attack psychiatry. As we now rush back to the bewildered embrace of lawyers who always thought we were against them, we should remind ourselves just what a tyranny the literal rule of law could turn out to be.[45]

This is pretty much what social workers have always claimed – without finding ways of doing a great deal about it. And from one point of view, it seems to say all that needs to be said. Surely nothing could be clearer to a Marxist criminologist, for example, than that 'the law is, perhaps more clearly than any other cultural or institutional artifact, by definition a part of the "super-structure", adapting itself to the necessities of an infrastructure of productive forces and productive relations'.[46] Indeed Richard Quinney, in the italicised assertions with which he sets about the 'demystification of the criminal law', declares that 'criminal law is an instrument of the State and ruling class to maintain and perpetuate the existing social and economic order' and that 'crime control ... is accomplished through a variety of institutions and agencies established and administered by a governmental élite, representing ruling-class interests, for the purpose of establishing domestic order'.[47] This point of view is more or less taken for granted elsewhere in the same volume, *Critical Criminology*. Taylor, Walton and Young, for instance, attack 'Fabian criminology' in their introductory essay exclusively on the grounds that it is deeply incriminated by its associations with positivism and ignore what Fabianism might have to say about the law.[48] They do not, therefore, have to confront the argument that, with the exception of a few bad laws, the criminal code reflects a broad consensus about what kinds of behaviour should be prohibited and that the main problem with the law is that many people do not have adequate access to the services of its practitioners. In general, it is the case that until quite recently radical criminologists have been too preoccupied with attacking the positivist tradition and the welfare institutions it created to pay much attention to law or the state. Their analysis did not usually go much beyond David Matza's cloudy references to Leviathan. Where the deficiency was recognised, it tended to be met by grand assertions like Quinney's or the traditional references to the Marxist scriptures. The problem with this position for our present purposes is that once again, as with the comparable view of welfare, it leaves very little room for manœuvre. If the law is simply an instrument by which the ruling class maintains its power, if its pretensions to justice are a mask and a hypocrisy, then there is no point in arguing for anyone's access to legal advice to be improved, and attempts to bring more justice into the juvenile courts, for instance, are clear evidence of a laughable naïveté.

It will be argued that this position is at best an oversimplification, at worst a very dangerous kind of abstraction. It could leave its adherents with no basis on which to distinguish a state in which the government itself is ultimately subject to the rule of law (for example, Kenya) from one in which the law is whatever government says it is, according to its immediate convenience (for example, Amin's Uganda). The crucial importance of the status of law and its institutions is what is left out in characterisations of such states as dictatorships on the grounds that they do not have a two-party parliamentary system. But, first, the element of truth in the schematic Marxist view should be acknowledged. There is good evidence for the idea that the law is far from being an impartial mediator of social relations and that instead it weighs most heavily upon the most defenceless and is hardly brought to bear against the illegalities of the powerful and well-connected. This is not the same as saying that it is exclusively directed against the working class: the low level of prosecutions in the hidden economy of workplace fiddles and pilfering suggests that a section at least of the working class is relatively immune from the law's most rigorous applications. It makes more sense to see its main target as still being, as it was more explicitly in the nineteenth century, the 'dangerous classes' – unorganised labour or the unemployed, marginal, transient and easily stigmatised groups, the non-respectable workers and the undeserving poor. Within this group working-class children are likely to be (and, according to criminal statistics, are) especially vulnerable, since almost by definition they are disorderly and unorganised and require surveillance and control, if only for their own protection, and in general their illegal acts are fairly unsophisticated and highly visible. With this qualification, some of the muck-raking by radical criminologists has been very effective in exposing the double standards which inform the operation of the criminal law.

For instance, one can contrast the treatment at law of social security 'fiddlers' and illegal tax avoiders. In 1972–3

there were only 17 prosecutions for false income-tax returns (as against some 80,000 cases settled without prosecution). But there were 12,000 prosecutions over that period by the Department of Health and Social Security for fraudulent claims by its (largely working-class) clients. The amount recovered in these 12,000 cases amounted to less than 15 per cent of the amount recovered by the Inland Revenue in its seventeen income-tax prosecutions.[49]

It appears that tax fraud has already been largely decriminalised, unless perpetrated on a truly gradiose scale. The penalties imposed by the criminal law are often by no means related to the damage done by an offence. Sometimes the absence of guilty intent appears to be the crucial mitigating factor, for example when one considers the nugatory fines imposed on companies whose negligence or disregard of safety or fire regulations results in the deaths of employees and compares the relative weakness of the fire and factory inspectorates with the strength of the police. But it is the police, we are constantly told, who require further strengthening and while crime remains a major preoccupation of the media there is a deafening silence over the far greater volume of death and injury which results from illegalities in the workplace. Evidently the police are meant to protect the public only from specific kinds of law-breaking. Similarly it is clear that while the sums of money abstracted from the community through underdeclared and illegal excess profits almost certainly exceed those lost in burglaries and thefts, the perpetrators of such business frauds are not subjected to the same penal sanctions as their more modest, but also more visible, working-class counterparts. The most spectacular evidence on this comes from the USA,[50] but it is probable that this is because of that country's more developed anti-trust legislation rather than because British businessmen operate with more exalted ethical standards. In the nature of things it is impossible to be sure how typical or otherwise are the occasional glimpses we are allowed, in spectacular cases of local government corruption or company fraud, of 'the unpleasant and unacceptable face of capitalism', of normal business practice; the record on health and safety at work does not in many cases suggest that its usual, everyday face is especially pleasant or acceptable. At a more anecdotal level, a week's perusal of any newspaper will provide an instance of differential treatment at the hands of a judge of a respectable citizen driven (by punitive taxes or a nagging wife) to bankruptcy or fraud and an evidently disorderly one wilfully and wickedly engaging in robbery or theft. Really wild discrepancies, like the forty-two-year sentence on George Blake and Anthony Blunt's immunity from prosecution, even arouse comment in the *Guardian's* letter page. Nevertheless, we are assured, all is fundamentally well, or at least for our own good; normal service is quickly resumed after the public scapegoating of a few crooked local government officials and corrupt senior policemen and the criminal law is restored to its usual and proper preoccupation with the crimes of the disorderly working class, and particularly of its children. The result is that of boys born in 1946, 15–20 per cent whose fathers were manual workers had been convicted of at least one offence by the age of 17, compared with 10 per cent from white-collar homes and only 5 per cent whose fathers were of the professional or salaried class.[51]

It is the children who are most at risk. It is juveniles and young adults who have supplied the media and – in a complex process of action and reaction – the police, sentencers and welfare agencies with their long series of postwar 'folk devils', from teddy boys to punks. Each new style has been subjected to fascinated scrutiny and generally been judged as the ultimate symptom of national decline, the degeneracy of youth, the failure of progressive educational methods, the undermining of parental authority, and so forth. Although their offences are overwhelmingly concerned with property and are modest in scale, it is the violence allegedly associated with these youth cultures which has preoccupied the media, penal policy makers and official agencies of control. Since the mid-sixties, at least, football 'hooligans' have been the most consistent and reliable folk devils, since however much the styles of dress have changed, working-class boys (and girls) have continued to assemble, most obviously and in the greatest numbers, at football matches. Cage-like fencing separating the crowd or sections of it from the pitch is now commonplace. Even ten years ago it was thought an undesirably oppressive measure, suitable perhaps for volatile Latin American crowds who were used to oppression anyway, but hardly for British conditions. Young football supporters are shepherded and policed all the way from their homes to the ground and back again and the massive police presence which is now taken for granted at big matches in itself generates delinquency. Many of the characteristic 'hooligan' offences – breach of the peace, insulting words or behaviour, disorderly conduct, obstructing the police, making an affray (the last a very serious charge) – are in practice only offences if the police define them as such. They are offences without victims, in the normal sense; they belong to the shadowy realm of disorder, in which a decision about whether an offence has been committed is by no means clear-cut. Here there are no real 'facts of the case', no material or forensic evidence, no clear definition of when behaviour becomes illegal; everything depends on subjective judgements, on context, on mood, on perceived dangerousness, on stereotypes and on gut reactions. This is not necessarily to condemn the police; although it is clear that their unremitting attention can sometimes provoke serious incidents and very often provokes verbal abuse, it is not clear that, with hooliganism so well established as a central social problem of youth, they could act otherwise. Certainly any change is likely to be gradual. The point is that from the time ten years ago when the police took to removing, under no known law, the bootlaces of skinhead supporters before they boarded football trains, to today's routine and accepted marshalling of crowds and assertive control by the police of the streets surrounding grounds, the behaviour of young football supporters has been a major focus of an offical preoccupation with youthful disorder. The history of this preoccupation and the possible reasons for it, have been well dealt with elsewhere.[52] For our purposes it is offered as the most striking example in recent years of the mobilisation of the criminal law against juveniles – not in the cause of detecting and punishing specific infractions but in the cause of social order, surveillance and regulation. It has been a most potent example, the classic and by now traditional point of reference for all who have argued over the past ten years for something to be done about the disorderly youth of today. It has had an incalculable effect upon the development of juvenile penal policy, the sentencing practices of juvenile courts and the responses of official agencies to the 'rising tide of juvenile crime'.

If, then, the law is less than it pretends to be and, far from dealing impartially with all classes, weighs most heavily upon the weakest, most visible and most vulnerable – what then remains of the 'back-to-justice' argument? Early in this chapter it was suggested that sentencing in the juvenile court had lost all sense of proportion in some cases. This can only be recovered by the partial restoration of principles of sentencing which are founded on the principles of law. It is quite clear that to speak of law is not to speak of justice. There are serious problems in advocating a sentencing policy based on 'just deserts in an unjust society'[53] and to advocate a return to the eighteenth century is clearly to advocate a return to a penal code of unbridled savagery and inequity. Nevertheless, the historian E. P. Thompson, at the end of a book which shows clearly how little justice there was in the eighteenth century, draws 'conclusions which may be different from those which some readers expect' and argues eloquently that 'the rule of law itself' is 'an unqualified human good'.[54] He has since shown what he means with reference to present events in equally eloquent attacks on the administrative convenience of rigging the membership of juries. His theoretical arguments are relevant to the issues dealt with in this book and will be taken up later. But, first, the idea that the law is an instrument of ruling-class oppression needs to be countered by some evidence rather than mere assertion. Most social workers dealing with offenders know anyway that, whatever radical criminologists write and they themselves might like to believe, working-class people are the main victims of crime as well as (supposedly) its main exponents. David Downes, in the course of a succinct critique of the excesses of the Marxist school of recent criminology, quotes some research findings which support this intuition. They come from a summary of research carried out for the 1967 President's Commission on Law Enforcement and the Administration of Justice in the USA: 'The risk of victimisation is highest among the lower-income groups for all Index offences except homicide, larceny and vehicle theft; it weighs most heavily on non-whites for all Index offences except larceny.' Downes comments:

> Moreover, even the larceny finding relates only to sums of $50 or more:
> if all larcenies had been included, that finding too may have tallied with
> the other offences in its distribution of victims, since the lower one's in-
> come, the less one is likely, presumably, to be in possession of sums of
> over $50. Indeed, this is partially borne out by figures showing median
> net property losses by income group, which for whites shows the
> average for those whose incomes were under $6,000 was $34, while for
> those whose income exceeded that sum it was $30, a result that could
> have occurred only if the lower-income group experienced a far higher
> rate of larceny of sums under $50 than the higher income group'.[55]

Downes is arguing against one of the higher lunacies of the Marxist school,
that an increase in crime reflects a rejection by sections of the working class
of the existing distribution of property. But these results equally show that
the working class has a considerable apparent interest in the enforcement of
the law. This applies to areas in which it is at present enforced – such as
petty thefts and burglaries – as well as to areas in which it is not – such as
breaches of safety regulations at work. For these figures show 'a massive
infliction of misery on those least able to protect themselves', and it is not
only the material losses which cause the misery. The effect of petty criminal
activity in a working-class neighbourhood can be utterly divisive,
producing anxiety, suspicion, isolation and unhappiness and undermining
any possibilities of creative collective action. It will be argued in a later
chapter that there are more constructive ways of dealing with juvenile
offending, at least, than having automatic recourse to the blunt instrument
of the criminal law which of its nature is impersonal and abstract and can
take no account of the human reality of an offence, as experienced by either
victim or offender. For the moment the point should be clear: that whatever
the ultimate social or economic basis of the law it cannot be supposed, in
practice, simply to protect the property of the rich. Potentially at least, it can
also be a source of protection to the poor. And, of course, these figures take
account only of property offences; the victims of offences of violence or
sexual offences are not usually strangers to the offenders. The idea that
whatever the irregularities of its operation, the existence of the law is in the
interests of ordinary people and that a community-based vigilante force,
perhaps modelled on recent initiatives in Northern Ireland, would not
necessarily be preferable, at least deserves serious consideration.

Is the law, then, more than a mask for the maintenance of ruling-class
power? E. P. Thompson's *Whigs and Hunters* is a study of the notorious
Black Act of 1723, which prescribed capital punishment for over fifty
distinct offences, mainly connected with poaching and what would now be
called armed trespass. Its scope was such that it 'constituted in itself a

complete and extremely severe criminal code'.[56] It was intended, as Thompson shows, to protect the newly acquired domains of the Hanoverian Whigs against the assertion of traditional rural rights – to take game or fish, to cut turf or gather wood, to quarry stone. It was administered with the aid of government informers and a deliberate carelessness about the normal rules of evidence. It seems, therefore, as likely as any Act of Parliament in history to bring discredit upon the law and to expose its pretensions to impartiality and neutrality as a hollow sham. Thompson is clear that it was 'a bad law, drawn by bad legislators and enlarged by the interpretations of bad judges'. But even to say this is to acknowledge that all laws are not equally bad, from the standpoint of the ruled, which is what one would suppose if law is simply 'a mystifying and pompous way in which class power is registered and executed'.[57] For Thompson, law is much more than this. He argues that 'law was often a definition of actual agrarian *practice*' and cannot, therefore, be separated off from the actual working life of a community and deposited in a notional 'super-structure'. Secondly, law

> has its own characteristics, its own independent history and logic of evolution ... Moreover, people are not as stupid as some structuralist philosophers suppose them to be. They will not be mystified by the first man who puts on a wig. It is inherent in the especial character of law, as a body of rules and procedures, that it shall apply logical criteria with reference to standards of universality and equity.

Thus, while the law has a function as ideology, in legitimating and thus reinforcing the power of a ruling class, it must do so in terms of its own logic and its own proclaimed standards:

> If the law is evidently partial and unjust, then it will mask nothing, legitimize nothing, contribute nothing to any class's hegemony. The essential precondition for the effectiveness of law, in its function as ideology, is that it shall display an independence from gross manipulation and shall seem to be just.[58]

And even, on occasions, actually be just. The paradox is that while this reinforces the existing power by according it legitimacy, it is also clearly in the interests of the ruled. It was suggested earlier that a crucial question to ask of any society is whether its government exercises arbitrary power or is, at least in principle, bound by the rule of law. The answer will inform us of the presence or absence of civil rights in that society. This is why the principles of law, for all their frequent absurdities of expression (which can make social workers very impatient), are a central cultural achievement, and one which needs to be defended against attempts to erode it in the name of administrative efficiency. It is their insistence that legal principles matter which social workers should take from exponents of the 'back-to-justice' school. It is a far clearer message than any which has yet emerged from Marxist criminologists, with their characteristically undeveloped references to such concepts as 'socialist diversity' and 'socialist legality'. It is a message which has particular relevance to the juvenile court in which, often for laudable humanitarian reasons, the principles of due judicial process have been most compromised and a sense of proportion in sentencing is least evident.

In Chapter 4 we demonstrate that children are generally made subject to care orders for offending very early in their delinquent careers. Our evidence is that this is usually on the recommendation of social workers. The care order is not only, on any comparative basis, a heavy sentence in itself: it can also, in effect, create for a child a subsequent institutional career. What seems to be involved here is a confusion of welfare and justice considerations. A child is recommended for a care order under Section 7(7), not in the great majority of cases because he evidently requires the kind of care which only the social services department can provide but because there are enough problems in his background, or his family is disorderly enough or well enough known to official agencies, for the social worker to conclude that it would be as well to obtain the considerable powers over a child which a care order gives. Since it is available as one sentencing option among the available alternatives, why not bring it in sooner rather than later to be on the safe side? The problem is that the care order is also an element in a sentencing tariff. It is not simply a welfare measure which gives the social worker useful powers (no irony intended); it is the last, most extreme sentence available to the court within the local authority child care system. Beyond are only the frankly penal measures of detention centre and borstal. Of course, it does not always work like this; courts continue, in general, to follow social workers' recommendations, and social workers often hold on to the children in care, with a series of recommendations for conditional discharges. What does seem to have a crucial effect is the child's placement during the care order: children placed in CHEs, the local authority's ultimate custodial resource, appear to be more likely than others to be sent to detention centre or borstal when they reoffend. They are placed in CHEs not because they are more delinquent than the rest but because they have more 'welfare problems'. Thus definitions made on the basis of one set of criteria can have a profound and surely unintended effect on subsequent decisions based on quite different criteria. Consideration of a child's needs or problems is reinterpreted by the juvenile court as an indication of his criminality.

A renewed sense of the importance of basic legal principles in juvenile justice is necessary if this elision of welfare-oriented intervention into punitive sentencing is to be stopped. Equally, there is a clear need for social workers to be better informed about, and pay more attention to, what the law actually says. Examination of local authority records shows that a surprising number of children are in care illegally; others are made subject to care orders when they are already in care; still others appear in the records under the wrong section of the Act. Social workers are frequently uncomfortable and inept in court, ignorant of or uninterested in the rules of procedure or evidence. It may be here that magistrates' more favourable opinions of the probation service are grounded.[59] The point is that if social workers themselves are uncertain of the law, and perhaps attach no great importance to it anyway, they will hardly be in a position to ensure that the legal rights of children are safeguarded. Since children are represented by a solicitor in only about 20 per cent of all cases[60] there will generally be nobody else in court to do the safeguarding. Anyone who has spent any time in a juvenile court, with its half-hearted attempts at informality and its sudden lapses into confusing legalism, will have noticed that children and their parents are often utterly confused about what is happening to them.

Thompson's theoretical position on the nature of law and the criticisms from the justice lobby of the dominance of the rehabilitative ideal, at the expense of legal principles, have, then, important implications for social workers operating within the juvenile justice system. They point to the importance of remaining sensitive to the very straightforward idea of fairness and to the rather less straightforward rules and procedures which have evolved within the law to help ensure that that idea stands some chance of being translated into reality. But the following questions remain. Where can change be most readily achieved? At what point is the existing system weakest? Where is there most room for manoeuvre? Not, in the present context, within the law itself. All the important forces are at present working against decriminalisation, against leniency or understanding, against any change which could be interpreted as a softening of official attitudes towards juvenile deviance. The next piece of legislation on juvenile offenders is far more likely to represent a negation of the principles behind the 1969 CYPA than an attempt to reinstate them. Yet the system is full of holes. The law itself may at the moment be unalterable, except in the direction of greater punitive zeal; in any case, changes in the law take time. The process by which the formal legislation is given actual life, the system which turns social policy into social reality, is by contrast rich in possibilities for change. A complex process of definition, discrimination and decision-making must be undergone before any child appears before a juvenile court. When he does get there what happens to him depends largely upon what both social workers and sentencers see as the range of choices open to them. It is in these areas − modification of the administrative processes which precede a court hearing, and the development of credible alternatives to the sentencing options now available − that the possibilities of change are clearest and the prospects

most hopeful. The theoretical position established in this chapter informs
the specific strategies, research findings and recommendations for practice
which occupy the rest of the book. Throughout we emphasise the
importance of setting very clear, limited and specific objectives. Without
these anything can be justified in the name of rehabilitation or treatment –
with disastrous results. But to discover your objectives you must first know
what is going on. The next two chapters deal with the theory and practice
of research in the juvenile justice system.

REFERENCES: CHAPTER 2

1   Foucault, M., *Discipline and Punish* (London: Allen Lane, 1977), esp. pp. 264–70.
2   Millham, S., Bullock, R. and Hosie, K., *Locking Up Children* (London: Saxon House, 1978), p. 28.
3   Cornish, D. B. and Clarke, R. V. G., *Residential Treatment and Its Effects on Delinquency* (London: HMSO, 1975), pp. 16–17.
4   Quoted in Cornish and Clarke, op. cit., p. 32.
5   ibid., p. 32.
6   ibid., p. 28. Cf. Millham, Bullock and Hosie, op. cit., pp. 48–9.
7   The title of a 1970 Home Office publication on the type of regime appropriate to the new CHEs.
8   *Prison Statistics 1977* (London: HMSO, 1978), p. 164.
9   ibid.
10 Tutt, N., editor's 'Introduction', in *Alternative Strategies for Coping with Crime* (Oxford and London: Blackwell and Martin Robertson, 1978), p. 11.
11 *Prison Statistics 1978* (London: HMSO, 1979).
12 *Sending Young Offenders Away* (London: leaflet published by New Approaches to Juvenile Crime, 1979).
13 Hall, S., *et al.*, *Policing the Crisis* (London: Macmillan, 1979), p. 323.
14 See Packman, J., *The Child's Generation* (Oxford: Blackwell, 1975), pp. 121–2.
15 Foucault, op. cit., pp. 276–82.
16 Young, J., 'Left idealism, reformism and beyond', in NDC/CSE, *Capitalism and the Rule of Law* (London: Hutchinson, 1979), pp. 13–16.
17 Ignatieff, M., *A Just Measure of Pain* (London: Macmillan, 1978), p. 220.
18 Jordan, B., *Freedom and the Welfare State* (London: Routledge & Kegan Paul, 1976), p. 55.
19 Cohen, S., 'Manifestos for action', in Bailey, R. and Brake, M. (eds), *Radical Social Work* (London: Edward Arnold, 1975), p. 83.
20 Scull, A., *Decarceration* (Englewood Cliffs, NJ: Prentice-Hall, 1977).
21 ibid., p. 2.
22 ibid., p. 57.
23 ibid., pp. 47–56, and *Report on Probation and After-Care Statistics 1975 and 1976* (London: Home Office Statistical Department, 1977, restricted publication), p. 2.
24 Scull, op. cit., p. 59.
25 ibid., p. 41.
26 ibid., p. 134.
27 ibid., p. 152.
28 Matthews, R., 'Decarceration and the fiscal crisis', in NDC/CSE, op. cit., p. 105.
29 See Rock, P., 'The sociology of crime', in Downes, D. and Rock, P. (eds), *Deviant Interpretations* (London: Martin Robertson, 1979), pp. 52–84.

30 Platt, A., *The Child Savers* (Chicago, Ill.: University of Chicago Press, 2nd edn 1977).
31 ibid., p. 97.
32 Quoted in ibid., p. 125.
33 ibid., p. xx.
34 ibid., p. 132.
35 ibid., p. 99.
36 ibid., p. 158.
37 Musgrove, F., *Youth and the Social Order* (London: Routledge & Kegan Paul, 1964), p. 47.
38 See Platt, op. cit., pp. 63–4.
39 Ignatieff, op. cit., pp. 50–1.
40 See Jordan, B., *Poor Parents* (London: Routledge & Kegan Paul, 1974) and *Freedom and the Welfare State*, op. cit.
41 See Mayhew, P., Clarke, R. V. G., Sturman, A. and Hough, J. M., *Crime as Opportunity* (London: HMSO, 1976).
42 Bean, P., *Rehabilitation and Deviance* (London: Routledge & Kegan Paul, 1976), p. 111.
43 ibid., p. 80.
44 Hardiker, P., 'The role of probation officers in sentencing', in Parker, H. (ed.), *Social Work and the Courts* (London: Edward Arnold, 1979), p. 133.
45 Cohen, S., 'Guilt, justice and tolerance', in Downes and Rock (eds), op. cit., p. 41.
46 Thompson, E. P., *Whigs and Hunters* (Harmondsworth: Penguin, 1977), p. 259.
47 Quinney, R., 'Crime control in capitalist society', in Taylor, I., Walton, P. and Young, J. (eds), *Critical Criminology* (London: Routledge & Kegan Paul, 1975), p. 199.
48 Taylor, I., Walton, P. and Young, J., 'Critical criminology in Britain: review and prospects', in Taylor, Walton and Young (eds), op. cit., pp. 9–14.
49 ibid., p. 32.
50 See, for instance, Pearce, F., *Crimes of the Powerful* (London: Pluto Press, 1976).
51 Douglas, J. W. B. *et al.*, 'Delinquency and social class', in Carson, W. G. and Wiles, P. (eds), *Crime and Delinquency in Britain* (London: Martin Robertson, 1971), pp. 91–8.
52 See, for example, Ingham, R. *et al.*, 'Football Hooliganism' (London: Inter-Action Imprint, 1978).
53 See Cohen, S., in Downes and Rock (eds), op. cit., pp. 36–9 for a discussion of this question.
54 Thompson, op. cit., p. 266.
55 Downes, D., 'Praxis makes perfect', in Downes and Rock (eds), op. cit., p. 13.
56 Radzinowicz, L., *A History of English Criminal Law and Its Administration from 1750* (London: Stevens, 1948), quoted in Thompson, op. cit., pp. 22–3.
57 Thompson, op. cit., p. 267.
58 ibid., pp. 262–3.
59 See, for instance, Priestley, P., Fears, D. and Fuller, R., *Justice for Juveniles* (London: Routledge & Kegan Paul, 1977), p. 88.
60 Anderson, R., *Representation in the Juvenile Court* (London: Routledge & Kegan Paul, 1978), p. 66.

3

Labelling and Social Work

It is no more possible to conduct atheoretical research than it is to practise social work without a theory, however unarticulated. In this chapter we therefore provide a brief account of our broader theoretical perspective on the object of detailed study – the juvenile criminal justice system. We attempt to situate this position within recent developments in criminological thought, with particular emphasis on what has come to be known as the 'labelling perspective'. This is appropriate because our interest is primarily in the workings of the juvenile justice system rather than in the peculiarities of juvenile offenders themselves, and it was precisely their insistence on the central importance of official agencies in defining and creating deviance which was (or seemed to be) new in the writings of labelling theorists like Howard Becker and his successors. It was this, also, which made the labelling perspective seem so relevant and appealing to social work practitioners: it was saying something about them. It held out the promise of new ways of understanding one's own work and the work of one's agency. We shall argue that this promise was flawed by the failure of the labelling perspective to take adequate notice of the inevitable continuities between the historical roots of welfare agencies and their present activities. Our present mismanagement of juvenile offending is not the product of the incompetence or malevolence of social workers; it has a long and formidable pedigree.

Those who concern themselves with research into delinquency find themselves in the middle of the theoretical equivalent of Spaghetti Junction. The ground here is confused, crossed with tracks from many separate and interconnected disciplines and concerns. Stan Cohen has given an outline of the relationship between positivist criminology and the new deviancy theorists in the British context, illuminating the development within sociology of an approach to the study of crime which was strongly critical of the traditional criminological approach, mainly for its almost total concentration on the causative factors of crime.[1] The objects of study for the traditional criminologists were, predictably, convicted criminals and the method was (more or less) the identification and description of pathological psychological or sociological characteristics.

The motivations of these traditional criminologists were diverse but essentially pragmatic. They were concerned not so much with the development of a perspective which located crime, its functions and its causes in the overall framework of society, but more with a pragmatic, everyday sense of the problems at the 'sharp end' of the criminal justice and penal system. Their individual concerns ranged, perhaps, from a desire to free society from the excesses of criminal behaviour to a desire to discover humanistic techniques which would free the convict from his own criminal behaviour and its consequences. Perversely, it is the latter approach, which shows some concern for the 'criminal' as an individual, rather than the former, which presents him purely as a threat to social order, that has proved the more dangerous in the long term. This may to some extent be explained by the fact that for the former, those concerned with social order, the nature and control of that order at least remained an accessible issue. For those concerned with more humane treatment of offenders, however, questions concerning social order tended to become obscured and submerged by those of pathology, personal development, need and treatment.

The development within British sociology of a thoroughgoing critique of traditional criminology did not take place in isolation. It was preceded by and developed from a period in which British sociology was heavily influenced by a succession of transatlantic imports. Perhaps the most influential and contentious of these American developments, and one which has been acknowledged in British social work as much as in sociology, is 'labelling theory'. Far from being a coherent theory, it is in fact a diverse and often conflicting series of perspectives developed, in large part, in reaction to the dominance in American sociology for many years of structural functionalism and related approaches. These focused on an analysis of the overall structures of society and were concerned with the development of sociology as an 'objective' science sharing common procedures and principles with the 'natural' sciences. A fundamental division (in American sociology at least) may be characterised as the opposition between those theorists who see the proper concern of sociology as the investigation of the social structures and institutions which constrain and determine the behaviour of individuals and thereby constitute 'society', and those who think of society as being created and constituted through the interaction of individuals, and for whom the proper concerns of sociology therefore centre on the creation and maintenance of social structures through the actions and interaction of individuals. In what follows we shall refer to the first group as 'functionalists' and to the second group as 'action theorists'.

Whilst American sociology was dominated for much of the earlier part of the century by the functionalists, the approach of the action theorists (such as G. H. Mead) did maintain a following. It is from this base, and particularly from symbolic interactionism, that the resistance to the hegemony of the functionalists developed. Initially the action theorists were seen as occupying a somewhat peripheral field of social sciences, on the borders of sociology and psychology and to some extent forming a bridge between the two — not that any of the mainstream theorists then, as now, felt there to be any need for such a bridge. Meanwhile the functionalists were occupying (if not creating) the space of sociology as a scientific discipline, located in a box separate from, but contiguous with, that of the other 'new' science, psychology, both of these being a little below the older natural sciences in a conceptual hierarchy of science. The movement of the action theorists from a peripheral position to the mainstream of sociology, where they challenged the established structural and functionalist theorists, could be seen as a limited politicisation of American sociology, although it would be more accurate to see it as an increased awareness of the inherently political nature of all social theorising.

It is no coincidence that this recognition of and conflict about the political significance and relevance of American sociology was paralleled by growing cracks in the hitherto consensual facade of the USA itself. The cracks came from an increasing awareness that all was neither well nor as it appeared to be in the land of golden opportunity. (Whilst the depression of the 1920s had shattered the security of many Americans, it had been seen as an almost completely external and abstract disaster that could be thought of as hitting all Americans, rich stock marketeers whose shares collapsed as much as the already impoverished.) It was beginning to be recognised in the 1960s that certain sections of American society suffered degrees of impoverishment and degradation as a result neither of their own actions or inaction, nor of those of external (malevolent) forces, but rather as a result of the day-to-day practices of their fellow American citizens.

The substantive core of labelling theory was by no means a staggeringly new theoretical development. That the measures society takes to control deviance may in fact exacerbate that deviance had long been acknowledged, albeit in less organised, non-professional contexts. Geoff Pearson[2] cites criticisms made of the idea of workhouses at the time of the Poor Law Amendment Act which refer explicitly to the danger not only of contamination, i.e. that those in the workhouse through no fault of their own might, through association, come to adopt the standards of those there through their own indolence, but also of identification: that reception into a workhouse might so demoralise people as to render them unable to extricate themselves from their predicament and thus liable to identify with the stereotyped inmate of the workhouse, thereby further removing the possibility of 'recovery'. What was new was that this perspective was being to some extent legitimated by its acceptance as a proper area of sociology, as part, ironically, of a scientific discipline (ironically because the status of sociology as a scientific discipline was desired by the functionalists against whom labelling theory was reacting rather than by the action theorists themselves). Furthermore, labelling theory became the focus of research which examined the interactional processes by which deviance is socially constituted.

This research was characterised by its focus on 'marginal' forms of crime, the more esoteric forms of deviance. There had previously been two main approaches to deviance in society: the specifically criminological and that of the functional theorists. The criminologists tended to accept without question official definitions of crime and criminality. The objects of their studies were convicted criminals. They either ignored or were ignorant of those cases that could be described as marginal, but which belied the taken for grantedness of their approach. There was no analysis of the practices of the control agencies, of the possibility of wrongful conviction, of the disproportionate representation of the working and impoverished classes amongst the clients of the control agencies, of the temporal and cultural variability of laws and sentencing practices.

The traditional schools of criminology certainly generated plenty of research, but research of a highly uncritical nature. Although they generally displayed a conscientious regard for the sophistications and qualifications of 'scientific' research technique, their aim remained the location of the causes of crime in the physiological, psychological or sociological pathology of the individual. For many of the functionalists, deviance and crime seemed to represent a rather awkward piece of the jigsaw of the 'system' that they were attempting to construct. Collins comments of the functionalist approach that it consists of assuming

> that whatever is, is good, and trying to justify it instead of stating the conditions under which particular arrangements exist. The notion of what society 'needs most' is a value judgement, not an explanatory concept. It does not need any particular arrangement. It simply gets whatever the existing social forces produce.[3]

Whilst Collins's comment would seem to be aimed at the structural functionalism of Talcott Parsons rather than at functionalism in general, it is true that functionalist theories cannot be either critical or supportive of any particular social arrangement.

Functionalists such as T. H. Marshall or Wilensky and Lebeaux[4] may talk in general terms of social equality and inequality, but they are unable to locate these in terms of the interests and conflicts, the practices and understandings of individuals and classes in society. They are unable to render an account of the broad structures and processes of society which is meaningful and informative for the members of that society. This point may be clarified with reference to the work of Merton, one of the few recent functional theorists who has attempted to come to grips with the thorny problems presented by a study of deviance in society.

Merton begins by characterising societies in terms of culturally approved goals and the means available for achieving those goals. This leads to this simple matrix:

		Culturally approved goals	
		Accepts	Rejects
Culturally approved means	Accepts	A	B
	Rejects	C	D

Individuals may adapt to these culturally approved goals either by accepting or rejecting them. Those who accept both goals and means (cell A) adapt by conforming. Those who accept the means, but reject the goals (cell B), for example they go to church on Sundays but are not quite clear why, adapt by ritualising. Those who reject the means but accept the goals (cell C), for example the student who wants to pass his finals and so cheats in the examination, adapt by innovating. For the final cell (D), those who reject both goals and means, Merton identifies two modes of adaptation: first retreatism, for example the hippies of the 1960s who simply dropped out; and secondly rebellion, for example the revolutionary who seeks to institute new means and goals in society.[5] This account of deviance, whilst it looks neat, is hardly satisfactory. It is a fine example of abstract theorising. Whilst the five modes of adaptation could be useful to an abstract structural account, one suspects that it would be difficult to find individuals who fitted these categories. This is not just because of an absence of research. It is because of a basic defect of functional theory, namely that it hinges on the existence in society of a series of norms and values (the cultural approval or disapproval of any given means or goals) without being able to offer any account of how these norms and values come to be constituted and changed through the actions of individuals.

It was in reaction to theories such as these that the labelling perspective and what Pearson has aptly named 'misfit sociology'[6] developed its own theoretical concerns. It was a reaction against the positivist domination of criminological research and the hidden politics of functionalism. Although labelling theory was politically 'a turning of the guns of social science on to the establishment', the shells that were to be fired seemed to be aimed at establishment personnel rather than at strategic points in the structure. Functionalism legitimated what existed; criminology provided cures for recidivists. Labelling theorists claimed, justifiably, to have radical implications for social and penal policy. Their reaction against positivist head-counting research (as much a source of stigmatising labels as the actions of the control agents who enforced those definitions) and a vaguely phenomenological stance, linked with Weberian notions of *verstehen*, directed labelling theorists to more radical and contentious research methodology, using participant observation and qualitative rather than quantitative research instruments. In keeping with the mood of the 1960s the focus of the research was on 'the moment', the present, and here and now.[7] In focusing on the moment, however, labelling theory lost sight of history. With ammunition acquired at the level of individual confrontations between hapless definees and hostile definers of reality and the minutiae of their interaction, it was inevitable that the guns appeared to be aimed at these interactions rather than at the policies which sustained them and the structure within which they existed. They wished to appreciate the situation of the deviant; they left that of the control agent largely unexplored. Labelling theory's explanations cast control agents in unfamiliar and unwelcome roles, holding them responsible for decisions about which they felt they had little choice, under pressure as they were from organisational and situational contingencies. Labelling theory's usefulness to those it defined as control agents was further reduced by its tendency to research the more orderly and less threatening deviants, schizophrenics, delinquents and drug takers, criminals without victims. There was no research into the subjects of conventional criminology, murderers or psychopaths, those whose behaviour, however it was socially defined, appeared to have very real effects on the lives and well-being of others.

Given the social and political climate in which labelling theory was engendered it is not strange that it should have so weighted the balance between a 'deviant' act and its subsequent definition towards the definition, the degradation ceremony. Its political associations were with movements in the interests of structurally deviant, disadvantaged groups in society, for whom the ascription of deviance was arbitrary, more a question of one's colour, the neighbourhood one came from, even one's marital status, than of anything one might actually have done. It was for these groups that the political thrust of labelling seems to have been more successful, the deprived rather than the depraved.

Pearson's 'misfit sociology' was in many ways characteristic of the 1960s. Functionalist sociology had begun to identify the coming of an age of affluence and envisaged the possibility of an onion-shaped society, with a very small élite of the wealthy and an equally small deprived class which sandwiched between them the growing mass of affluent, if privatised, workers. For those who responded most enthusiastically to the labelling perspective, it was almost as though, for the first time since the war, if not since the inception of the welfare state, there was time for reflection and an assessment of the directions in which paths chosen in times of crisis had taken us. In Britain a supposedly socialist government was in power, and yet the mood was not one of complacency. The issues raised by an assessment of the disadvantages of the structurally deviant groups, the victims of the lean years, were not to be settled by bland and unconvincing promises about the redistribution of resources. Affluence did not produce a conciliation of political conflict; on the contrary, it appeared to exacerbate it. The 1960s were a decade of 'revolutionary' conflict and a proliferation of deviant solutions, in sharp contrast to the conformity and submission which in retrospect appeared to have characterised the previous fifteen years at least and to have made possible the glib assumption of an age of affluence and apathy. Paradoxically, this age of apparent material affluence created the conditions for a critique and rejection of the very ideals most sacred to it. That this rejection took place in the universities and in 'youth culture' generally was seen by some as cause for optimism; the vanguard was forming, social revolution was at hand. The dialectical materialist and the mystical anti-materialist sat together in the sunshine of revolution and spectacle, politics and dope, protesting in the gardens of the campus.

This was the climate of the misfit sociology, the sunshine of radical optimism. Yet the very contradictions that facilitated it were inevitably built into it. With the coming of the 1970s the sky clouded over and depression settled on radical optimism. Suddenly the assumptions of affluence were irrelevant, and the end products of the 1960s revolution were revealed as nothing more than minor liberal reforms and gestures. Social change turned out to be not that simple. The revolutionary vanguard was fragmented. Many went back to work, carrying fond memories of the holidays and a controlled despair, as they locked away within themselves the seeds of hope to await a spring for which there was neither prospect nor promise. A few stuck with revolutionary action, but this was no longer the spectacle and display of the surrealists and anarchists, the brotherly demonstrations of the white dwarfs and situationists. For these few love had sold out, and force and power had cornered the market of change; they turned to covert organisation and explosive and violent attack on those who symbolised the domination of the oppressed. For sociology and social policy, misfit sociology had embodied the promise and optimism of the 1960s. In the fields of criminology, deviance and delinquency, which had become generally synonymous with regard to the theoretical issues they raised, the apparent failure, for the most part, of labelling theory to fulfil its promise of real social policy changes prompted a movement towards more overtly Marxist explanations of and prescriptions for dealing with 'the problem of delinquency'.

The problem is that this reaction created a vacuum in the space which had to some extent been filled by labelling theory. The critique of deviance and welfare presented in the new criminology, the second generation of 'new' deviancy theory, was not just of the traditional conceptions of crime and criminality; it was, at least in intention, a more fundamental critique of the institutional technocracies which surrounded the identification and control of deviance in society. The experts, the psychological, criminological and sociological theorists whose ideas were used to inform the practice of the professionals of social policy and were seen as clarifying and rationalising the tasks of the professional agencies of control and welfare, were exposed as agents of mystification whose scientific and professional objectivity served only to legitimate the practices and classifications of control.[8]

This critique presented the welfare and control professionals with a dilemma. Many of these professionals experienced a certain sympathy, an uneasy accord, with the principles and substance of the new criminological and deviancy theories. Indeed, they shared a common starting point with the proponents of these theories. Their response to the failure of the radical optimism of the 1960s had led them to seek practical solutions in working with the deprived and depraved at the sharp end of social welfare policies. Yet they were lost. The criminologists and deviancy theorists, with whom there had been not only the traditional technocratic affiliation through the provision of answers by experts, but also a more recent political affiliation through a common critical perception of the welfare state and criminal justice, provided answers that could not be reconciled with the organisational and practical contingencies with which the practitioners were faced.

This feeling of frustration was very neatly crystallised in the subtitle of Stan Cohen's contribution to *Radical Social Work*: 'It's all right for you to talk'. In his chapter Cohen highlighted the dilemma produced for the social worker by the conflict of radical theory with his daily experience of the liberal ideology of welfare organisations and attempted some resolution of that conflict through Mathiesen's strategy of the 'unfinished'. Mathiesen's argument is that systematic change is hindered by attempts to produce detailed and deliberately 'acceptable' definitions of alternatives and prescriptions for policy change. He argues instead that those seeking changes should adopt an 'abolitionist' perspective. The strategy demands that the ultimate goal – abolition of whatever you have defined as intolerable – should be kept clearly in view, but that you should never allow yourself to be defined as unrealistic, and therefore not worth talking to by those who control the existing system. One problem with this, which Mathiesen partly recognises, is that social policies are not discrete entities or units which can be taken out and replaced with new units. Development takes place by modification and adaptation in practice rather than by replacement. Furthermore, there is ample evidence to suggest that policies exist not in isolation but as parts of ideological networks, so that even where it is possible to abolish a particular policy, that policy's functions may well be taken over and continued in adjacent areas of the policy network. Another ramification of this 'organic' aspect of policy, which is clearly demonstrated by the 1969 CYPA, is that even where there is some substitution of new policies for old, the integration of those new policies into the existing network may cause the reversion in effect of the new policies to the functions of the old, abolished ones. Mathiesen knows this and suggests that the abolitionist movement must develop a 'defensive' policy to prevent new systems of the kind you are opposed to from being introduced; but this requires constant vigilance and efficient organisation. Mathiesen himself constantly emphasises the difficulty of his strategy.[9]

It was perhaps because, rather than in spite of, the contradictions of labelling theory which were identified by its radical critics that it was able to offer some promise to social work and social control agencies. These contradictions enabled it to identify the political nature of the traditional conceptions of crime, deviance and delinquency. Simultaneously it had a message for the agents of welfare and control about specific areas of their 'professional' discretion and decision-making — which, although it was by no means uncritical, had a recognisable practical relevance to that discretion and its organisational contingencies.

The 'new' criminology encompassed the macro-structural sociology of the functionalists and the micro-interactional sociology of the subjectivist schools. It attempted to combine in a single perspective the broad structural movements which determine social consciousness and the local conflicts of interests and individual definitions which power those movements. Its exponents not only eschewed the traditional 'scientific' role of experts; their theory tended to imply that no actions on the part of individual social workers and similar agents of control could, whatever the organisational and administrative contingencies, have outcomes other than individualised control and class oppression. This tendency is only occasionally relieved by enigmatic and unhelpful qualifications, such as Bailey and Brake's view that even in a post-revolutionary society there would be a need for some form of social work.[10] Jock Young, considering the social responsibility of a new criminology, is not much more helpful:

> It does not rule out interim demands but it insists that such demands be part of an overall strategy. Thus, it does not lecture social workers and mental nurses that their function is *necessarily* as an instrument of social control, nor does it deny intermediate solutions, tentative graspings for survival on the part of the deviant.[11]

With criminology's rejection of an 'expert', 'scientific' role which consisted of the construction and dissemination of legitimated knowledge in the form of objectifications of people and groups, and its subsequent assumption of a role consisting of the demystification of deviance, the 'separation of desperation from solution' and the relation of the 'deviant solution to its effect on others',[12] social work is thrown back on its own resources. It must begin to think for itself. For a technical, 'painting-by-numbers' body of knowledge constituted around the performance of a series of routinised and ritualised procedures it must substitute a critical awareness of the historical and political contingencies through which those procedures have developed and of the network of policies which they constitute.

In terms of social work with young offenders the procedures are the contributions that social workers make to the processing of delinquency, its causal identification and classification, the preparation of social enquiry reports, the distribution of offenders to a variety of institutions and the monitoring of their progress in those institutions. The conceptual field underlying these procedures may be delimited through three general areas of debate: welfare *v.* justice, treatment *v.* punishment and the deprived *v.* the depraved. It would be convenient if these three debates could be defined as three dimensions of a matrix, facilitating neat and rapid classification and analysis; but these poles do not represent three symmetric continua; each identifies a series of themes; they serve as an access to a library of discourse. Furthermore, the significance of these themes, woven and tangled together like briars, does not lie in their substantive issues alone, but also in the conceptual field in which they are embedded, the soil in which this thicket is rooted.

Two stereotypes generally represent the two poles between which much of the current debate about young offenders is carried on. On the one hand, there are those – generally identified as the social workers and perhaps the probation officers – who see juvenile offending as the result of problems and deprivations experienced by the young offender. They are consequently concerned with the offender's welfare and the treatment of the problems which result from his deprivation. On the other hand, there are those – identified as the magistrates, the judiciary and the police – who see juvenile offending as resulting from depravity, from badness. They are consequently concerned to bring the young offender to justice and to punish him for his misdeeds. We have seen how uneasily such radically contradictory ideologies coexist within the one system of juvenile justice. In public debate both sides give the appearance of a frenetic struggle to maintain their positions and ideologies. Chief constables describe in their speeches the failure of justice under the increasing intervention of the agencies of do-gooders. Patricia Morgan[13] describes the liberal ideologists as 'the new establishment', concerned to maintain their power and professional status. This 'new establishment' meanwhile expresses its own sense of powerlessness and frustration before the almost mediaeval concern with retribution which, they feel, dominates the courts. They feel unfairly treated and misunderstood. How can society expect them to deal with the cause of crime and the consequences of judicial decisions if it does not give them sufficient power? It can be argued that in reality this debate masks a deep consensus. We have seen that the victories of the liberals in the field of juvenile justice have not reduced but have rather increased the severity of that system. This is less surprising than it seems because despite their contradictory appearance, the institutions of welfare and justice have a common historical and conceptual base. The call for a return to justice has come not only from apparently conservative ideologists such as Morgan but also from some of the more radical critics of the liberal ideology. It would seem clear that, despite some of the stereotypes held of the 'conservative ideologists', they do not mean us to return to the inquisitorial and punitive practices of mediaeval justice. The era of justice they have in mind is presumably the era of 'rational enlightenment'.

Together with the juvenile justice system, the modern institutions of social welfare were founded in the mid to late nineteenth century. The common perception of that foundation was of the equitable distribution of the fruits of rational scientific thought and development according to the precepts of the schools of rational social philosophies. From sewerage to education the technology of rational science paid its dividends to man. But this rationality was not always obviously benevolent:

> In the sixteenth century children were provided with better food and clothing and a higher boarding out allowance was paid to orphans than was customary later, even in the mid-nineteenth century. Justices and overseers of the poor were required to set to work, to apprentice and support all children whose parents were unwilling or unable to support them and the expenses of this welfare were paid out of the rates. It was a remarkable achievement and there was nothing comparable with the first Elizabethan concern for poor children until the mid-nineteenth century.[14]

The Poor Law Amendment Act of 1834 is, of course, the best-known example of a piece of reforming legislation in which traditional humanitarianism was barely allowed to contaminate the overriding principle of scientific rationality. In general, the reforms of the nineteenth century might be better described as being concerned with the regulation of welfare rather than its implementation. And this regulation was achieved through the law:

> In the reign of Queen Victoria more than 100 acts were passed specifically concerned with the welfare of children. Indeed the Children's Acts of 1894 and 1908 had to elbow their way through an avalanche of benevolent legislation for children in a way that makes the 1969 Act look positively lonely.[15]

In the previous chapter the work of Michel Foucault was dismissed as a version of 'left idealism'. This may have struck some readers, justifiably, as somewhat cavalier and incautious. Foucault's work is too important and too cogent to be left out of account. The emphasis of the previous chapter on the ambiguities and complexities of law and welfare was intended to undermine the grounds for the large generalisations which have characterised much recent radical writing on social policy. We must now redress the balance a little. In emphasising ambiguities and discontinuities one may lose sight of the connections and continuities which are Foucault's concern. In particular, his claim that our contemporary institutions of law and welfare stem from a single historical root enables us to explore a further ambiguity, based on a hidden consensus rather than a hidden conflict. It is a difficult one for social workers, but we must face it squarely.

The following discussion, then, is based on Foucault's account of the development of modern penal practice. Before what he terms the 'epistemological thaw', which enabled the development of economic rationality and thus of industrial capitalism, the law was the law of the sovereign. Whilst the forms of the law – the judiciary and a formally codified body of prohibited behaviours – resembled those of modern judicial institutions, its structures and dynamics were very different. Order was maintained through exemplary punishment. The populace, the subjects of control, were seen not as a collection of individuals but rather as a single entity, the mob, the rabble. Without the means to detect and report infractions, prosecution was by no means a likely consequence of the commission of offences. Much like the general of an army of occupation, the sovereign maintained control by selecting from time to time an offender, conducting a 'show' trial and then, with the mob assembled in a public place, demonstrating his awful power physically on the body of the unfortunate offender by branding it, flogging it, tearing it limb from limb and otherwise displaying the ingenious technology of torture – all before execution was formally carried out. Such a method of maintaining law and order had serious disadvantages. It was inefficient: prosecution was only occasionally a consequence of infraction, and the vast majority of offences were concealed within the mob. Further, the public nature of the punishment could all too easily have the opposite of the intended consequences. Such occasions were often treated as public holidays; the mood of the mob was generally one of excitement, of arousal and anticipation, and if the intended victim was at all a popular member of the community that excitement and arousal could all too easily turn to rebellion. It was not uncommon for the mob to rescue the intended object of punishment and turn upon the agents of the sovereign. Finally, a system of law and order characterised by excess was intolerable to an age of economic rationalisation. Foucault has identified three ways in which the inefficiencies and excesses of the old relations of power, the means by which law and social order were maintained, were transformed in the late eighteenth and early nineteenth centuries. He has epitomised the dynamic of this transformed, newly economic and rational system, this 'soft machine', in one word: discipline. Its main components are:

HIERARCHICAL OBSERVATION

The structure of the old, 'unenlightened' system had meant that conviction and punishment were only an occasional and by no means a probable outcome of infraction. For the efficient practice of control it was necessary that they became a probable outcome. Some modern critiques regard the inception of the police forces as the development which enabled, through surveillance, the automatic connection of offence and prosecution. But they were a late development. The first model for surveillance lay in the internal structures of armies. The geometry of military camps permitted unimpeded views along their aisles and ranks. This ordered geometry served as a model for similar developments in the arrangement of desks and beds in classrooms and dormitories, in the arrangement of machines in the early factories and in the exemplary design of post-revolutionary Paris, whose broad avenues and geometric blocks were intended to ensure the failure of any future revolution in the streets. The rigour of surveillance was further ensured by the pyramidal development of hierarchies. The performance of one group or of one task became the responsibility of a particular monitor, clerk or supervisor. The supervision of a group of these superordinates was in turn monitored at another level of the hierarchy to which they were subordinate, and so on, with each superordinate level subordinate to a higher one.

NORMALISING JUDGEMENT

It is in this aspect of discipline that the connection may be seen between the modern conception of punishment and that of the old mediaeval systems. But the new form of punishment was no longer of an excessive and exceptional nature, neither did it refer only to behaviour formally prohibited by law. Within social institutions were developed highly specific sets of regulations which prescribed as much as they proscribed behaviour. Punishment ceased to be an exceptional and exemplary demonstration and became one pole of a continuum, one aspect of a routinised response to all behaviour. No longer the awful demonstration to the mob, it became a continuous spur to each individual to conform.

THE EXAMINATION

This third aspect of the dynamic of discipline, Foucault describes as combining the elements of hierarchical observation and normalising judgement: 'It is a normalising gaze, a surveillance that makes it possible to qualify, to classify and to punish. It establishes over individuals a visibility through which one differentiates them and judges them.'[16] Taking its form from the development of medical science and with a brilliance of economy reminiscent of Japanese Zen art, the examination performed three processes simultaneously. It combined hierarchical observation and normalising judgement to individualise, to classify and to spur to conformity; in this it broke down the unitary mob into a structured and differentiated collection of accessible individuals. It permitted the constitution of an objectified body of knowledge, using the precepts and classifications of the human sciences, about each individual; in this it formed the basis of the archive, the file, the case record. Finally in its very performance it referred to, reconstituted and reinforced the relations of power; the visible and individualised examinees displaying themselves under the silent gaze of an ideally invisible examiner.

These transformations instituted the dynamic of a new machine of social order, a machine at once economic and its nature invisible. A more visible rendering of this machine may be seen in the balance of social and architectural elements constituting Bentham's 'panopticon', which he introduced in the following fashion: 'Morals reformed — health preserved — industry invigorated — instruction diffused — public burthens lighted — economy seated, as it were, upon a rock — the gordian knot of the Poor Laws not cut, but untied — all by a simple idea in architecture.'[17] The structure which embodied these ideals of rational social philosophy was indeed quite simple: a round building, its outer walls formed by tiers of cells and in the centre of the circular space enclosed by these walls, a tower. Each cell was to have a window in the outer wall and its inner wall was to be as open as possible. Thus the disciplinary requirements of visibility and individualisation were embodied. The central tower, meanwhile, was to be so arranged as to have an invisible means of entrance and exit and was to conceal as far as possible both the presence and the object of any supervisory surveillance. The inhabitant of each cell was isolated from his neighbours and yet his every action, profiled by the outer window, could be observed from the central tower. At the same time, the arrangement of the central tower meant that he could never know whether he was being watched or not. The discipline of this establishment did not have to be enforced; it was self-imposed as a result of perpetual uncertainty. To this concrete embodiment of the disciplinary machine Bentham added a further possibility, that the arrangement of the observation tower should enable the public to inspect the functioning of any particular establishment. Thus the machine could be rendered transparent to society at large. The legal and welfare reforms of the nineteenth century, however, gave the disciplinary machine a rather different sort of transparency. It did, indeed, become transparent to society at large, but with the transparency of glass. Although it continued to function, probably more efficiently than ever before, it became invisible, camouflaged beneath the surface conflicts of the developing systems of justice and welfare, which are expressed in debates about the deprived or the depraved, treatment or punishment, justice or welfare.

In fact the concerns displayed by the polarities of these debates differ semantically rather than in substance. They are expressions not of fundamentally conflicting ideologies of social order, but rather of preferences for different forms of peripheral technology. This is rather an extreme way of putting it and we remain clear that there are good grounds for preferring some technologies to others. If we did not think so this book would not have been written. It is important, however, that the social worker in making such choices is aware of the mechanics of the disciplinary machine in which such alternatives and preferences are located.

Whilst the superficial forms of the modern juvenile justice system – the trial or hearing, the presiding presence of the judge or magistrate and the formalities of the sentence – resemble those of the mediaeval juridical systems, such similarities obscure profound differences. Spencer Millham and his colleagues have referred to the profusion in the nineteenth and early twentieth centuries of legislation for children. Platt's study of the 'child-saving' movement and its development of institutional provision for children hints at the connection between the regulations and codes of conduct enacted in those institutions and the formally legislated body of children's law. The interaction between legal provisions and children's institutions has extended the regulations and relations of normalising judgement into the wider community. The consequence of a child's infraction of the legal codes is, too often, the submission of his behaviour to the minute observations of institutional regulations.

But the mechanics of the law itself have also changed. As the human sciences have developed methods for the classification and observation of conduct, they have, apparently in the interests of social justice, been integrated into the legal system in an 'advisory' role. In effect they have come to constitute a parallel system of adjudication. Whereas the judge or magistrate conducts his investigation according to the rules of juridical evidence and procedure, professional advisers conduct their own investigation according to rules of scientific evidence and procedure. (Or at least they are supposed to, and sometimes claim actually to be doing so.)[18] In the sphere of juvenile justice, then, the social worker is both the descendant of the early 'child savers' and the professional, scientifically informed adviser of legal judgement. In the professional establishment of social work, the codes of regulations of the child care institutions are superimposed on the classificatory expertise of the human sciences. In the case record are detailed the minutiae of behaviour, expanded by psychological, psychiatric and sociological speculation. At any given time, most commonly following the occurrence of an offence, however severe or trivial it may be, that record of behaviour may be reviewed in the light of the details of institutional regulations to produce 'scientific' classifications and prognoses.

It is impossible for social workers to change overnight the time-hallowed procedures and practices of their agencies, or suddenly to begin serving different class interests and agendas. Those practices and procedures are firmly locked in place by those of contingent agencies; social workers are themselves imprisoned in pyramidal hierarchies of supervision. Yet an awareness of their historical situation, of their roots, may enable them to adjust the focus of their concerns in the performance of those practices and procedures, to move from a professional to a social ethic, and thereby to adjust and redirect the policies which will be focused on in the following chapter. The research findings reported there seem striking enough to justify our claim that this task is urgent. The implications of Foucault's argument need not be that social workers should despair, or find other jobs. What they do mean is that social workers should begin to look very critically at the historical origins, the social functions and the immediate effects on individual clients of their traditional conception of professionalism.

REFERENCES: CHAPTER 3

1 Cohen, S., 'Manifestos for action', in Bailey, R. and Brake, M. (eds), *Radical Social Work* (London: Edward Arnold, 1975), pp. 78–85.
2 Pearson, G., *The Deviant Imagination* (London: Macmillan, 1975), pp. 149–51.
3 Collins, R., *Conflict Sociology* (New York: Academic Press, 1975), p. 421.
4 Marshall, T. H., *Social Policy in the Twentieth Century* (London: Hutchinson, 3rd edn 1976); Wilensky, H. L. and Lebeaux, C., *Industrial Society and Social Welfare* (New York: Free Press, 1965).
5 Merton, R. K., *Social Theory and Social Structure* (New York: Free Press, rev. edn 1957), p. 149.
6 Pearson, G., 'Misfit sociology and the politics of socialisation', in Taylor, I., Walton, P. and Young, J. (eds), *Critical Criminology* (London: Routledge and Kegan Paul, 1975), pp. 147–64.
7 For example, Goffman, E., *Frame Analysis* (Harmondsworth: Penguin, 1975) or *Interaction Ritual* (Chicago, Ill.: Aldwin, 1967); Garfinkel, H., *Studies in Ethnomethodology* (Englewood Cliffs, NJ: Prentice-Hall, 1967).
8 Schwendaiger, H. and Schwendaiger, J., 'Defenders of order or guardians of human rights', in Taylor, Walton and Young (eds), op cit., p. 134.
9 Mathiesen, T., *The Politics of Abolition* (London: Martin Robertson, 1974), esp. pp. 100–9.
10 Bailey, R. and Brake, M., 'Social work in the welfare state', in Bailey and Brake (eds), op. cit., pp. 1–12.
11 Young, J., 'Working class criminology', in Taylor, Walton and Young (eds), op. cit., p. 88.
12 ibid., pp. 87–8.
13 Morgan, P., *Delinquent Fantasies* (London: Temple Smith, 1978).
14 Pinchbeck, I. and Hewitt, M., *Children in English Society*, quoted in Millham, S., Bullock, R. and Hosie, K., *Locking up Children* (London: Saxon House, 1978), p. 11.
15 Millham, Bullock and Hosie, op. cit., p. 17.

16 Foucault, M., *Discipline and Punish* (London: Allen Lane, 1977), p. 184.
17 Bentham, J., *Panopticon*, p. 1, quoted in Ignatieff, M., *A Just Measure of Pain* (London: Macmillan, 1978), p. 112.
18 For example, Perry, F. G., *Reports for Criminal Courts* (Ilkley, Yorks.: Owen Wells, 1979).

4

Demystifying the System

Social services departments form one part of the network of agencies which constitute the 'juvenile justice system'. The agencies involved in this system are those that process young offenders: the police force, the probation service, the juvenile courts with magistrates and their clerks as well as the social services department. The current role of each of these agencies is based on a series of intra- and inter-agency developments reaching back to their historical inception. Within this system each agency performs different roles; the police are the 'referring' agents; they apprehend juveniles and commence the process of differentiation by referring some to probation and social services departments. Some they caution, while with other cases, for a number of reasons, they take no further action. The rest are then referred to the courts for hearing. The probation service and social services department are the professional advisers to this process of juvenile criminal justice. Ideally they provide 'expert' judgements based on their respective bodies of professional knowledge to inform and assist the adjudications of both the police, during the stages of initial referral, and later the courts in making sentences. It is through the recommendations made by these two services that they have come to represent a system of 'scientific', professional adjudication parallel to the more traditional processes of legal adjudication. Historically these two agencies, whilst they may perform similar 'servicing' functions for the juvenile criminal justice system, have very different roots and orientations.

The probation service is closely linked to the courts; its individual agents are seen as officers of the courts. Like the social services department, the probation service's expertise is used both to recommend and to carry out certain sentences of the courts. The resources it uses to carry out sentences are represented by its officers. Traditionally the probation service is seen as the supplier of resources both for the supervision of community-based sentences and for the rehabilitative and welfare aspects of penal sentences, although it has no direct control over the penal institutions. Social services departments, however, whilst they operate within a similar structure in their recommendations to courts, have developed very different disposal resources. With roots more firmly in the provision of social welfare and child care as opposed to criminal welfare and rehabilitation, social services hold within their ambit the whole range of child care institutions developed since the mid-nineteenth century, from hostels and the small community homes to the large community homes with education on the premises. Apart from this very different historical base, social services departments have been further diversified in recent years through the amalgamation of the old child care, mental health and welfare services into one department, and the composition of the generic social worker from the three separate agents of the old departments.

Figure 4.1 represents diagrammatically the connections between the various agencies involved in the system. The route from apprehension to sentencing and disposal of a young offender is by no means direct and automatic. At each stage of the process each agency makes decisions within its own sphere of discretion which have the effect of directing and redirecting the offender to different processes and outcomes.

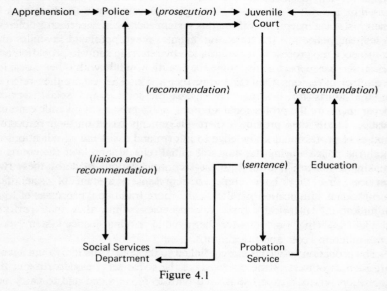

Figure 4.1

Even before the juvenile is apprehended, differential policing of certain geographical areas comes into play. The young offender is more likely to be caught in the back streets of large urban areas than in the peripheral areas of private housing estates or in rural areas. Once the juvenile is apprehended by the policeman 'on the beat', each police force has different procedures for the management of decision-making thereafter. Depending on the offence and the behaviour and disposition of the juvenile when he is caught, the constable may decide not to take the matter any further. If he does, however, make out a report on the offence, then depending on the force, the offender may be referred on to a juvenile bureau or the community involvement branch of the force. If he is referred to such a branch, then that branch is likely to request information and recommendations as to how the case should be handled from either the probation service or the local social services department. Whilst the police will ultimately take a decision whether to take no further action, to caution or to prosecute, that decision will have been strongly influenced by the organisational structures of the force concerned and may have been further influenced by information and recommendations from probation or social services departments which will, in turn, have been influenced by the internal structure and organisation of these departments. Even before the young offender arrives in court for prosecution he has already been selected at several levels of decision-making, decision-making influenced by the orientation and ideology of each agency, its organisational practices and variations in local liaison procedures.

In the court, the child may be found guilty or not guilty of the offence. If he is guilty, then again dependent on local agency practice and court administration, reports may be submitted for consideration at the sentencing stage. These reports are likely to be submitted by the two 'central' professional agencies, probation and social services, and also by the education authority in the form of a school report. Reports may also be submitted from more 'specialist' professions, for example psychiatric and psychological reports, observation and assessment reports. Once again the process is subject to considerable variability, dependent on the organisation and ideology of the recommending agency as well as local variations in the practices of these agencies. Some indication of the extent of these variations may be seen from the results of a study of six months' proceedings in the area covered by one court. This study is offered solely as an example of a local study rather than as a basis for generalisation about differential practices.

The basic data for this analysis, the background data for all offenders who had appeared in the local juvenile court within a specified six-month period, was gathered *en masse* from the local police in the area who were encouragingly willing to offer any help which could improve liaison in a situation about which they too, despite stereotypes, were critical. The basic information which they had, in any case, routinely collected, consisted of data on family size, previous convictions, the charge, damage done, recommendations and sentences made on the juveniles who appeared before the local court in the specified period.

The total population of the area covered by the court studied was some 50,000–60,000, serviced by one social services area office, with three social work teams (two intake and one long-term). This data forms a profile not just of a group of young offenders but also of the policies of the agencies involved in the system and the interconnections between those policies. From it we may make limited inferences about the various levels of selection and discretion that constitute the juvenile criminal justice system in this area.

Table 4.1 shows the number of cautions that these juveniles had received prior to their appearance in the six months studied.

Table 4·1. *Number of cautions received by juveniles appearing in court in period of study.*

No. of previous cautions	No.	%
0	77	58·8
1	34	25·9
2	13	9·9
3	7	3·3
	131	100

Note: Percentages in this and the following tables are approximate and may not always add up to 100.

As can be seen, nearly 60 per cent of the juveniles appearing had never been cautioned before being prosecuted. Cautioning was originally introduced in the late 1960s as a form of diversion. Since the majority of first offenders do not appear again, it was intended that cautioning should replace the trauma and stigmatisation of a court appearance, particularly for these 'one-off' offenders. It is difficult to compare these figures with the cautioning statistics presented in the Home Office's national *Criminal Statistics*. Those national figures are worked out on the basis of juveniles cautioned as a percentage of all juveniles dealt with by the police, whereas Table 4.1 shows the proportion of those appearing before courts who have previously been cautioned. Table 4.1 can be interpreted in two ways; on the one hand, it could be said that the relatively low number of previously cautioned offenders in the sample was indicative of the success of cautioning; while on the other, it could be suggested that, since less than half of those appearing before the court had been cautioned, the diversionary strategy was being used for a different category of juvenile – those whose offences would never have been considered for prosecution before the existence of cautioning, but for whom there now existed a 'softer' option. The results of the Home Office's recent study of cautioning would suggest that the latter interpretation is correct (see Ditchfield, J. A., *Police Cautioning in England and Wales* (London: HMSO, 1976).

During the six-month period studied, 131 juveniles appeared before the court in question. Table 4.2 shows the distribution of these cases by the service preparing the social enquiry report.

Table 4·2.   *Distribution of cases by service preparing social enquiry report.*

Service preparing report	No.	%
Probation	46	35·1
Social services	36	27·5
Sentenced without enquiry report	49	37.4
	131	100

This table throws some light on the differential involvement of probation and social services. The original intention of the 1969 CYPA was that as the age of criminal responsibility was increased, social services departments should take over the probation departments' involvement with juveniles so that they would ultimately deal with all offenders up to the age of 17. It may be seen here that, some nine years after the 1969 CYPA passed through Parliament, the probation service, in the area under study, was still dealing with the majority of those juveniles who received social enquiry reports.

The greatest proportion of these juveniles, however, appeared without any social enquiry report. This raises the question of how and where it is decided that any particular young offender should have a report prepared for his court appearance. The system which was supposedly operating in this area was that juveniles charged with minor offences unlikely to result in sentences more severe than fines (such as offences against the Road Traffic Act) were not referred for reports. Where the offence was seen as being relatively grave, however, and particularly where it could result in supervision or a custodial sentence, reports were requested. If the juvenile was over 14 and unknown to the probation service then he was referred to the social services department. In practice the system did not appear to operate in exactly this way. Column 1 of Table 4.3 shows the sentences received by those who appeared without court reports. It may be seen from this column that by no means all offenders in this group received 'light' sentences such as fines and conditional discharges; eight received supervision orders; there was one care order; and five received detention centre orders.

Columns 2 and 3 of Table 4.3 show the distribution of the recommendations made by the social services and probation departments. There are some considerable differences between the two. Although the two populations are relatively small, too small to produce results of any significance for most statistical tests of comparison, some of the differences are big enough to merit consideration. Proportionally social services recommended three times as many conditional discharges as probation, but only half as many fines, fewer supervision orders, but three times as many

Table 4·3. *Comparison of recommendations and results on social enquiry reports (SERs)*

	1		2		3	
			Recommendations			
	Results no SER		SER by probation		SER by social services department	
	No.	%	No.	%	No.	%
		Not known				
No recommendation	14	28·5	2	4·3	4	11·1
Case dismissed	2	4·1	—	—	—	—
Conditional discharge	4	8·2	2	4·3	6	16·6
Sentence deferred	—	—	1	2·2	—	—
Adjourned	1	2·0	—	—	—	—
Fine	13	26·5	14	30·4	6	16·6
Attendance centre	—	—	—	—	1	2·7
Supervision order	8	16·3	6	13·0	3	8·3
Supervision order with intermediate treatment	1	2·0	3	6·5	8	22·2
Interim care order	—	—	1	2·2	2	5·5
Care order	1	2·0	—	—	2	5·5
Detention centre	5	10·2	—	—	—	—
Referral for borstal	—	—	1	2·2	2	5·5
Plea for leniency	—	—	3	6·5	1	2·7
Court sentence inappropriate	—	—	13	28·3	1	2·7
TOTALS	49	100	46	100	36	100

intermediate treatment orders. Somewhat more puzzling only 2·7 per cent of social services recommendations as opposed to 28·3 per cent of probation recommendations were for a nominal sentence, on the grounds that the offence would be more appropriately dealt with in a context other than that of the court. But the most germane difference between these two sets of recommendations appears when we sum the recommendations for custodial sentences, i.e. interim care orders, care orders, detention centre orders and referrals to crown court for borstal sentencing. In these categories social workers made three times as many custodial recommendations as probation officers.

One explanation for these differences would be that the population dealt with by social services and the population dealt with by probation are in fact qualitatively different from one another. Thus the processes that lead a juvenile to be reported on by one service or the other actually select out different types of young offender. One problem with this explanation is that these processes make some rather arbitrary selections, for example a juvenile over 14 may be reported on by social services if he is already known to them but in practice it could be that he is known because he or another member of his family has been in touch with social services for reasons completely unconnected with the 14-year-old's offending, such as Part III accommodation for elderly relatives, or child-minding referrals for a younger sibling.

If it is accepted that the official criteria for selection to one service or the other are in operation, contradictory arguments are raised; it would be necessary to say that, although the social services recommend the more severe sentences, probation deal with the older clients, so it must be that social services clients are the more disturbed and disturbing offenders if it is the case that they merited these recommendations. This raises the question of where social services get these cases from, since there is nothing in the criteria of allocation to one service or the other which differentiates on the basis of gravity of offence or degree of disturbance. The only way of maintaining the argument that there is a difference between children receiving social services and children receiving probation social enquiry reports must finally come down to saying that the circumstances or problems that lead people to become clients of social services departments, the range of problems that social services deal with other than delinquency, generate or give rise to more severe forms of delinquency and disturbance than one would normally find. Thus, those juveniles that are already known to social services for reasons beyond the sphere of delinquency are likely to be more than 'normally' delinquent. Ultimately this argument comes to constitute a theory of causative factors of delinquency, a theory which, as is argued elsewhere in this book, has little of value to say about delinquency, but says rather more about the agencies adopting such perspectives.

We come then to the second possible explanation for the different distribution of recommendations by the two services, that rather than demonstrating differences between the two groups of juveniles, they demonstrate differences between the two services. On the one hand, the probation service with a history of close connection to juridical processes, the law and justice and little in the way of resources apart from its own agents, the probation officers. On the other, the social services departments, relative newcomers to the processes of criminal justice, with ideologies rooted in welfare, treatment and social problems and with extensive residential resources to inform the social worker as to the functions of his department.

Table 4.4 shows the sentences received by the 131 juveniles in the sample, broken down according to the services providing the social enquiry reports.

Again, substantial differences may be seen between the sentences received by the clients of the two services, one of the most prominent features being that 50 per cent of probation clients received fines. Custodial sentences were received by 9·1 per cent of probation clients, 17·2 per cent of those who

Table 4.4. Results – Services providing reports

	Total appearances in court		Probation reports		Social services reports		No. recommendations		less those unknown			
	No.	%	No.	%	No.	%	No.	%	total	Probation	Social Serv. dept.	No SER
Not known or not yet heard	18	13.7	2	4.3	2	5.5	14	28.6	3.5	2.2	2.9	5.7
Withdrawn/Dismissed	4	3.1	1	2.2	1	2.7	2	4.1	0.9	—	2.9	—
Absolute Discharge	1	0.8	—	—	1	2.7	—	—	—	—	—	—
Conditional Discharge	19	14.5	8	17.4	7	19.4	4	8.2	16.8	18.1	20.5	11.4
Sentence deferred	1	0.8	1	2.2	—	—	—	—	0.9	2.2	—	—
Adjourned	2	1.5	—	—	1	2.7	1	2.8	1.8	—	2.9	1.9
Fine	42	32.1	23	50.0	6	16.6	13	26.5	37.2	52.3	17.6	37.1
Attendance centre	2	1.5	1	2.2	1	2.7	—	—	1.8	2.2	2.9	—
Supervision order	16	12.2	5	10.9	3	8.3	8	16.3	14.2	11.4	8.8	22.9
Intermediate treatment	8	6.1	1	2.2	6	16.6	1	2.0	7.1	2.2	17.6	2.9
Care order	6	4.6	—	—	5	14.0	—	—	5.3	—	14.7	2.9
Detention centre	10	7.6	4	8.7	1	2.7	5	10.2	8.8	9.1	2.9	14.3
Crown court	2	1.5	—	—	2	5.5	—	—	1.8	—	5.9	—
Total	131	100	46	100	36	100	49	100	100	100	100	100

Custodial sentences:
13·7 of total sample
8·7 of probation
12·2 of No SER cases
22·1 of social services

Less those sentences unknown:
Total sample   15·9
Probation   9·1
Social services department   23·5
No SER cases   17·2

appeared without reports, and 23·5 per cent of social services clients. Social services clients tended therefore to receive more severe sentences than either the probation clients or those who appeared without reports from either service.

This study was not intended to produce generalisable results; the numbers it deals with are relatively small and the time-span short and, in this sense, any interpretation is liable to a bias produced by exceptional circumstances. For example, it was suggested that the high proportions of juveniles appearing without social enquiry reports, but who received custodial sentences in this sample, could be the result of one group of juveniles committing an exceptional offence, being held overnight and the case being heard the next day. It does, however, give some idea of the often arbitrary contingencies of the local system by which young offenders are processed. This example, at a local level, creates the basis for a renegotiation of the juvenile liaison system centred on the use of cautioning which can be informed by discussion about specific cases. It highlights the processes by which a client is selected, if at all, for reports and recommendations by one service or the other and raises questions about the effect of that selection. Despite the common perception that the probation service is more authoritarian and more 'punitively' oriented as a result of its closer connections with courts, while social services are seen as more welfare oriented, the 'soft option', it would seem that in this area, the juvenile who receives a social services report is likely to receive a more severe sentence than the one who receives a probation report. At the same time as it presents some form of critique of the local administration of juvenile justice, the study also indicates likely levels of demand for community-based services. The various intensities of a proposed intermediate treatment programme may be matched against specific sentences to define the client group for the service and identify potential demand. From the above study, one might identify the eighteen recipients of custodial sentences as indicating potential demand in six months for high-intensity programmes, and the twenty-four supervision order sentences as indicating demand for medium-intensity programmes.

The analysis of the system described so far allows the planning of an alternative community-based service for young offenders. It indicates the location and function of diversionary, gate-keeping systems and estimates demand for services. To implement an alternative, however, it is important to do more than create these preconditions. The target group at which these alternative services are aimed is subject to the range of current services. It is important to begin with the clients currently in residential institutions, primarily because the justification for community-based services is that for many offenders residential care is unnecessary. Despite the welfare orientation of the system, many of those currently in residential care are there against their best interests. The first step in the provision of an alternative is the removal from care of those who are already there. The identification and decarceration of juveniles currently in care serves to demonstrate: (1) the type of client at whom community-based alternatives are aimed, and (2) that the alternative to custody is viable and possible.

The following Section 7(7) care order studies serve to identify the clients for the first step of a community-based alternative. They also highlight the processes and procedures which lead social workers to sustain the use of residential care. The undertaking of Section 7(7) care order studies with social workers analysing their own files can therefore provide pressure for change.

One of the intentions of the 1969 CYPA was that of preventing the unnecessary committal to care of children and young people found guilty of criminal offences. Thus the 1968 White Paper *Children in Trouble* suggested that 'proceedings will be possible only if the test at (a)(i) can also be satisifed'. The test at (a)(i) was that the child 'is not receiving such care, protection and guidance as a good parent may reasonably be expected to give'. The procedure indicated by these proposals in the case of a child brought before a court for the commission of offences was that:

> If the child denies having committed the offence it will be necessary to prove this in the same way as at present. It will normally be for the police to bring forward the necessary evidence. If the court is not satisfied that the child committed the offence, that will be the end of the proceedings. If the offence is admitted or proved, evidence will then be brought forward by the local authority or the police, in the same way as in existing care, protection or control proceedings, that the child is not receiving such care, protection or guidance as a good parent may reasonably be expected to give, or is beyond control.[1]

These suggestions were implemented in Section 1 of the 1969 CYPA, a finding of guilt following prosecution for a criminal offence standing alongside the other, welfare-oriented grounds for care proceedings. Following proof of any of these grounds, a court could make an order on a child only if it was further satisfied that 'he is in need of care or control which he is unlikely to receive unless the court makes an order under this section in respect of him'.

According to this section, a child could be made subject to a court order for the commission of an offence only if there were no other way that the necessary care and control could be provided for him. It seems logical that amongst the alternatives to be weighed against residential care at this stage of court proceedings, the provision of other forms of supervision, statutory and otherwise, by the social services department would have to be considered.

According to this procedure, before a child for whom one of the

conditions outlined in Section 1(2) of the 1969 CYPA had been proved
could be committed to care, it would have to be established that there was
no other way that either the parents, the social services department, the
probation service or any other agency − voluntary or statutory − acting
alone or in combination could provide a sufficient degree of support or
control necessary for the child to remain at home. Given these conditions, it
would have been an indictment of the local agencies had any but the most
serious of young offenders come into care.

In the final draft of the Act which was eventually passed by Parliament
there was, however, a brief subsection towards the end of Section 7 of the
Act which, when it was implemented, completely undermined the
intentions of Section 1 care proceedings for juvenile offenders. Section 7(7)
said simply that when

> a young person is found guilty of any offence by or before any court, that
> court or the court to which his case is remitted shall have the power, (a) if
> the offence is punishable in the case of an adult with imprisonment, to
> make a care order (other than an interim order) in respect of him.

This section constituted the provision for juvenile courts to make custodial
orders on juveniles in (explicitly) the same way as an ordinary magistrates
court might pass a custodial sentence on an adult. There was in this section
no consideration of the child's demonstrated needs, no consideration of
alternative courses of action, no implicit consideration, by comparison, of
the long-term consequences of such a sentence on the young offender.

Somehow, probably because of their sense of victory at the
implementation of Section 1, professional social workers failed to notice the
importance or even the existence of Section 7(7). Despite the fundamental
differences, in the procedures for hearing cases and passing sentence,
between Section 1 and Section 7(7), social services departments have for the
most part failed to recognise that all children committed to care following
criminal prosecution are committed under Section 7(7) and not under
Section 1.

In 1978 a study was conducted into young offenders subject to care in
one authority.[2] Of 112 cases, 79 were recorded by the authority as subject
to care orders under Section 1(2)(f) of the 1969 CYPA and 33 as subject to
care orders made under Section 7(7). Further investigation revealed that all
112 care orders were made under Section 7(7). This pattern of
misinformation has persisted in all the authorities in which we have been
involved.

The local juvenile criminal justice system study described earlier in this
chapter was made in an area where a policy of decarcerating juvenile
offenders in care was being developed. While the system study enabled
social workers to have a clearer picture of the context in which they were

working, the Section 7(7) care order study in the same locality helped them to discover the processes whereby such orders came to be made, as well as to identify potential clients for the high-intensity intermediate treatment programme.

The mere identification of the Section 7(7) care order cases for the study was in itself a fraught and lengthy task. In that locality, thirty-five such cases were identified during one visit. Subject to a sudden attack of human fallibility, the researchers neglected to bring the names of the identified cases on their next visit, with the result that the social workers with whom they were working had once more to go through the long process of identifying the cases. This time they found thirty-six. When the old list was found and compared with the new one it was discovered that the first search had produced eight names unidentified in the second, and the second search nine names unidentified in the first giving a grand total of forty-four cases – only two of which were actually filed as subject to Section 7(7) care orders.

Once the delinquents subject to care orders had been identified, their case files were gathered together. Since these children had been committed to care under Section 7(7), the next step was to apply a 'care or control test' to see how many of them would have been committed to care had they been taken to court under Section 1 of the 1969 CYPA and their needs for care and control given consideration in the courtroom. The general method for administering the care or control test was to pair researchers with the most senior child care staff available at the time in the social services department. Each pair screened each case on three criteria demonstrating the need for care and control at the time the care order was made. Thus each pair sorted the files into three piles, (1) no need for care or control demonstrated, (2) need for care and control demonstrated, and (3) uncertain. Each case was recycled through the pairs of screeners until the panel arrived at a common agreement and the files had been sorted into two piles, those who demonstrated a need for care and control and those who did not. The three criteria used in this screening process were as follows:

BEHAVIOUR

Is the child a danger to himself and/or the community?

A child would be deemed to present such dangers if there were any record of or reference to self-destructive or violent behaviour such as attempted suicide or convictions for unwarranted assaults or grievous bodily harm. Or if there were records indicating a pattern of dangerously irresponsible behaviour such as persistent taking and driving away of motor cars which endangered other road users, or offences of arson.

FAMILY BACKGROUND

Does the child have a home in the community which can, with appropriate support, provide an adequate degree of care and control?

In the earlier discussion of Section 1 of the 1969 CYPA it was mentioned that when a court addresses itself to the question of whether or not a child is in need of care or control that he would not receive without a court order, it should weigh the merits of residential care for the child against not only his home and parental circumstances, but also against levels of community-based support and provision available to the family. In considering this criterion, the panel was concerned to see if there was any information on the files which would demonstrate or imply that, even with an appropriate level of social work support, the child's home could not provide adequate care and control. Two obvious examples of situations where the need for residential care would be demonstrated under this criterion would be where the child has no home in the community (in which case he is likely to have been in care before his committal under Section 7(7)) and those cases where the child or young person is the target of persistent parental hostility.

DEVELOPMENTAL NEEDS

Does the child have any specific medical, educational, vocational or psychiatric needs which can be dealt with only in a residential context?

For this particular criterion the panel was concerned with severe disabilities such as psychosis, brain damage, epilepsy, or physical illness or handicap, which required forms of containment or specialised treatment that could not be effected in the community. There is a point worth noting here with regard to remedial education. It was not unusual for children in the Section 7(7) care order samples studies to be recommended for residential care in CHEs primarily because they were a year or two behind their peers at school (sometimes as a result of truancy). Such cases were not seen as meriting residential care under this criterion for two reasons: first, that there is no reason why remedial education should not be provided in the community (indeed many education authorities have established community-based remedial and truancy units), and secondly, because this form of educational 'retardation' is primarily an *educational* problem; its 'treatment' is the responsibility of education departments. By acceding to recommendations for the placement of such children in CHEs, social services departments are merely taking the pressure off education departments to increase the limited provision in community-based units and, in some cases, to examine the extent to which such problems may be generated by the curricula and structure of their schools.

To date, Section 7(7) care order studies have been conducted in three separate local authority social services departments. A similar study was undertaken in a fourth social services department, but only in respect of delinquents who were placed in CHEs.[3] Table 4.5 shows the results of the care or control tests applied to the Section 7(7) care order samples in these three departments. Local authority 1(a) is a 100 per cent sample of all such orders (132 cases), while 1(b) represents an area office within that sample which was studied in greater detail twelve months later. Local authority 2 is again an area office sample, while local authority 3 is a 100 per cent sample from another part of the country.

Table 4·5.   *Section 7(7) care order studies and the application of the care or control test*

Authority	No. of 7(7) orders	care appropriate	care inappropriate	% inappropriate
1(a)	132	13	119	90
1(b)	28	3	25	89
2	44	13	31	70·5
3	112	12	100	89
Totals	316	41	275	87

The methodology applied in these studies has since been used in one London social services department, but without the assistance of the authors and using a panel drawn from that authority of senior and advisory staff from both the residential and fieldwork sections. From a sample of eighty-four Section 7(7) care order cases, fifty-four (64·3 per cent) were found to be inappropriately subject to such orders and not in demonstrable need of residential care.

The results of these studies speak for themselves. The large proportions of delinquents who were not in demonstrable need of care or control under any of the criteria outlined above lead inexorably to a questioning or investigation of the patterns and contingencies of decision-making which result in so many delinquents receiving inappropriate care orders.

The Section 7(7) care order differs from the Section 1 care order in terms of its retributive emphasis, for it is the nature of the offence which is the only determining criterion under Section 7(7) – i.e. one for which the maximum penalty for an adult would be imprisonment. The benefits or otherwise of residential care are not considered. Given that so many of these delinquents were not, therefore, apparently in explicit need of care or control when the order was made, but that they had committed offences imprisonable in the case of adults, then there is a suggestion that the care orders were made as a result of serious and frequent offending.

In authority 1(a), the mean cost of property damaged or stolen by the 119 delinquents who 'failed' the care or control test was £20. This does not seem particularly high considering the inaccuracies and distortions introduced by police methods of recording the cost of theft or damage, regardless of whether or not stolen property, for example, is actually returned or recovered. Furthermore, where two or more delinquents are involved in the same offence, the full value of the property is recorded against each individual rather than divided between them. Thus it is not uncommon for a group of children who have taken a car to have the full value of the car recorded separately, once for each child involved, even though the car will probably have been recovered and returned to its owner. It is not difficult to see how a few such incidents can easily inflate the recorded cost of delinquency out of all proportion.

In authorities 2 and 3 the offences for which the children received inappropriate care orders were recorded according to the classification in Table 4.6 (since some children were charged with more than one specific offence, the number of charges exceeds the number of children in the 'inappropriately committed' sample).

Table 4·6.   *Distribution of types of offences committed by children inappropriately committed to care under Section 7(7) of the 1969 CYPA*

Charge	% 2	% 3
Attempted offences against property	1·5	90·0
Offences against property	91·0	
Traffic offences	3·0	4·9
Offences against persons	8·0	2·1
Offences defined by police	1·5	3·0
	100	100

The first three categories of this classification – attempted offences against property, offences against property, and traffic offences – are clearly identifiable and self-explanatory. Offences against persons included any form of assault, from the minimal charge of assault itself which could mean a tap on the shoulder, to charges of grievous and actual bodily harm, of which there were no more than one or two in any of the populations studied. A further consideration here is that in any case where the nature and circumstances of the assault indicated the possibility that this was more than just an isolated occurrence and was likely to recur, the child would automatically have been selected into the 'appropriately committed' population rather than the 'inappropriately committed'.

Since over 90 per cent of these children's delinquencies were associated with property rather than endangering other people, and very few of these property offences, even according to official figures, were what might be described as 'big time', then perhaps, rather than the severity of particular offences, it was the public-nuisance value of persistent petty offending which led to justifiably retributive sentencing decisions for these children. Table 4.7 shows the number of court appearances on separate charges that these children had before their committal to care.

Table 4·7. *Number of previous court appearances made by children inappropriately committed to care under Section 7(7)*

Previous number of appearances	Authorities							
	1(a)		1(b)		2		Total	
	No.	%	No.	%	No.	%	No.	%
0	40	33	7	28	10	31	57	32·5
1	33	28	8	32	9	29	50	28·5
2	27	23	6	24	8	26	41	23·4
3	10	8	2	8	2	7	14	8·0
4	7	6	—	—	—	—	7	4·0
5	2	2	2	8	2	7	6	3·4
Totals	119	100	25	100	31	100	175	100

Note: All percentages are rounded to the nearest whole number.

This table only includes data from authorities 1(a), 1(b) and 2 since information was not collected in the same way for authority 3. Nevertheless, the results from authority 3 were in line with those in the other areas studied.

The 1978 study mentioned earlier[4] produced a figure of 33 per cent of committals to care without previous court appearances. A later, independent study in an inner London borough produced a figure of 44 per cent for the same group. In all the other authorities for which figures are available over 30 per cent of children in care under Section 7(7) are committed on their first court appearance. The evidence would seem to suggest that the inappropriate committal to care of these children cannot be explained by either the severity or the frequency of offending. Of all cases studied to date from authorities 1(a), 1(b) and 2 who received inappropriate Section 7(7) care orders, 32·5 per cent had no previous court sentences, 28·5 per cent had less than two, and 23·4 per cent had less than three. Over three-quarters, therefore, had three or less previous court appearances.

If this high number of inappropriate committals cannot be explained by reference to characteristics of these children's offences and offending, we must question the decisions that both constituted and created the conditions for the making of the orders; primarily the sentencing decisions of the magistrates. Very significantly contingent on these decisions, however, would be the recommendations made to the magistrates by the social workers.

It is common for social workers to argue that inappropriate sentencing decisions stem from the primarily retributive concerns of magistrates. If this were to be the case with regard to these inappropriate disposals, then one would expect to find considerable differences between the recommendations made by the social enquiry reports presented on these delinquents and the sentences made by magistrates. In other words, one would predict that the majority of recommendations would be for disposals other than care orders. Table 4.8 shows the recommendations made to magistrates in social enquiry reports at the court appearance when the care order was made. (Unfortunately the form of analysis used for authority 3 does not permit compilation of recommendations at committal.)

Table 4·8. *Recommendations made by social workers for court appearances at which children were inappropriately committed to care*

Recommended Sentence	Authorities							
	1(a)		1(b)		2		Total	
	No.	%	No.	%	No.	%	No.	%
Unclear/not available	26	22	3	12	6	21	35	20
Conditional discharge	4	3	—	—	1	3	5	3
Adjournment	—	—	—	—	2	8	2	7
Fine or attendance centre	2	2	—	—	1	3	3	2
Deferred sentence	—	—	2	8	—	—	2	1
Supervision order	8	7	1	4	—	—	12	7
Supervision order with intermediate treatment	5	4	2	8	—	—	7	3
Interim care order	12	10	—	—	4	14	16	9
Care order	61	51	17	68	15	51	93	53
Detention centre	1	1	—	—	—	—	1	1
Totals	119		25		29		176	

Note: All percentages are rounded to the nearest whole number.

The first category of recommendation in this table, 'unclear' or 'not known', covers three distinct possibilities. (1) Those cases where a social enquiry report had been supplied but could not be located at the time of the study (although the organisation of case files considerably hindered the collection of data, it was relatively rare for a social enquiry report to be missing from the file). (2) Those cases where a care order had been made without the submission of a social enquiry report. (3) Those cases where the report was available but inconclusive in its recommendations. Approximately half of the 20 per cent of recommendations that fell into this category were cases where the recommendation was inconclusive. Far from being at odds with the SER recommendation, the majority (53 per cent) of these inappropriate care orders were made in direct concurrence with social workers' recommendations. In fact if the question is slightly rephrased to ask in what proportion of cases did magistrates' sentencing decisions conflict with social work recommendations, the answer is about 25–30 per cent.

For two of the local authorities studied, 1(a) and 2, further data was available on the recommendations made by observation and assessment centres. In both authorities considerably more children received observation and assessment than were recommended by social workers for inappropriate care orders (see Table 4.9).

Table 4·9.   *Inappropriate care orders and the use of observation and assessment.*

	Authority					
	1(a)		2		Total	
	No.	%	No.	%	No.	%
Recommended for interim care order	12	12	4	24	16	13
Received assessment	96	88	13	76	109	87

Note: All percentages are rounded to the nearest whole number.

Whilst more delinquents received observation and assessment than were recommended for it in both authorities, the figures reflect a considerable difference between the authorities in terms of the overall proportions receiving observation and assessment. It may be tempting to explain this difference in terms of a stated policy that all children coming into care should receive observation and assessment as part of their 'treatment' to enable the development of rational plans and objectives, but in fact it is authority 2 which has the most explicit policy. It seems more likely that the high proportion of children receiving observation and assessment, compared with the relatively low proportion recommended for it, reflects the pragmatic development of observation and assessment centres as clearing houses for children committed to care.

Table 4.10 shows the recommendations of observation and assessment reports in authorities 1(a) and 2. Over 85 per cent of recommendations on inappropriately committed children were for some form of residential care, the majority (42 per cent) being for placement in CHEs, the ex-approved schools.

The evidence of the Section 7(7) care order studies at this level indicates that the majority of children studied who were committed to care under this section of the 1969 CYPA did not show any 'needs' for care or control, but were not, for the most part, committed in retribution for either the frequency or the severity of their offending by punitive magistrates. On the

Table 4·10.   *Distribution of recommendations made by observation and assessment centres*

Recommendation	Authority 1(a) No.	%	2 No.	%	Total No.	%
Home on trial	11	12	—	—	11	10
Further observation and assessment	1	1	—	—	1	1
Supervision order	1	1	2	14	3	3
Supervision order with intermediate treatment	2	2	—	—	2	2
Care order	6	6	2	14	8	7
Community home	26	27	1	7	27	24
Community home with education	39	41	7	51	46	42
Other residential placement	10	10	2	14	12	11
Totals	96	100	14	100	110	100

Note: All percentages are rounded to the nearest whole number.

contrary, juvenile court decisions seem to have been largely due to the recommendations and judgements of the 'treatment' oriented professional advisers to the juridical process. Despite the apparent contradiction between the retributive form of Section 7(7) and the concern of social workers for children's welfare, together they have created a short cut into the residential care system and perhaps even acted to escalate rather than terminate the careers of young offenders. In authority 1(a), the 119 children who 'failed' the care or control test and did not demonstrate any need for residential care had between them 155 court appearances before the making of the care order. They had 200 appearances altogether subsequent to their committal. It would be contentious to suggest that increases in offending (or at least conviction) were generally a consequence of committal to care, but it is almost a matter of common sense that once a child has received a care order, subsequent offences are likely to be dealt with more severely by juvenile courts. Tables 4.11(a) and 4.11(b) show the distibution of sentences in court appearances before and after committal to care under Section 7(7) in authority 1(a).

It is easy to see from these tables the shift in sentences from the 'lighter' conditional discharges, fines, attendance centre orders and supervision orders before the care order, to the more severe detention centre orders and committals to crown court for borstal sentencing subsequent to the care order. Before care committal there were two detention centre orders; subsequent to committal there were thirty-six detention centre orders and crown court referrals – an increase in these sentences of some 1,700 per cent. Whilst it has not been possible in these studies to establish a common 'tariff' of sentencing leading to a care order, it certainly seems to have been

Table 4·11 (a). Sentences received before committal to care under Section 7(7) in Authority 1(a)

Sentences		Conditional discharge	Fine	Attendance centre	Supervision order	Supervision order with intermediate treatment	Care order	Detention centre	Crown court	Prison	No.
Sentences before committal to care	1 No.	18	4	17	39	1	—	—	—	—	79
	1 %	22·7	5·1	21·5	49·4	1·3	—	—	—	—	100
	2 No.	6	4	16	17	2	—	1	—	—	46
	2 %	13	8·7	34·8	37	4·3	—	2·2	—	—	100
	3 No.	3	3	6	7	—	—	—	—	—	19
	3 %	15·8	15·8	31·6	36·8	—	—	—	—	—	100
	4 No.	2	2	2	3	—	—	—	—	—	9
	4 %	22·2	22·2	22·2	33·4	—	—	—	—	—	100
	5 No.	—	—	1	1	—	—	—	—	—	2
	5 %	—	—	50	50	—	—	—	—	—	100
Totals	No.	29	13	42	67	3	—	1	—	—	155
	%	18·7	8·4	27·1	43·2	1·8	—	0·6	—	—	100

Table 4·11 (b). Sentences received after committal to care under Section 7(7) in Authority 1(a)

Sentences	Conditional discharge	Fine	Attendance centre	Supervision order	Supervision order with intermediate treatment	Care order	Detention centre	Crown court	Prison	No.
1 No.	23	5	17	—	—	26	4	1	1	76
%	30·3	6·6	22·4	—	—	34·2	5·3	1·2	1	100
2 No.	14	4	12	—	—	12	8	1	—	51
%	27·5	7·8	23·5	—	—	23·5	15·7	2	—	100
3 No.	5	7	6	—	—	5	6	1	—	30
%	16·7	23·3	20	—	—	16·7	20	3·3	—	100
4 No.	5	3	—	—	—	4	5	1	—	18
%	27·8	16·6	—	—	—	22·2	27·8	5·6	—	100
5 No.	4	4	—	—	—	1	2	2	—	13
%	30·8	30·8	—	—	—	7·6	15·4	15·4	—	100
6 No.	1	1	—	—	—	—	2	2	—	6
%	16·7	16·7	—	—	—	—	33·3	33·3	—	100
7 No.	—	3	—	—	—	—	1	—	—	4
%	—	75	—	—	—	—	25	—	—	100
8 No.	—	—	—	1	—	—	—	—	1	2
%	—	—	—	50	—	—	—	—	50	100
Totals No.	52	27	35	1	—	48	28	8	1	200
%	26	13·5	17·5	0·5	—	24	14	4	0·5	100

Sentences subsequent to committal to care

the case for the 119 children in Table 4.11 that committal to care triggered a
new tariff on subsequent conviction. It is somewhat disturbing to consider
that committal to care on the grounds of the welfare of the child may, far
from rescuing him, expose him to ever more 'punitive' sentences and the
use of prison department establishments.

Further analysis of post-care-order delinquent careers in authority 3
revealed that the type of placement is a significant factor in determining
sentencing. Out of the 100 delinquents in that authority subject to Section
7(7) care orders, 54 were placed in CHEs for an average period of fifteen
and a half months each. The CHEs were no more successful in preventing
reconviction than any other type of placement, including home-on-trial,
family group homes, hostels and maladjusted schools. The reconviction rate
was 66 per cent regardless of placement. However, the sentences received
by the delinquents who were reconvicted during or after a CHE placement
were far more severe. No less than 20 of the 54 CHE-placed delinquents
subsequently went to detention centre (out of a total of 28 detention centre
orders given to the 66 who got into further trouble). Equally striking was
the fact that out of 16 of the reconvicted care order delinquents who
received borstal sentences, 14 were inmates or ex-inmates of CHEs. It
would appear then that while CHEs were no more successful than any
other type of placement in preventing further delinquency, the delinquents
who were placed or had been placed in such establishments were much
more likely to be sent on to penal establishments than those placed
elsewhere. In that authority, moreover, the CHE-placed delinquents were
no more seriously delinquent than the non-CHE children.

The Section 7(7) care order studies served to indicate that things were not
working in the way that had been assumed. At the same time, they
contained an implicit direction for the development of policy. They detailed
a number of specific children who were being maintained in residential care
against their best interests. At the time of the 7(7) studies those children
subject to 7(7) orders were at various stages of their careers. A large number
had already been through 'the system' and were home on trial: the rest
were scattered through a variety of institutions. Table 4.12 shows the
placement of those subject to inappropriate 7(7) care orders in authorities,
1(a), 1(b) and 2 at the time of the study.

It may be seen that a little under half of these children were already in the
community, some boarded out in hostels, the majority back at home. About
one-eighth were in establishments beyond the realm of social services.
Some 43 per cent were still in social services establishments: community
homes, CHEs, and observation and assessment centres.

The previous chapter concluded by referring to the superimposition
within social work of the child savers' institutional codes and regulations
on the classifications and legal recommendations of the professional adviser
to the juridical process. The use of the Section 7(7) care order is by no

Table 4·12. *Current placement of children subject to care orders under Section 7(7) at the time of study*

Placement	Authority							
	1(a)		1(b)		2		Total	
	No.	%	No.	%	No.	%	No.	%
Home-on-trial	52	43	15	47	11	40	78	45
Boarded out	4	3	—	—	—	—	—	—
Hostel	3	3	—	—	—	—	3	1
Community home	14	12	7	22	3	11	24	14
Observation and assessment	7	6	2	6	—	—	9	6
Residential special school	7	6	—	—	1	3	8	4
CHE	22	19	7	27	11	40	40	23
Detention centre and borstal	3	3	—	—	1	3	7	3
Other placements	4	3	1	3	1	3	6	3
Prison	2	2	—	—	—	—	2	1
Totals	118		32		28		177	

Note: All percentages are rounded to the nearest whole number.

means an exception to this. One of the principles of curriculum development referred to in Chapter 7 is that when presented with two contrasting perceptions of the same event, the individual is forced to develop an explanation. Social workers are no exception to this. When social workers were presented with the results of Section 7(7) care order studies in their own authorities, with the apparent punitiveness of their own recommendations despite their good intentions, the explanation most frequently offered was that their recommendations were not punitive because they were not concerned with the severity or otherwise of the offence, but with problems presented for the child either by his own behaviour or in his family. This explanation could take several forms. The first may be characterised in terms of inaccessibility; the social worker was aware of serious emotional or psychodynamic problems in the family but was unable to get the family to recognise this and allow him to work with them. In this light, the child's offence allows the social worker access; he may recommend care on the grounds not of the severity of the offence or of previous offences, but rather to enable him to remove the child from the disturbing influences of his home life or to give him rights of access to the family. From this point of view the child's removal from his family may be seen as allowing him to settle down or as preventing further inhibition of his development.

The second explanation may be characterised in terms of crisis. In the Section 7(7) care order study in authority 1(b), although the sample of Section 7(7) care orders was in fact quite small, (twenty-eight, including both 'appropriate' and 'inappropriate' committals), it was found nearly half (twelve) of those children were committed to care at the time of a severe crisis in their families, most frequently due to marital breakdown, or friction between the young offender and one parent or step-parent. The result of the court appearance – committal to care – seemed almost inevitable given the presentation of such background information in the social enquiry report. Once in care, however, the average length of stay in an institution for these children was just over two years, whereas the family crisis would often be resolved in some fashion within a matter of weeks or at the most a few months. This resolution would be the stabilising of the dynamics of the family but with an important difference: the child was, if not absent from the new dynamics, for the most part unable to participate. The family had stabilised without him, creating the possibility that his return could generate the conditions for a new crisis and would at least involve considerable shuffling amongst the family.

The third explanation encountered was educational. It was argued that the child, frequently as a result of truancy, was behind at school and therefore would benefit from placement in a CHE.

These explanations for inappropriate committals to care all hinged on the linking of problems to offending. The child's court appearance following an offence created a focus, for the social worker at least, not on the specific offence which had brought the child before the court, but rather on the disorderliness, the problems in the child's background which were seen as generating the offence. From this perspective the court becomes a source of remedies for problems; the social worker is no longer seen as an agent of control, but instead as an agent of welfare who explains children's offences. The hidden contortions of this view are exemplified by the case of a social worker in one authority who returned to the office from court angry that a child had been found not guilty of an offence, not because of her feelings about the offence but rather because, believing that the child would plead guilty, she had prepared a social enquiry report in which she had argued for a care order. She was angry because the 'not guilty' finding had denied her access to the child and his problems. There is here some explanation of the reasons why social work agencies are for the most part unaware of the distinctions between Section 1(2)(f) and Section 7(7) of the 1969 CYPA. Although the wording of Section 7(7) is retributive, it would seem that many, if not most, of the children who are committed to care under that section are so committed on the grounds of their own welfare, as a remedy for problems rather than because they have committed offences for which adults would receive imprisonment. Problems are perceived in an ambiguous relationship to offending. On the one hand, they are used as explanations, even as mitigations for the type of behaviour which constitutes offending; on the other, more subtly, they are seen as preconditions indicating the tendency to, or likelihood of, further offending.

It is this ambiguity which supports the connection between problems and offences rather than theoretical clarification and explanation of the ways in which childrens' problems lead them to commit offences.

In all the areas where it was carried out, the Section 7(7) care order study formed part of a strategy not of research, but of policy development and change. Its effect was to confront practitioners with the results of their practice.

Historically, social work research has tended to be characterised by its focus on the individual – the client. Studies intended to inform practice have been subject to the same deficiencies as the 'positivist' criminological and sociological research mentioned in the previous chapter. They have tended to take the client as their focus and have assumed rather than clarified the client's 'problem' status. Such research has had the effect of extending rather than questioning the classifications routinely used by social workers.

That social workers are aware of the deficiencies of such research would seem to be indicated by the rejection, together with the labelling theorists and misfit sociologists generally, of head-counting research. The research of the labelling theorists has tended to focus exclusively on the social constitution of meanings in interaction, the construction and maintenance of labels, a tendency shared by the other radical perspectives with which it was associated, for example Laing's studies of schizophrenia.

As a profession, social work has taken a somewhat ambiguous stance with regard to research. Whilst it has historically been informed by 'positivist' studies, it has developed a resistance to statistical research. Although this resistance appears similar to, and indeed has been associated with, the resistance of the labelling theorists, its roots lie in the individualising tendencies of professional social work.

Social workers are themselves part of a hierarchy. Their professional status places on them a responsibility to their authority, their supervisors, seniors, area officers and ultimately social services committees, to supervise the cases allocated to them. At the same time, it confers on them certain rights to control the 'style' of supervision. The uneasy tension between a social worker's responsibility and his rights is evidenced by the conflict, endemic in social services departments, between the levels of fieldwork and management.

The image of this conflict is that of the social worker attempting to fight off the bureaucratic demands of his hierarchy in order to meet the personal needs of his clients. The services provided in social work are conceptualised as 'personal'; the needs of clients are unique and antithetical to quantitative analysis and management. The professional judgement of the social worker is secure and unassailable. These inclinations of social work are reflected in the way that information is organised within social services departments. In conducting the Section 7(7) care order studies it appeared at times as though the filing and information systems of departments were organised to obscure rather than record. In none of the authorities studied were figures on anything other than financial dimensions collected and collated at local level. As was mentioned above, the figures that were available at the level of central administration often proved very suspect. In no authority was it possible to collect comparative information on cases, for example details of previous cautions and offences, without a painstaking study of case files.

The inaccessibility of such data could be described as beneficial from one point of view in that it limits bureaucratisation of social work and underlines the centrality of the social worker as opposed to his supervisory hierarchy. This view is, however, somewhat limited since it appears to assume that 'personalisation' as opposed to bureaucratisation ensures the ethical performance and benevolent outcome of the social work task. Yet this very personalisation appears in practice to undermine in some ways the interests of the social work clients it seeks to protect. The Section 7(7) care order studies demonstrated that most of the inappropriate committals made resulted from the recommendations of the social workers. These recommendations were based on conceptions of personalised need. It would appear that social workers have reacted against both the bureaucratisation of departments and their identification as 'control' agents by personalising their task, stressing their commitment to the needs of individual clients rather than the control of an identifiable group. The effect of this reaction has been to mystify and obscure from themselves the results of their own practice.

The Section 7(7) care order studies were, in many ways, the first step in a programme of development. They provided a critique of practice at the local level. Even more importantly, the studies provided an insight into a key sector of the juvenile criminal justice system, for local authorities currently spend vast sums of money on CHE provision for juvenile offenders. It is clear from the studies presented in this chapter that these residential services, far from preventing delinquent careers, actually promote them at eventual considerable cost to both the community and the individual delinquent. Moreover, such provisions and expense often prevent the development of vital intermediate treatment services in the community which are needed to prevent career development. The ease with which Section 7(7) care orders were made is, at least in part, a reflection of the absence of such intermediate treatment services in the authorities studied. Policy developments can only be based on factual appraisal, not on impression. The muddled and confusing evidence presented to the House of Commons sub-committee, described in Chapter 1, is merely a reflection at the highest professional levels of the confusion at local levels where the police, magistrates, probation and social services blame each other for mishandling juvenile delinquents. The evidence seems to suggest, however, that a remarkable degree of collusion actually exists, and this collusion is maintained by the operation of sets of procedures by different professional bodies who do not in fact possess either clear policy guidelines or clear criteria for the delivery of services to delinquents.

One of the criticisms made of labelling theory in the last chapter was that it tends to characterise the labelling process in terms of the hapless definee and the hostile, mechanical definer of reality. At the level of brute statistics alone, the Section 7(7) care order studies show a similar deficiency, tending to identify the recommending social worker as the 'hidden baddie' in the system whose overt conflict, but hidden collusion, with the retributive leanings of Section 7(7) entraps young offenders at random. It is important to go beyond this level to understand the contingencies that enable social workers to sustain perceptions so divergent from what is demonstrated by the statistics. There are three areas here which share a broad correspondence with the more abstract and theoretical dynamics of the last chapter. They are the connections between welfare, problems and delinquency; the individualising perspective of social work; and the massive institutional commitment of social services departments. The implication for practice is that it is not sufficient merely to collect information about individual delinquents and aggregate it into global statistics. It is the decisions which are made by the professionals on these individuals which reveal that delinquent careers are not merely a direct result of a series of individual delinquent acts, but also very much a result of decisions made about the actors.

REFERENCES: CHAPTER 4

1   Home Office *Children in Trouble*, Cmnd 3601 (London: HMSO, 1968).
2   Thorpe, D., Dunsby, E. and Green, C., 'Services received by juvenile offenders subject to care orders', in *Children and Young Persons' Act 1969* (Birmingham: BASW, 1978).
3   Thorpe, D., 'Managing juvenile delinquents – the Wakefield method', *Social Work Service*, no. 20 (June 1979), pp. 45–9. (Published by DHSS, London.)
4   Thorpe, Dunsby and Green, op. cit.

5

A New Framework for Social Work with Juvenile Offenders

It is tempting to say that we are at a watershed. After nearly ten years of conflict and confusion – apparent conflict, genuine confusion – it is at last time for a reappraisal. The pragmatic philosophy of peaceful coexistence between two opposed systems has engendered too many contradictions and, with the rhetoric of punishment swiftly re-establishing itself, it has become necessary to reorganise and redefine the abolitionist alternative. This will mean rejecting, or at least substantially modifying, some principles that have long been identified with social work – principles which many social workers believe distinguish their approach from the more 'punitive' enemy. But it is precisely these principles – in their present form – which have done the damage for, paradoxically perhaps, they are embedded in the same framework of beliefs and assumptions that currently sustains the re-emerging philosophy of deterrence and the short, sharp shock. Indeed, it is this shared framework which, arguably, has made the ironic tragedy of peaceful coexistence possible.

In this chapter and the next we shall attempt this task of redefinition before going on to describe, in rather more detail, some of the implications for social work practice. If the past decade has shown anything, it is that 'good ideas' and new techniques are simply not enough. It would be easy to write a handbook of method, an inchoate list of activities, games and therapeutic stratagems, but it would change nothing. Techniques are meaningless if practised on the wrong people, in the wrong setting and for the wrong reasons. This is not to say that that rare individual, the 'charismatic nut',[1] cannot make an impact. But it is an inevitably transient one. The dividing line between what makes sense and what does not is so teasingly narrow that once the new ideas have been absorbed into the established corpus of knowledge, the established framework of concepts, they lose both their colour and their effectiveness, and the achievements that might once have been claimed for them are successfully undermined. We are trying to bring about a fall from grace. It is time to bite the apple and realise that there is more to social work with delinquents (or anyone else) than the latest activity fad or the most recently imported therapeutic cult. In these two chapters, therefore, the necessary rebuilding of conceptual foundations will be carried through. It will be a long but essential argument. This chapter will attempt to establish the outline of a new framework, while the next discusses the various parts of this framework in greater detail. Both should be read with great care because it will be all too easy to mistake what is being said for something that is not being said, despite the many disclaimers and qualifications along the way. The social work vocabulary is vague enough, at the best of times, to make communication a problem, and nowhere more so than in talk about delinquency whose field of discourse is currently defined by two concepts whose meanings have been all but emptied of content. It is with these two concepts – care and control – that we begin.

CARE AND CONTROL

When concepts become clichés there is good reason to think that they have outlived their usefulness. The very ubiquity of the 'care or control' dilemma in social work, the fact that it is regularly invoked to explain, justify or merely define, suggests that it has become just another piece of empty terminology whose contribution to the understanding of real problems is quite nugatory. Whether we are presented with a puzzle – how to reconcile the conflict between the two – or whether we are reassured that they are merely opposite sides of the same coin, there is always a sense of unreality, a feeling that, whatever it is that is being said, it does nothing more than reflect the formal polarisation inherent in a particular vocabulary.

As soon as we inquire what this vocabulary is based on, it collapses. In one of the social work versions of the dilemma, care is identified with the individual's needs, control with society's. One need only state the matter in these terms to see how sociologically naïve the distinction is. If radical criticisms of social work – of its 'consensus' thinking, its functionalism – are justified anywhere, they are justified here. Whose society (or whose image of society) are we talking about? And in terms of what social theory are we defining individual needs? These questions are inescapable.

We have already suggested in an earlier chapter that the social worker's traditional unease about 'social control' is, to some degree, misplaced. But let us interrogate this unease on its own terms, taking as an example the more specific concepts of 'treatment' and 'punishment' – just one aspect of the field of discourse apparently defined by the opposition between care and control. If social workers tend to be anxious about their own 'social control' role, they are positively hostile towards that of other agencies and 'punitive' is still one of the most damning accusations in the repertoire of professional invective. But what is the real significance of the distinction between treatment and punishment? Whatever the emotional connotations, it is not simply that one is nice and one is nasty, or that one is coming to terms with the individual's problems while the other is society's reminder that he has erred. When we analyse the difference between their objectives, and when we actually look at the regimes with which they are associated, it becomes apparent that what we have here are two distinct modes of socialisation, each attempting to inculcate different kinds of virtue, different habits and attitudes, and each embedded in a particular view of the wider social structure.

The regimes associated with 'treatment' and 'punishment' are both designed to shape the personality: they differ in that they aim to produce different types of person. The personal qualities, the virtues, which they prize and seek to inculcate fall into two distinct groups, each associated with a particular image of society, and with political and social beliefs about the individuals who ought to populate it. They differ, too, in the psychological theories that underlie them, theories about how people learn different modes of behaviour or acquire different virtues – theories, in short, which explain how the basic socialisation trick is worked. And although both try to produce controlled and controllable behaviour, each identifies a different mechanism, a different concept, of control. If the key idea of punishment is *'obedience* to *authority'*, the key idea of treatment is *'conformity* to social *norms'*.

Consider: punishment almost invariably takes place in settings characterised by explicit hierarchies, formal modes of authority and address, and highly organised frameworks of space and time. In contrast, treatment is associated with implicit, understated hierarchies, informal modes of authority and a much more flexible organisation of the spatio-temporal framework. Punishment works by command, coercion, habituation and instruction; treatment involves the use of social-scientific knowledge to diagnose problems and bring about change through various kinds of interpersonal pressure. Consequently, while punishment emphasises the virtues of discipline, obedience, routine and respect, treatment has more to do with conformity, urbanity, pragmatism and tact.[2]

The very use of words like 'maladjustment' (and other less question-begging terms) implies that treatment seeks to bring about not a proper respect for authority but an ability to read social cues, adapt to social norms and conform to social pressures. In that sense, it is as much a form of 'control' (or attempted control) as punishment, the difference being that the conception of society which underlies it conflicts at all points with the conception of society which underlies punishment. It is evident that talk about 'social control', independently of the kind of 'social' we want to control for, is almost meaningless.

It is, of course, possible to classify theories of delinquency in a way that corresponds to the distinction between treatment and punishment.

Someone who favours punishment is likely to attribute delinquency to all or some of the following: lack of discipline in the home or at school; lack of respect for authority; permissive morality; a society gone soft on crime. Theories of this kind permit the inference that in order to stop delinquency it is necessary to expose offenders to the rigours of a punishment regime which will restore a sense of discipline, increase respect for authority, and draw a strong distinction between right and wrong.

Conversely, someone who favours treatment needs to be able to justify an emphasis on interpersonal pressure. Accordingly, he is likely to take the view that delinquency is a result of poor social development; absence of social skills; inability to communicate; maladjustment or immaturity. The inference which these theories permit is that young offenders should be placed in an environment which allows them to develop properly. It should provide them with the opportunity to become like everyone else and should encourage the growth of social awareness (i.e. that necessary insight into implicit cues and expectations) and social skills (i.e. the ability to respond to these cues in an appropriate manner).

Despite appearances, however, the inference usually goes the other way: not from a theory of delinquency to the best method of coping with juvenile offenders, but from a preferred mode of socialisation to a suitable explanation for delinquency. What really underlies the preference for one regime or another is a general image of society whose structure is isomorphic with the regime in question – so that the type of person that a particular regime is intended to produce fits the corresponding vision of what society ought to be like. The product of a 'punishment' regime would be suited to a strongly hierarchical society, in which inequalities of status and power are the price that must be paid for the goods and services it provides. The product of a 'treatment' regime would be more at home in an apparently egalitarian society where the same goods and services are exchanged for bureaucracy, increasing homogeneity and a high level of mutual surveillance.

It follows that a person's approach to dealing with juvenile crime (and, of course, much else besides) cannot be prised apart from his general view of society – his political philosophy. Political and social beliefs are unavoidably implicated in whatever thoughts he has about the most 'effective' kind of regime. The problem of delinquency, therefore, is not simply a matter of technique. It is a matter of values and ideals, aims and objectives which are rooted in the most fundamental beliefs about the kind of society we ought to have.

Within the current framework of social work discourse, then, there is an implicit symmetry, a set of structural equivalences, between 'treatment' and 'punishment'. The difference between them is not so much one of form as of content. They are opposed and incompatible, it is true; but if their objectives differ they are, at least, objectives of the same kind. It is this that

makes possible the banal but commonly accepted thesis that one must
control in order to care, while at the same time it sustains the chronic but ill-
defined unease which social workers feel about their work with young
offenders. It explains both the identity and the contradiction.

It is necessary, however, to identify the common structure rather more
precisely, even if it means stating the (apparently) obvious. If 'treatment'
and 'punishment' are alternative modes of socialisation, what are the
conditions to which both of them must conform? What is the logic of the
conceptual framework to which they both belong? We shall suggest three
concepts which, taken together, represent the basic nexus of this
framework. They are individuation, transformation and anticipation, and
they form the subject of the next section.

INDIVIDUATION, TRANSFORMATION AND ANTICIPATION

Both 'treatment' and 'punishment' seek to *transform* the *individual* in
anticipation of his future actions. This fact would be obvious, and would
not require emphasis, were it not for a vocabulary which tends (and
frequently *in*tends) to mystify. Consider the following definition: 'any
measure taken to change an offender's character, habits, or behaviour
patterns so as to diminish his criminal propensities'.[3] This definition
articulates the three concepts very precisely; but von Hirsch offers it as a
definition of, specifically, 'rehabilitation' and throughout *Doing Justice*
there is an ambiguity between rehabilitation as a general goal of the
correctional system, including custody, and rehabilitation as a narrower set
of treatment options — which may or may not be available in custodial
settings.

But the goal of transformation, the attempt to 'change an offender's
character, habits or behaviour patterns', is common to both 'treatment' and
'punishment'. It is in this sense that their objectives are of the same kind,
even though the virtues which they seek to inculcate — and the methods that
are used to inculcate them — are very different. Change the nature of
something and you change its subsequent behaviour: this is a principle at
the very heart of the penal system we have inherited from the nineteenth
century, as Foucault has convincingly argued. It is a mistake to believe that
'punishment' was ever purely a matter of 'retribution' or 'deterrence'. It has
always sought to alter and transform, and the increasing significance of
'treatment' has only served to diversify the range of techniques and
objectives. It is this that makes the use of the American term, 'correctional
system', so very appropriate.

The common goal is further signalled by the manner in which the
various techniques are evaluated. The prevention of recidivism is a central
feature of the positivist approach to crime — or, at any rate, the criminal —

which underlies both 'punishment' and 'treatment'. We anticipate further offences unless something is done and so our intervention (whatever form it takes) is assessed in terms of future crimes committed or not committed. Correctional measures are inherently forward-looking. Not that there has ever been conclusive evidence that one method of intervention is any more effective than another.[4] It is the fact that *this* is taken to be relevant evidence that is significant. Later, we shall suggest that our inability to distinguish between the success and failure rates of different methods of intervention should be interpreted not as a technical so much as a conceptual difficulty. Current thinking about the penal system collapses together two aims that are separable in theory and ought to be separable in practice.

If people differ as to the ways in which we should be trying to change the offender's personality, they are more or less agreed as to the point. A dose of the right kind of virtues should make him less inclined to commit offences in future. For example, if we make him properly respectful of authority or more sensitive to other people's needs, he is less likely, all in all, to commit further crimes. How plausible this is, is another matter. Compare the concept of 'moral education' (which has never become as fashionable as its 'social' counterpart). The assumption seems to be that there is, or ought to be, a form of education which makes people 'better'. In view of the very reasonable doubts that might be expressed about this, one might equally well say that it is an attempt to define such a form of education into existence. The question we might pose is this: Is there really a generic frame of mind which makes people less inclined to break the law in specific situations? And the answer we give to this question may well resemble the answer we give to another, similar one: Is there really a generic mental ability – 'intelligence' – which equips people to deal more effectively with any task or problem? If the answer to both these questions is in the negative, as it appears to be,[5] the implications are far-reaching. We shall explore them later in this chapter.

Of the three concepts we are considering, it is easiest to lose sight of individuation, although it is, at the same time, the one most taken for granted. Again, this is partly the result of a misleading vocabulary. Certainly, we speak of the impersonality of large institutions and custodial regimes, as if the individual becomes lost and somehow less important as soon as he enters one of them. We speak, too, of various forms of situated therapy – within a group, within a family – as if the individual's membership of an ensemble were the only reason for taking an interest in him. But in neither case may it be inferred, necessarily, that the individual is not the primary object of intervention or the definitive unit of knowledge. If there were no other means of telling, the way in which documentation is organised – in 'case' files – would indicate as much, as would the various criteria of success and failure, the modes of assessment and the individualised 'treatment' plans. What 'depersonalisation' and situated

therapy represent is not any lack of interest in the individual. Rather, they
are different forms of interest in the individual: different ways of knowing
him, different methods of controlling him. Each individual, in his own
right, is a 'case'.

It is tempting to redescribe individuation as 'casework', since it is the
concept of a case which 'at one and the same time constitutes an object for a
branch of knowledge and a hold for a branch of power, it is the individual
as he may be described, judged, measured, compared with others, in his
very individuality; and it is also the individual who has to be trained or
corrected, classified, normalised, excluded'.[6] And one might succumb to the
temptation were it not for the fact that the term already has a (misleading)
identity of its own. For the social worker, 'casework' is one of a set of
alternatives which, despite recent attempts at theoretical integration, remain
opposed or at any rate methodologically different. Certainly, casework and
group work would not normally be identified, although they might well
form two different aspects of one intervention strategy. In view of the
significance of the individuation concept, therefore, and the popularity of
'group work' in intermediate treatment, it might be as well at this stage to
make a few parenthetical comments about some of the issues involved.

What is the role of groups in social work activity? If we turn to a recent
British text on group work,[7] some of the ambiguities become apparent even
on the contents page (our emphasis): 'Group work as a *Process* of Social
Influence'; 'The Family Group as a *Medium* for Change'; 'Choice of the
Group as a *Target* of Intervention', and so on. Three titles, three different
models (apparently) of the group: that which brings about change; that in
the context of which change takes place; and that which is to be changed.
While the first and second of these models imply that it is still the individual
who is to be changed, the third does at least suggest a possible alternative.
However, the chapter in question[8] begins as follows: 'Consumers of social
work are not often given a choice as to the form in which they are to receive
a service. In certain agencies workers seldom ask: "Can this client be helped
best with an individual relationship or would a group offer him a better
chance?" ' – which makes it sound as if the group is being offered as a tool
for change rather than a target. Admittedly, the project described in this
particular chapter does not really conform to the 'tool' model; but the
authors do not seem to be at all clear about the conceptual equipment they
are using. They appear to identify '*working* with groups' and 'group work
skills' as the chief (group work oriented) conceptual components in their
'unitary' model, and they do not successfully distinguish between the
different *functions* that groups may be regarded as having.

The vocabulary of the 'unitary perspective' does, however, afford one
way of identifying a difference that is implicit in these chapter headings. We
can distinguish between the group as 'action system', a 'resource' which is
'mobilised' in order to induce change in the target individual; and the group

as 'target system', an object of action and change in its own right.

At least, it seems that we can make a distinction of this kind. But there is a difficulty – a difficulty that emerges when we come to consider what it means to describe the group itself as a target. The question is this: Is describing the group in this way different from saying that the real targets are the individuals of whom the group is, in fact, composed? And if it is different, in what way is it different? For example, it would not make a great deal of sense to describe an artificial group – people chosen by the worker and not previously conscious of themselves, or identifiable, as a group – as a target system. What is the point of creating a group simply in order to change it (unless, of course, by 'it' one really means the individuals who comprise it)? At the very least, if we are talking about groups as target systems, it is 'natural' groups we ought to be referring to (though, even in this case, there are problems in identifying such groups and in specifying the criteria which must be fulfilled if we are to be able to say that the group, as such, has changed).

It will become clear later in this chapter that we do want to be able to describe some groups as target systems. In such a case, the act of transformation cannot be equated with the socialisation of a collection of individuals. The 'change objectives' will be of a different order, even though they will be equally forward-looking, and equally concerned with the future incidence of crime. In this respect, they will differ from the objectives normally associated with 'intermediate treatment', which are as individualised as any other form of punishment or therapy. In the vocabulary of the unitary perspective, intermediate treatment groups are usually 'action systems'. They are ways of 'getting at', or bringing 'social influence' to bear on, the individuals who make up their membership. And in the sense that they are organised around the fundamental concept of the individual 'case', they may be accurately described as 'casework', even if, in the liturgy of social work, that term has quite different connotations.

INTERMEDIATE TREATMENT AND PREVENTION

We are now in a position to consider an interesting symmetry which the concept of individuation makes possible, and of which the development of intermediate treatment provides an illuminating example. It is the symmetry between 'prevention' and 'cure', between backward-looking and forward-looking approaches to the juvenile offender. If the object of 'rehabilitation' (in the broad sense) is to change the individual's 'character, habits, or behaviour patterns so as to diminish his criminal propensities', it is, in principle, a matter of indifference as to whether he has already committed offences or not, provided – if he has not – it is thought likely that he will do so. If it is possible to identify people who have criminal propensities, even if they have not yet committed an offence, the act of transformation, the socialising task, the objectives of treatment, will have exactly the same form. After all, an actual offence is only an indicator – admittedly the best indicator – of criminal propensities liable to be realised in future. And there may well be other ways of identifying such propensities independently of, and prior to, the committing of a crime. So it is that the conceptual framework to which both 'treatment' and 'punishment' belong calls into being an idea with which intermediate treatment, in particular, has been associated – that of 'prevention'.

In the next section, we shall need to distinguish very carefully between different concepts of 'prevention'. But here we are concerned with only one variation – what might be called the 'individuated' concept of prevention: the prevention of (further) offences on the part of individuals. We are also concerned with how the rhetoric associated with this concept of prevention helped to determine the shape of intermediate treatment during its formative stages. In considering this point, it will be helpful to recall the summary account at the end of Chapter 1, and the image of two opposed systems of juvenile justice gradually working towards a mutual accommodation, and arriving at a state of peaceful coexistence.

The development of intermediate treatment coincided with the rise of 'prevention theory'. If the child who appeared in court more than once was going to remain within the jurisdiction of the old system, as he clearly was, the proper function of the new system might plausibly be interpreted as intervention at a much earlier stage. In this way, the two systems might be accommodated to each other. Instead of reading *Children in Trouble* as an abolitionist document, social workers took its concepts to imply a treatment strategy appropriate to a younger, or at any rate a less delinquent, population. Instead of challenging the old system on its own ground, the new system would aim to identify 'children at risk' and take steps to prevent them realising their full, delinquent potential. No doubt the success of this strategy could not always be guaranteed, but it was likely to be more effective than attempts to intervene when it was already 'too late' – that is at a stage when, with several court appearances behind him and with custodial sentences in the offing, it could reasonably be argued that the delinquent was beyond social work help.

It was not difficult to persuade social workers of the validity of prevention theory. The view that vulnerable children are exposed to some of the causes of delinquency from a very early age is sometimes overlaid with quasi-Freudian beliefs about the formation of personality. Consequently, there is frequently a pessimistic tinge to what is basically an optimistic outlook: the sources of delinquency are identifiable and treatable – but only if you get the child early enough. If you do not, you may well find that in the meantime he becomes inured, set in his ways and impervious to treatment – in short, a member or potential member of the 'hard core', about whom the magistrates are so concerned. Add to this general perspective the liberal platitude that 'prevention is better than cure'. It is surely better to combat delinquency at its source rather than try to eradicate it only when it has taken root. Admittedly, it does not follow from this observation that we should not try to 'cure' it at all, but there is a strong implication that we ought to concentrate what few resources are available where they are likely to do most good.

Prevention theory, then, was a convenient theoretical framework for many of those who found themselves assuming responsibility for the development of intermediate treatment. But it had a rival – the 'alternative to care' lobby which emerged during 1974–5. Whatever the merits of this rival view – and it could be said to have missed the point – it did help to polarise the ensuing debate: prevention *v.* cure, heavy-end *v.* light-end, 'intensive' intermediate treatment (the Personal Social Services Council invention) *v.* everything else. Even the optimistic, and all-embracing, 'continuum of care'.[9] For a long time this debate was conducted at a rather superficial level: endless attempts, for example, to define 'intermediate treatment' – as if this would somehow resolve the issue – or those somewhat groundless and inconclusive arguments about where priorities ought to lie.

It should be clear that in no sense did this debate break out of the conceptual framework associated with individuation. There was little disagreement – except in matters of detail – about what you should do with the individual-as-target-system once he was in your hands. The only question was at what point you should identify him. Moreover, the grounds on which different answers to this question were offered were primarily technical. It was more efficient either to identify the child – the 'pre-delinquent', the child at risk – as early as possible, because the act of transformation, the miracle of socialisation, was more likely to be effective if he was still relatively young and law-abiding, or to identify him as a labelled offender, the 'secondary deviant', because that was when the need (his need, society's need) was greater.

One can visualise individuation as the thread on which both 'preventive' and 'curative' (or 'reactive') beads are hung. At one end, the red-coloured beads: social workers attempting to identify and treat individuals before they commit offences (in the hope of preventing them from doing so). At the other end, the blue ones: policemen, social workers and magistrates attempting to treat or punish (i.e. transform) the same (?) individuals afterwards. What this image and the example of intermediate treatment make clear is that, in current penal thinking, the reaction to crime and the anticipation of it are essentially the same thing. Backward-looking and forward-looking approaches are collapsed together into one conceptual framework and a single act of transformation. Agreed: there are differences of opinion as to what this act should consist of – 'punishment' or 'treatment' – and these disagreements are particularly rife, or at least more overt, at the point when an offence has actually been committed. But there is no fundamental difference of structure. Whether the (likely) offender is identified before or after his offence, the main point of doing whatever it is that is done to him is to stop him doing-it again, or at all.

It is sometimes argued that the present system of juvenile corrections embodies a contradiction between 'justice' and 'welfare',[10] and that this contradiction accounts for the conflict and confusion associated with the 1969 CYPA. But this contradiction is arguably less important than the conflation between backward-looking and forward-looking approaches embodied in the conceptual framework which accommodates both 'justice' and 'welfare'. For one thing, the conflict can be exaggerated – we have already argued that, at the level of practice, an accommodation between the old system and the new system has been worked out. For another, a network of concepts – which is partly a cause and partly a consequence of this working accommodation – can now be discerned which holds the apparent conflict together. Rather than arguing about the relative merits of 'justice' and 'welfare' – and we have alluded to the dangers of this in an earlier chapter – we ought, perhaps, to take a step backwards and survey the framework which effectively supports them both. The beads may be of different colours and situated at opposite ends. But they are on the same thread.

SOME CONCEPTS OF PREVENTION

We shall consider the forward-looking function first, and some of the things that might be meant by 'prevention'. In the previous section, we dealt with the individuated concept of prevention: the assumption that something can be done to, or with, an individual that makes it less likely that he will subsequently commit an offence. But the question is: Why should the individual be the 'unit of prevention'?

There are three alternatives, each of which focuses on one dimension of the sequence of events which constitute a crime. We can characterise these dimensions, very roughly, as circumstance, author and definition: three ways of looking at how offences are committed which suggest that 'preventive work' need not be vested in the individual.

First possibility (circumstance): we might treat offences as 'subjectless', abstracting from the fact that they are committed by individuals. Other circumstances do characterise offences. They are committed at certain times, in certain places and in certain social contexts. They are events of a certain type. Why should not the unit of prevention be one of these factors? Instead of trying to ensure that a specified individual does not commit offences of unspecified type in unspecified times and places, we could be trying to ensure that events of a certain kind do not occur in such-and-such a place or at such-and-such a time.

Second possibility (author): we might give a more liberal interpretation to 'subject'. Who, or what, is it that commits an offence? If we really believe in the 'causes' of delinquency and crime, why not regard these causes as acting through the individuals concerned and for this reason as the true authors of the offence? Again, a number of candidates suggest themselves (depending on one's causal preferences): a peer group, the family, a neighbourhood, an environment. Why not treat one of these as the unit of prevention, rather than an individual whose role can only be that of an intermediary between the offence and the real criminal? Why not work towards ensuring that such a unit is responsible for fewer offences in the future than it has been hitherto? In view of remarks made in the brief interlude on group work, it is worth pointing out that these 'indirect subjects' are natural groups, and that to undertake preventive work with a unit of this kind might be to identify the group in question as a target system rather than an action system.

Third possibility (definition): whether or not an action which constitutes an offence is actually recorded as such sometimes depends on the degree to which the person who committed it is already defined as an offender (or as someone who is likely to become an offender). In someone already regarded as criminal, almost anything can be taken to be a crime. Similarly, of course, with the consequences of arrest and prosecution: the habitual or persistent offender is likely to be treated far more severely than someone in whom an offence is perceived to be a temporary aberration. The third possibility, therefore, consists in trying to relax these conditions: we might try to prevent individuals from being seen as habitual or 'career' offenders by intervening in whatever part of the machinery threatens to represent them as such. In doing so, of course, we might also hope to avoid the consequences which may sometimes flow from the offender's own internalisation of this label.

The first of these possibilities is the one we shall say least about, since it is recognised to be, pre-eminently, a police function. Indeed, it is what most police officers would recognise as 'crime prevention', since they tend to interpret this term rather narrowly, restricting it largely to technology, information and advice — what precautions to take against burglary and car theft, what equipment to install in order to detect shop-lifters. To distinguish it from other kinds of prevention, we shall refer to it as 'techno-prevention'.

The second possibility represents a broader, and more ambitious, concept altogether. Ironically, most of the thinking about it has come from the police world, although even there it is very much a low priority and the preoccupation of only a few. Indeed, Alderson's notion of 'pro-active policing'[11] has been greeted with suspicion and hostility. The modern police force has an image of itself as, in Alderson's terms, a reactive agency, its primary functions being investigation and arrest ('collar-feeling'). This image, which it has successfully transmitted to the rest of society, is yet another example of individuation. Policing is defined not as a general 'anti-crime' service but as the identification and apprehension of individuals who have committed offences.[12] Even in those few areas which have experimented with 'pro-active' and 'community policing' schemes, their reputation, among officers of all ranks, is not high. The general consensus tends to be that these 'hobby bobbies' are not doing real police work, but are carrying out functions which properly belong to social services.

It would seem that individuation is well established both in social work and in policing, so much so that neither can recognise a non-individuated preventive function as its own. But there seems to be no reason why this kind of prevention should be any less (though certainly no more) a social work function than a police one. If certain features of a particular social environment (no matter how broadly or narrowly conceived) are seen to encourage various kinds of juvenile delinquency – and all the things that are a consequence of it, such as fear and anxiety, unusable public services (telephones and lifts), and physical deterioration – it is hardly eccentric to claim that changing some of those features might be a task for social work. Indeed, in the case of an individual's immediate social environment, his family, social workers already attempt to do this.

It is the existence of these other factors which makes it possible, and necessary, to conceive of the 'change objectives' much more broadly. If a community is, in some cases, the indirect author of delinquent behaviour, it is also, in many more cases, the main sufferer. The two aspects may even be connected – people's fear of crime, for example, even when it is exaggerated may discourage them from taking active, though still common-sense, measures to prevent it. In such instances, the police or social work task may not simply be to try and reduce the number of offences being committed; it may also be to come to terms with the affective consequences of offending and to try and lessen the fears and anxieties which do as much to impair the quality of life as any other form of disablement. In fact, this part of the task may be the more important of the two: an objectively smaller amount of crime may do a community of little or no morale more social harm than that suffered by a confident community with a higher crime rate. They have at least equal claims, these 'objective' and 'subjective' components of the preventive task. For the community itself (though now in a slightly different sense) is both subject and object. It must be admitted, of course, that, given a broader conception of 'change objectives', the criteria for success and failure become much more nebulous. This is one reason, perhaps, why individuation is so firmly entrenched in both social work and policing – individuals are so much easier to count.

The third possibility is, of course, the diversion option and one of the ironies of the 'prevention' concept is that this option seeks to reverse some of the consequences of individuated prevention. The main idea is that 'prevention theory' (the individuated version) may have a number of unpleasant side-effects which need to be carefully monitored. For example, in creating an additional population of clients it helps to widen the funnel of entry into the system, drawing in ever more candidates for incarceration. At the same time, the experience and information it generates may render a child even more vulnerable when he does arrive in court, thus speeding his progress towards care and custody. Secondary themes in the attack are more familiar: the impossibility of identifying 'children at risk' with any certainty; the dangers of over prediction; and the lack of any real knowledge about how the business of prevention ought to be conducted.

This attack yields a distinction between two different approaches to 'prevention': intervention designed to prevent further offences (we cannot do this, and we do not know how to try); and intervention designed to prevent the development of a delinquent career (which may be feasible). The distinction turns on the fact that while we may not be able to do a great deal about a child's subsequent actions, there is something we can do about the consequences of those actions. And the something is to lengthen the route to care and custody and to create various diversions along the way.

At least one diversionary mechanism already exists – cautioning – and others are built into the 1969 CYPA, for example, Section 5. However, this section was, of course, never implemented and recent research also implies that cautioning may have back-fired in some areas,[13] increasing, rather than decreasing, the numbers of children coming before the court. In the next chapter, we shall make a number of suggestions as to how this particular balance could be redressed.

In this section, then, we have distinguished four different modes of 'crime prevention'. It may be worth summarising them briefly:

(1) The individuated concept (the anticipation of future offences by individuals).

(2) Techno-prevention (the anticipation of certain types of crime at certain places or times).

(3) The pro-active approach (working to reduce crime in groups or communities).

(4) Diversion (trying to reduce the career-promoting propensities of the juvenile criminal justice-system).

Broadly speaking, if task (2) has been regarded as a police function, task (1) has been regarded as the only feasible social work function. Except for a small number of experimental projects, no agency has attempted to come to grips with tasks (3) and (4).

Both these tasks, however, cut right across the division of labour implicit in the vertical integration of the two systems of juvenile justice. As we have already suggested, the reason that the 1969 CYPA (what is left of it) is not 'working well' is precisely because the two systems have become integrated, the new one functioning partly as a feeder mechanism for the old. But neither of the preventive tasks identified as (3) and (4) functions in this context: one is not concerned with individualised justice at all, the other tries to keep the justice system at bay. If either of them can be accepted, at least partially, as a social work task, other issues arising out of the 1969 CYPA are raised. One of these issues is both urgent and practical. Is there any way of reconstructing the social work task in such a way as to prevent it from becoming integrated with the old system – given the very strong likelihood that the latter will remain as the well-established incumbent in the foreseeable future? An equally important, but more philosophical, issue is this: Was the new system of juvenile justice well conceived in the first place? In the long run, is 'social work' the best concept to have at the core of society's treatment of the offender? It may not be possible or desirable to remove it from the field altogether, but need it be quite so close to the centre? *Children in Trouble* may have been an abolitionist text: Was it right to be so? In the final section of this chapter, which moves towards a more comprehensive framework for social work with juvenile offenders, we shall begin to address ourselves to some of these issues.

THE FRAMEWORK

Do the non-individuated concepts of prevention suggest that there is a role for social work which does not assist and encourage the (old) juvenile justice system to expand? Do they also suggest that a social work alternative to the old system was in any case misguided? There are two questions here, but a number of different, overlapping issues. Some of them – medical models of social work intervention, the unjust consequences of 'individualised justice', and so on – have been well raked over in the literature and by various pressure groups. We shall not say a great deal about these issues directly, preferring to stick to themes more closely related to this book. For the most part we shall be trying to disentangle ideas and concepts which appear to have got themselves conflated.

The first and most crucial distinction is that between treatment of the offender and the prevention of crime. At first sight, this seems banal and obvious. But the important point is that prevention need not be conceived as relating solely to individuals. The 'pro-active' approach, for example, as opposed to 'prevention theory', does not take individuation as a premise. It transcends that concept by treating the offences it seeks to prevent either as 'subjectless', or as committed, and suffered, by 'indirect subjects'.

Each of the two terms involved in this initial distinction can be broken down into further components. Let us take treatment of the offender first. It has been the central theme of this chapter that the usual distinction between 'treatment' and 'punishment' hides another distinction between two different modes of socialisation. The question therefore arises: Is socialisation all that is important in society's response to those who commit offences? Or is there any other idea that might be taken as the core concept in 'what to do about offenders'? After all, socialisation is not unique to treatment/punishment settings. Is there anything else which is?

The rhetoric of punishment at least suggests an answer to this question. The idea of a 'penalty', and of 'paying the penalty', is firmly embedded in most people's thinking on this subject. Traditionally – for the last 150 years, at any rate – punishment = imprisonment = deprivation of liberty (deprivation of liberty being the 'price' one has to pay for crimes committed). The rhetoric of treatment is not so unsubtle – though it could be argued that treatment makes its own demands on people's time and on their mental, if not their physical, liberties. Perhaps the question was wrongly phrased. Perhaps we are not looking so much for something unique to treatment/punishment settings (which can be separated out from socialisation), as for a reasonable criterion – a criterion which would permit a distinction between what an offender must do in order to atone for his offence, and the context in which he atones for it. If, in a particular case, atonement means deprivation of liberty, the context is provided by the regime (implicit or explicit, 'treatment' or 'punishment') enforced in the place of his 'incarceration'.

'Atonement', despite its Biblical sound, is a useful generic term covering most of the available possibilities – all the way from imprisonment to community service and the recently canvassed 'reparation'. The basic idea is that if to commit a crime is to take something away from somebody (a private individual, or 'society' at large), it follows that one should be made to give something up in exchange (whether that something is useful to somebody else or not: one's liberty, presumably, is not). The adoption of this concept would make it possible to discuss something of great importance, something which is separable, and ought to be separated, from socialisation and various other conditions under which atonement would take place. We are arguing, in other words, that instead of penology and the philosophy of punishment we ought to have the 'theory of atonement'.

Next, preventive or 'pro-active' social work. It is a consequence of abstracting the concept of individuation from this idea that social work with individual offenders is not included in it. Social work with offenders is not equivalent to the social work of offenders. Or, in other words, social work with offenders is not, or ought not to be, an intentionally 'preventive' act. Of course, offenders, as much as anybody else (and perhaps more than some), may often be people in need of social work help. And some of the problems they need help with may have much to do with the fact that they have offended. Nevertheless, it is possible and necessary to distinguish between two disparate social work tasks. First, social work with individuals (and their families) who are – i.e. they happen to be – offenders. Second, pro-active police/social work with various (natural) groups and communities – i.e. the non-individuated prevention of crime, focused on an identified target system which is both the object and the indirect subject of juvenile delinquency.

The advantages of this distinction are two-fold. At the level of functions, it takes social work – in both its roles – out of the juvenile justice system. And as a consequence it may help to overcome the unfortunate side-effects of 'prevention theory', and the all-too-obvious ill effects of the vertical integration of two incompatible systems. It may also help to relieve the role-conflict from which many social workers have suffered in the past decade. At the level of concepts, it seeks to provide a conceptual framework in which the identification of different target systems (individuals and their families, on the one hand, the indirect subjects of criminal offences, on the other) can be related to the identification of appropriate change objectives (problems only contingently related to offending in the first case, the experience of crime, and its possible prevention, in the second). Again, we shall say more about each of these two functions towards the end of the next chapter.

Finally, suspended between the theory of atonement and these two social work tasks, is diversion. Its relation to each side of the equation is as follows. It shares with the pro-active approach the fact that it is a reasonable preventive strategy, designed to divert children from the penal system rather than draw them in (as the conventional, individuated concept of prevention has tended to do). Whereas the pro-active approach means intervening in communities, diversion means intervening in the justice system itself, in order to reduce its career-promoting tendencies. On the other side, the theory of atonement makes possible one range of diversionary strategies in a way that the theories of retribution, deterrence and rehabilitation do not. For in its informal mode, atonement suggests that there are ways of reconciling offender and victim without resort to the penal system. If the sacrifice of time, as a bare penalty, is ultimately wasteful, the undertaking of reparation to an individual, or service to a community (victims may be either or both) is not only more constructive, it is also less dependent on the time-consuming ritual of the court appearance. Resistance to the encroachment of the penal system and diversion through informal methods of service and reparation provide the link between a court system based on atonement and the pro-active approach to crime prevention.

By way of summary, the five separate themes identified in this section are illustrated in Figure 5.1. It is clear that while all of them are analytically separable each has its closest conceptual links with the concepts immediately adjacent to it. In the next chapter, each of these five themes will receive a more detailed discussion.

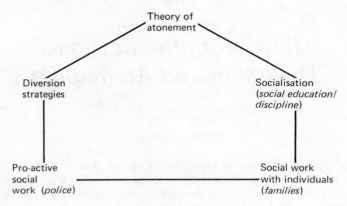

Figure 5.1

REFERENCES: CHAPTER 5

1 Millham, S., 'Intermediate treatment: symbol or solution', in *National Intermediate Treatment Forum Conference Papers 1977* (Leicester: National Youth Bureau, 1978).
2 See Paley, J., 'A Participant Study of Intermediate Treatment' (unpublished research report, University of Lancaster, 1979).
3 von Hirsch, A., *Doing Justice: Report of the Committee for the Study of Incarceration* (New York: Hill & Wang, 1976).
4 For example, Brody, S. R., *The Effectiveness of Sentencing* (London: HMSO, 1976).
5 See McClelland, D., 'Testing for competence rather than for intelligence', *American Psychologist*, vol. 28, January 1973, p. 107.
6 Foucault, M., *Discipline and Punish* (London: Allen Lane, 1977), p. 191.
7 McCaughan, N. (ed.), *Group Work: Learning and Practice* (London: Allen & Unwin, 1978).
8 Vickery, A., Rawcliffe, C. and Ward, U., 'Choice of the group as a target for intervention', in McCaughan (ed.), op. cit., pp. 32–45.
9 Paley, J. and Thorpe, D., *Children: Handle with Care* (Leicester: National Youth Bureau, 1974), pp. 84–93.
10 For example, Morris, A. and McIsaac, M., *Juvenile Justice?* (London: Heinemann, 1978).
11 Alderson, J., *Communal Policing* (Exeter: Devon and Cornwall Constabulary, 1978).
12 See McKane, D. J., 'An Evaluation of the Community Policing Scheme in West Yorkshire' (unpublished M. Sc. thesis, Cranfield Institute of Technology, 1979).
13 See Ditchfield, J., *Police Cautioning in England and Wales* (London: HMSO, 1976).

6

Beyond Individuation: Diversion and Atonement

SOCIAL WORK

People who are (happen to be) offenders are as likely to have problems amenable to social work help as anyone else, and there is no reason why they should not be offered it on the same terms as anyone else. The fact that someone is an offender should not make any difference – that is what being 'non-judgemental' amounts to. These are platitudes, of course. But in our view, social workers are rarely 'non-judgemental' in the case of offenders. It is not easy for them to resist the temptation to let their approach be determined by the fact that the individual in question is an offender – not in a 'negative' sense, however. We are not suggesting that they are always making adverse 'value judgements'. Rather, they are inclined to assume that the individual's problems and his offences are – perhaps must be – connected in some way. Very often, no doubt, they are connected; but by no means always. And even when they are, it does not follow that social work intervention needs to take the form of 'treatment' – that is an attempt to resolve problems in order to reduce the level of offending.

This is true even of statutory cases, even of probation. The idea of social work help must be separated out from the concept of 'treatment'. Bottoms and McWilliams[1] have recently made a very similar point and have gone some way towards establishing the framework of a 'helping', as opposed to a 'treatment' paradigm. A number of simple consequences follow. We must drop the assumption that delinquents and/or their families must have problems amenable to social work. If it turns out that they do have such problems, we must not assume that these problems are connected with the fact that offences have been committed. And if it turns out that there is some reason for thinking they are connected, we must not assume that the aim of social work intervention is to prevent further offences. The resolution of the problems, in and for themselves, is a worthwhile and important enough objective without that. Finally, we must not judge the effectiveness of intervention by the subsequent occurrence or non-occurrence of criminal behaviour. Whatever social work goals have been identified will determine their own, more relevant, criteria. The implication – that social work must in this sense withdraw from the juvenile justice system altogether – is one that has to be accepted. Sometimes it is not at all clear what it was doing there in the first place.

No doubt this kind of social work will be vulnerable to all the usual doubts, reservations, qualifications and criticisms. In some quarters it will be regarded as unnecessary do-gooding, an expensive and misplaced indulgence. In others, it will be said to be a cosmetic, patching up (nay, reinforcing) the public ills of capitalism in the social problems of private individuals. But it will be no more vulnerable to this kind of criticism than any other form of social work. And it will unburden itself of the role-conflict, anxiety and guilt which is endemic to a treatment-oriented approach. Having divested itself of this 'extra expertise', it will have to take its chances as 'just another' manifestation of social work. But if any kind of social work is worth doing, this kind is.

One might ask: Is there nothing, then, that the social worker can do with the individual that is directly relevant to his being an offender? Has not the case been somewhat overstated? Perhaps it has – but the statement needed to be forceful in order to make the distinction between offence-related and other problems as sharp as possible. We do, in fact, think that certain kinds of intervention may be helpful in this respect; but these forms of intervention have not been widely practised as yet and they must be carefully defined.

It has become fashionable in social work to speak of 'social skills'. Frequently, all that is meant by this term is a sort of generalised social-education experience of the kind provided by some forms of intermediate treatment. The previous chapter indicated that this approach usually collapses into one pattern of socialisation, an attempt to inculcate a particular constellation of virtues and a general conformity to social norms. As we have already suggested, there is little reason to think that such general patterns of socialisation are at all effective in transforming delinquents into law-abiding citizens. But it may be possible to conceive of much more highly specific skills, the absence of which is connected with the fact that some children get into trouble in certain situations. If it is, then introducing these children to the skills in question – and doing this in the right context – could well be a positive contribution.

What might these skills be? It is important to realise that there is no general answer to this question. We are not about to offer a general theory of delinquency which identifies skills appropriate to any child in trouble. The assumption that there is such a theory and that there are, as a consequence, certain forms of treatment or training which are (almost) universally applicable seems to us completely unfounded. This is not to say that some well-known theories cannot prove helpful in understanding a given case: the example outlined below does, in fact, draw on some ideas associated with David Matza. But it should not be assumed that any theory covers all cases or that, with respect to a single case, some relevant theory already exists.

For us, the tautology of 'client-centredness' means that theory must be client-centred as well. Each individual is, in principle, a singular personal universe, a unique theoretical domain which may or may not be comparable with others. It is worth noting the implication of this: the social work practitioner must, in effect, be a research worker too. Any social inquiry is, in principle, a small-scale research project, and the questions that are asked in the course of such an inquiry need to be framed accordingly. Ironically, however, the 'art of asking questions' is not highly developed in social work and the business of skilled 'personal research' is left to the (psychology) experts. This is a pity. Research methodology is not always as esoteric as it is sometimes assumed to be and if research-like activity represents so large a proportion of the professional task, there is no reason why the appropriate skills should not be part of social work training.

To inquire how and why a child gets into trouble calls for exactly this kind of skill. The simple, perhaps simplistic, question, 'How and why do you get into trouble?' is not necessarily the best means of eliciting this information: the answers are not guaranteed to be illuminating. But there are other ways – the authors have, for example, experimented with cartoons, projective exercises, repertory grids and role-plays. A series of pictures, depicting a recent 'incident' may tell us a lot more about 'getting into trouble' than the lengthiest and most comprehensive of interviews: and the child is likely to enjoy drawing them a lot more than answering a list of boring and tedious questions.

But let us consider an example of the kind of usable theory such a 'research project' might produce and the kind of offence-related social work help that might be appropriate as a result. It should be remembered that, although it draws on David Matza's ideas, we are not implying that these ideas are generally applicable or that, in a real project, Matza's work would be the source of them (as we have explained above, the client is the source).

The 'situation of company' is one context in which delinquent incidents occur. It is an inherently ambiguous situation in which miscues and misunderstanding abound. It is certainly not a situation in which delinquent activity, an offence, is consciously decided on. Instead, the children involved in it allow themselves to be carried along by an ill-defined sequence of events and 'discover' that an offence has been committed only after that 'invitational edge' has been crossed.[2] In many cases, the situation is best described as one of play. Another analysis, that of Bateson, suggests what the connection between play and delinquency might be. Play is itself inherently ambiguous. In some contexts, when people confront each other it is not clear – it is not a decidable question – as to whether what they are doing is 'playful' or 'serious'. This may become clear only in retrospect, when the sequence of events emerging from the ambiguous situation has been resolved in some way.

Suppose, then, that we have someone who has represented his own delinquent activity in this context: a group of mates playing, 'messing about', enjoying the ambiguity of a situation over which none of them has complete control. At some point, however, an action which was innocent when it was performed – or at any rate, was not deliberately intended as a delinquent act – reveals itself, in retrospect, to be an offence. We would argue that there is a role here for 'social work help' – of a kind, and provided it is welcomed by the individual concerned. It is certainly a case in which one could argue that specific social skills – that is skills relevant to this kind of situation – might be helpful. If the child were able to recognise such a sequence of events as soon as it began, and if he had had some practice either in withdrawing from it or in exerting some control over it, then he might be able to avoid getting into trouble on at least some future occasions. Both the training in recognition and the opportunity for 'practice' might be offered through such exercises as role-play and other forms of 'social skills' training. (Chapter 7 contains a more detailed account of this example.)

Another area in which similar training might be appropriate is that of demeanour. It is well known that some children make themselves more vulnerable to arrest and prosecution by the manner in which they conduct themselves when apprehended by the police. Sometimes, no doubt, this is deliberate and the chase makes for an exciting game. At other times, however, it may result from a genuine inability to 'turn on' the appropriate demeanour at the appropriate moment – and make it convincing! Again, practice at this kind of thing may improve things and make the child less liable to arrest on trivial or technical charges.

We shall close this section by re-emphasising two points. The first is that we are talking of specific skills in relation to specific individuals. 'Demeanour-training', for example, might not be appropriate for all offenders (though, for a court appearance, it might well be suitable for a high proportion). Deciding what is and what is not appropriate – formulating a theory as to how and why a particular person does get into trouble – can be a difficult task, and one for which social workers are not as well equipped as they might be. The second is that what distinguishes this form of training from generalised socialisation is precisely its specificity – and the fact that it has more to do with making certain skills available than with inculcating certain values. It is a matter of extending the child's options in specified situations, rather than a general attempt to provide discipline or 'social education'. It follows that the child himself must decide whether he wishes to make use of this kind of training.

SOCIALISATION

If socialisation, as we have already insisted, must be distinguished from atonement, the 'treatment' of the offender, it must also be distinguished from the social work function just discussed – although it is more regularly confused with the latter (and with the preventive function) when the juvenile offender lies at the focal point of intervention. The routine conflation of social work, socialisation, treatment and prevention is more noticeable in our approach to delinquency than it is in any other sphere, and this partly accounts, perhaps, for the great intellectual interest in that field. It is a virtue of that otherwise somewhat tautological concept, 'client-centred' social work, that it directs the attention towards problems which the client himself can recognise and away from the virtues and values which the social worker, albeit unconsciously, may be trying to reproduce in him. Unfortunately, while this is something that one may try to control for in the case of adults, it is less easily submerged in confrontation with children, and particularly 'difficult' and 'delinquent' children. The inference that the child's problems are identical with the fact that he is not being 'brought up' properly is a very tempting one, and if it is made, then of course social work and socialisation become one and the same thing. But this is to assume that certain child-rearing practices are 'abnormal', 'deviant' or 'pathological', rather than – as may possibly be the case – part of an unfamiliar and perhaps unattractive cultural pattern which many other, non-delinquent children suffer but survive.

The issue is further confused by the 'treatment' objectives usually associated with work with offenders. Not only are the child's problems identified with faulty child-rearing, but it is further assumed that correct child-rearing – proper socialisation – will result, or should result, in fewer subsequent offences. So that, whatever one's socialisation preferences – strong discipline and respect for authority, on the one hand, social skills and urbanity, on the other – the claim tends to be that not only are these virtues excellent in themselves (which no doubt they are), but that a good dose of them makes offenders less inclined (less able?) to offend. The empirical evidence for this extra claim is, of course, every bit as thin as one would expect it to be. Not that the paucity of the evidence is likely to stop people being thoroughly committed to the ideals of discipline, social education, or whatever else. Hence, one of the only two jokes that the serious business of intermediate treatment has ever sponsored: the image of the 'well-adjusted delinquent'. (The other is the one about the hitherto non-delinquent child who commits an offence just to get on an intermediate treatment outing.)

No doubt, however, these virtues are excellent in themselves – at least some of them are, as they are not all compatible with one another. And there is space for a discussion of socialisation in abstraction from its misleading relationship with social work and treatment. After all, we must raise the next generation. But on what criteria do we make the relevant choices? Which virtues ought we to emphasise and which insist on? We do not pretend to know the answers to these questions (we suspect that, in this form, they do not have answers at all), but we can make a few comments on some of the issues that might be thought to have a bearing on them.

We began the previous chapter with the distinction between care and control, the child's needs and society's, and commented on how naïve this distinction can be. When we begin to identify more of the interested parties (parents, children, social workers, teachers, relatives, passers-by and other representatives of this ambiguous concept, 'society'), some of the knots into which intermediate treatment workers sometimes tie themselves (trying to decide on the 'standards' which the group should maintain) become even more intelligible. Specific issues, such as whether to allow smoking, swearing, fighting or chip butties, are only symptoms of much more deeply seated differences of philosophy, culture and politics. It is only the reduction of everything to a matter of 'technique' which serves to conceal this fundamental point. The social workers' 'treatment' regime, for example, emerges from a nexus of social and professional considerations. Its ideology of (social) education reflects the origins of the 'new middle-class' in the 1944 Education Act, while its prevailingly 'feminine' ethos is rooted in the partial female emancipation signified by roughly parallel social trends. Its emphasis on 'small groups' is a projection of the standard work situation to be found in most of the helping professions (the social work team, for example) and its insistence on the value of talk, the importance of discussion, matches the significance of linguistic exchange and control (endless team meetings, supervisions and case conferences) associated particularly with social work. Or so it could be argued: an argument whose central theme is that those factors which most accurately depict both the origins and ethos of the new professions are those which are most clearly embedded in the mode of socialisation it prefers.

Such an argument would help to explain why the intended objects of this mode of socialisation frequently neither understand nor appreciate it. Children tend to insist on fairness and exchange, as well as on 'knowing where they are'; none of which concepts are central to the treatment ideology, though they may function as peripheral accretions. Many 'working-class' parents, as not a few cultural and ethnographic studies have indicated, actively disagree with the child-rearing practices of the 'new middle-class', tending to prefer modes and practices more closely related to the (old middle-class's) 'traditional' socialisation methods. In the end, each group has preferences not necessarily based on – though frequently justified by appeal to – theories of what a child 'needs', or how it should 'develop'. In the end, one might say, crudely and no doubt sweepingly, each group is trying to reproduce itself.

It just is not possible to balance or integrate all these conflicting demands, though social workers sometimes try. But it is anxiety about 'social control' and fears of imposing 'middle-class values on working-class people' that leads them to make the effort. A knot that cannot be loosened, a contradiction which cannot be resolved. It is tempting to say: social workers should stay well clear of the socialisation business. They should leave it to people who are a lot more confident about the values and virtues that children should be taught, and who are more certain that their vision of society is the right or the best one. One might add: parents have the right, within certain limits, to bring up their children as they choose; various brands of evangelist, religious and secular, have the right to put their visions and practices on (voluntary) offer. In a pluralist world, social workers should not compete. They have services of their own to provide without getting involved in the battle for children's minds.

And yet is this not an evasion? Is it not to let pluralism slide into relativism and make a virtue out of being uncommitted? Is there no prospect of a more positive conclusion? Perhaps there is, though it would mean abandoning any commitment to the child's needs or to society's. The only plausible alternative is something over which neither 'care' nor 'control' has any jurisdiction.

The alternative we have in mind is represented by a list of virtues which belong neither to 'treatment' nor 'punishment', discipline or social education – virtues such as the ones involved in being critical, sceptical, inquisitive, candid, dispassionate, even insouciant. These are the virtues neither of the leaders nor the led. Furthermore they are not the virtues of conformity or virtues which have ever found their way (so far as we know) on to any list of intermediate treatment 'objectives'.

Such virtues, we believe, strike a number of theoretical chords: Gouldner's 'culture of critical discourse'; Habermas's 'communicative competence'; Sennett's 'disinterested' society.[3] To foster and encourage them would be to appeal to values and criteria other than those embedded in social education and discipline. A critical and dispassionate nature fits neither a disciplined and obedient respect for authority, nor a warm and gregarious, socially skilled conformity. It is content neither with having a certain kind of role, nor with being a certain kind of person. Its primary concerns are disinterested inquiry, cogent argument and critical assessment. But this does not make it a cold, unfeeling, unsociable monster. Rather, the adoption of critical virtues transforms the nature of sociability. The interpersonal ideal ceases to be 'narcissism', 'psychic strip-tease', the externalisation of what is inside.[4] It becomes, instead, impersonal but expressive, distanced but playful, conventional but protean. It creates, in the place of externalised privacy, a genuinely public space.

In no sense do the critical virtues serve either the 'needs' of the child or the 'needs' of society. They are not intended to serve 'needs' at all. Even to identify them suggests the possibility of irresolvable conflict with more obviously personal considerations. Ignorance, for example, is bliss – it can certainly be argued that assimilation into the 'culture of critical discourse' would not make people any happier, any more content with their own lives. Knowledge may be power, but it can also be despair. At the same time, the persistence of critical virtues does not guarantee that the interests of 'society' will be preserved. While some 'intellectuals' are prepared to restrain their critical powers in exchange for power, wealth and status, others, evidently, are not. Apart from the pursuit of learning for its own sake, and the promotion of technological change, criticism of 'society' is the most obvious use to which critical discourse is put – nothing else is so worth criticising.

How does one go about developing the critical virtues in young people? The task is so very rarely attempted that there are no obvious models to which one can point. There are two main reasons for this. In the first place, there are very few things that manage to combine both the critical and the playful/dispassionate elements. Criticism, for example, can be a very serious business indeed, embedded in a pompous, academic style and signifying a much greater attachment to ego and career than to genuine curiosity and bewilderment. Much of academic life is devoted to the domestication and routinisation of critical ideas. On the other hand, what is lacking from most play situations is genuine criticism.

We do know of one intermediate treatment group which concentrated on play and met at least some of the criteria. It managed to create a public space in which private troubles were set aside rather than minutely examined, a space which could become saturated by convention, fantasy, role-playing, satire, parody, and many other forms of play. But it was not inherently critical. Although it parodied various forms of social work, although it even invented a game called 'intermediate treatment', it did not, even in play, develop a critique of social work, much less anything else. It did not set out to develop the parody or the game beyond certain well-defined limits – limits imposed by the style and the setting as well as by the group worker's own understanding of what intermediate treatment should be. And this, of course, is the problem: how to combine criticism and play at a mundane level – working with children rather than in the worlds of politics, art and philosophy.

The development of critical virtues should not, of course, be confused with the sort of 'democracy' often found in intermediate treatment groups – those meaningless 'decision-making' exercises whose scope is so narrow and whose outcomes are so carefully manipulated – any more than Habermas's 'communicative competence' should be confused with the distorted communication which is used to threaten, manipulate and exercise power. 'False democracy' in an intermediate treatment group may be a good preparation for certain kinds of society – those in which a universal franchise and the 'ballot box' conceal the inequitable distribution of real power — but it does not water the seeds of a critical persuasion. Indeed, it may have the opposite effect. Once the children have seen through the power structure and the limits of 'decision-making', they are likely to abdicate from shared 'responsibility', retreat to their own subculture, and concentrate on getting what they can from the exchange mechanism that remains. This brings us to the second reason why there are no models available — what we may refer to as the 'autonomy dilemma'. Is it even possible to introduce autonomy and the critical virtues inside a framework which in the last resort denies autonomy and inhibits criticism? A 'decision-making' framework whose very existence depends on the decisions made by someone else? A framework which must characterise any setting in which adults seek to pass on their accumulated wisdom to children. A setting, in other words, in which adults know better.

In the modern world — as in other societies — the adult–child relation symbolises and reflects other, large-scale relationships of power and authority. There was a time when it could be said that the sovereign was the father of his people; we might now say that the state — by which we mean all levels of government — is, like the school, *in loco parentis*. The nineteenth century invented adolescence — and we are all adolescents now. Is it possible — a wild question — to reverse this trend? To bring children, young people, adolescents (as we think of them) back into the society from which they have been so carefully excluded? It may be that this question and the previous one — 'Is it possible to develop and encourage the critical virtues? — are virtually the same. Only by permitting autonomy and criticism to count, only by giving them scope beyond the narrow limits prescribed by special groups and institutions — safe and controlled — can we give them any meaning at all. But we have scarcely begun to think about what this might imply — if, indeed, it can truthfully be said that we have begun.

Bringing children back into society does not necessarily mean closing down schools — even though schools were one of the instruments of their exclusion. People may come to appreciate education more when it is not identified with childhood and a state of dependency. But why, for example, is there an eight-year gap between the age of criminal responsibility and the age of majority? If, by the age of 10, we have learnt the difference between right and wrong, what more do we have to learn in order to be able to vote, and why does it take another eight years? Many other questions could be asked about the ages at which, legally speaking, various other rights and duties may be invoked. It is ironic that many of those who genuinely believe in granting adult functions to young people continue to deny them adult status. Young people ought to participate, etc. in society; but youth is still a time for learning and preparation. The parental version of this contradiction is wanting them to behave like adults and treating them like children.

We have drifted some way from the social worker's problem as it was initially formulated. But having come via a discussion of the critical virtues and the role of young people in society, we have reached a point at which it can be formulated in a new and perhaps surprising way.

Let us treat adolescent status as a social problem. Social workers deal in problems and to possess adolescent status is to have a big one. Ameliorating this problem, overcoming this disablement, is at the same time to create the conditions in which the critical virtues can flourish. Rather than forming safe enclaves in which the child can 'learn' decision-making, we should be inviting children to take decisions which affect their (real) lives, and especially their 'public' lives, their lives outside the family. Rather than attempting to socialise children, we should be trying to resocialise the adults who deal with them outside the home: teachers, policemen, other social workers. (How about intermediate treatment groups for education welfare officers?) The scope may appear to be limited − and we are certainly not underestimating the practical problems. But in two of the next three sections there will be examples of the kind of thing we mean. We shall suggest, first, that if a child has to atone for an offence, he should decide the penalty himself; secondly, that if the pro-active function is to be taken up, children should help to conduct the necessary research, decide on the objectives and monitor the outcomes. Rather than treating children as the problem, let us turn to them for solutions.

ATONEMENT

It will not, of course, be possible to develop a theory of atonement at any length here. A few remarks on some of the central issues will have to suffice. For reasons that will become obvious, it is necessary to begin with some comments on the philosophy of punishment − a rather odd subject, in many respects, as we shall see. The discussion, while necessarily speculative, does, we believe, help to clarify some of the fundamental issues confronting penal policy.

Philosophers have given a great deal of attention to the justification of punishment, but have made very few attempts to state what punishment consists of or ought to consist of. Not that they have avoided 'definitions' of one sort or another − definitions of which the following is probably typical: '*authority's infliction of a penalty*, something involving deprivation or distress, *on an offender*, someone found to have broken a rule, *for an offence*, an act of the kind prohibited by the rule'.[5] The point of such definitions is usually (as in this example) to specify with some care the circumstances in which punishments are legitimately carried out, and to build these circumstances into the definition. One reason for this is that some theories seem to imply absurd (to say nothing of unjust or immoral) possibilities: in the case of extreme utilitarianism, for example, the 'punishment', so-called, of people known to be innocent. If such possibilities can be defined away, the task of justification becomes somewhat easier.

The nature of the penalty, however, is rarely discussed, although Rawls (who carefully avoids the subject of punishment in his *magnum opus*) does refer to people being 'deprived of some of the normal rights of a citizen'.[6] But which rights? And why? Nor is it anything other than a taken-for-granted assumption that the 'authorities' who 'inflict the penalty', or at least authorise it, should also decide what form it is going to take. But there are clearly some very difficult philosophical problems here which need a much more detailed discussion than we can give them.

For example, let us say that the punishment of imprisonment is intended to deprive an offender of his liberty. What is meant by 'liberty' here, and is it possible to deprive him of that and nothing else? If it means simply to incarcerate him, to restrict his freedom of movement (to deprive him, colloquially, of 'time'), then the answer to the second part of the question is, in practice, if not in logic, 'no'. The loss of too many other freedoms is implicit in the loss of 'geographical' liberty, freedoms which, in the case of this country, include political freedoms (the right to vote), economic freedoms (the right to provide for one's family) and social freedoms (the right to dress as one pleases, and so on). So the question becomes: Which liberties should/does imprisonment deprive an offender of, and which liberties should he be allowed to retain? And on what basis should this question be answered?

The concept of 'regime' involves a reference to some of the restrictions which deprive an offender of his rights. Different regimes suspend different rights in different combinations. Being 'incarcerated' entails being subjected to some kind of regime, so one way of picturing the situation is to see 'removal from home' as the 'core' deprivation, the 'bare' penalty, and the regime as the experiential context in which this deprivation is carried out. It is not possible, in this sense, to abstract the core deprivation from the regime for the same reason that it is not possible to abstract form from content. The penalty must be realised, but its realisation entails some regime, some set of circumstances and restrictions. And so, on this view, another form of the above question is: On what basis ought the particular realisation of the 'bare' penalty to be chosen?

Currently, in the case of juvenile offenders, a number of considerations apply: tariff, no doubt, and the form of 'training' or 'treatment' which the child is alleged to need are among them. But if we reject the images of 'need' and socialisation, and if the concept of 'core deprivation' is acceptable, presumably the amount of time during which an offender is deprived of his liberty is the key variable. The circumstances in which deprivation is maintained are immaterial. In which case, why not permit the offender himself to choose? Why not take the rhetoric of autonomy and decision-making seriously and invite him to decide – from a range of options – the circumstances in which he will be detained, the regime under which he will serve out his 'time'? The options would include those – at least those – which are available now: different structures (explicit and implicit), different opportunities, different skills – from trade training and military discipline to therapeutic communities and group discussion.

It is tempting to suppose that if such a choice were offered some establishments would go out of business. Some, no doubt, would argue that it is obvious that offenders would take the 'soft' option. We cannot agree. Many young people actually prefer traditional discipline and routine; they appreciate the physical rigour of 'life conducted at a brisk tempo'. Why else do they join the armed forces? But there is, of course, something else behind this argument and a reason for looking at it more closely. The something else in question is this: the thought that the penalty which the young offender pays must also be something which he suffers. In other words, the 'core deprivation' must be inherently disagreeable. It should be measured not just in terms of time, but also in terms of the pain or discomfort it imposes.

We shall not pause here to discuss one interesting point – that the amount of pain or discomfort which any given penalty causes will vary from person to person (and that, therefore, this concept of penal justice is, in principle, as individualised as any other). Instead, we shall deal with the argument by reorganising our own. Let us drop the concept of 'core deprivation' altogether – it was only one way of picturing the situation anyway – and replace it with the idea of a 'constellation' of restrictions, a constellation which would include the deprivation of liberty (for a period of time), the infliction of pain or discomfort (measured appropriately), and a number of other restrictions limiting normal rights and freedoms. Now such restrictions can obviously be combined in variously different ways to form distinctive 'constellations'. But from among the indefinite number of constellations that could be identified, there will be various groups that can be regarded, roughly, as equivalents – even though their components are of different shapes and sizes, they effectively balance each other. At which point we return to a different version of the original question: On what basis do we choose between constellations that are, approximately, equivalent? We can see no reason why this version cannot be answered in a similar way: let the offender decide.

(We are ignoring here problems which have to do with how 'calculations' of equivalence are made. But this does not seem to be a task that can be shirked, if only because young offenders already do it for themselves. The rhetoric of the current debate tempts one to believe that two months in a detention centre is more 'punitive' than a possible two years in care. Many children do not agree. It is not unusual for youngsters awaiting a court appearance to commit more offences in the hope of going to a detention centre, or even borstal, rather than risk the indefinite sentence of a care order. Clearly, for such children, 'time' is a more significant variable than the supposedly harsh and unwelcome treatment they are likely to receive in custodial institutions. It would be simpler, perhaps, to revert to a generic sentence based on 'time' — as recommended by the Advisory Council's report on young adult offenders and accepted in the 1978 Green Paper — than to attempt complicated calculations in the first place.)

At any rate, the suggestion that the young offender should decide for himself the form in which a penalty is realised meets at least one of the criteria specified in the previous section: instead of 'preparing' young people for decision-making, we should be trying to create conditions in which they can take decisions which actually influence their 'public' lives. Choosing the context in which a penalty is to be paid seems to us a far more significant exercise than deciding on 'rules' in artificially created (and artificially sustained) groups. Admittedly, the suggestion does presuppose that certain other conditions are met. One, for example, is that we abandon the nonsense of 'assessment' — or that we let the child do the assessing. Which leads to a second — the availability of information. We cannot make reasonable decisions without knowing what the likely consequences will be. Visiting various kinds of institution might, for example, take up the space vacated by 'assessment' (although in the case of Home Office establishments this would, of course, require a significant change of policy). And a third condition: a change in the use to which most local authority residential establishments are put — for example, making use of CHEs on a short- and fixed-term basis.

But what of non-residential, non-custodial alternatives? Our discussion began with the philosophy of punishment and led naturally to the concept of 'time', the deprivation of liberty, as a standard form of penalty, the 'core deprivation'. But this is only the limiting case and we have said nothing as yet about fines (money as another 'bare' penalty), community service, corporal punishment or anything else. Clearly, however, the same principles apply, only much more widely. The calculation of equivalences remains a problem, but the principle of real choice for the offender opens up the possibility of negotiation between him and the 'authorities' as to the exact nature of the penalty or penalties. The range of options is almost limitless and many of them — community service, reparation, compensation — are in marked contrast to the relatively useless and unproductive sacrifice of 'time'. The success of the community service order, though it does not imply a universal model for atonement, does at least indicate one of the more promising directions.

We shall not attempt to elaborate these ideas any further — there are plenty of ideas around — since our primary objective is to outline a basic conceptual framework for generating them. But before closing this section, two more connected points need to be made. The first brings us back to the idea that any penalty, any form of atonement, should be inherently disagreeable or unpleasant – an idea that is likely to resist the principle of offender-choice. Suppose the offender gets to enjoy his atonement – one can hardly call that a penalty! What lies behind this anxiety? The fear that the penalty will not act as a deterrent? The fear that many of the men who populate British prisons enjoy – or at least are dependent on – the experience of imprisonment. Lurking behind this doubt is the concept of individuated prevention again: the idea that, whatever form treatment of the offender takes, it should do something to him that ensures he will never (want to) offend again. This concept is simply incompatible with the theory of atonement (it does not rest easily with theories of retribution and denunciation, either). Whether they like it or not, even those who voice this principle in the name of harsher punishment are making use of a 'medical model'. The annulment of past crime is different from the prevention of subsequent crime. Whether or not the offender enjoys the act of annulment is a matter of indifference.

Connected with this is the following: by the theory of atonement, penalties are not evaluated by their 'success' rates – that is their effectiveness in reducing recidivism (however this is defined). This is a simple corollary of the first point. If atonement is not intended to prevent subsequent offences then it cannot be evaluated in these terms. In our view, the way in which the community service order has been evaluated (to take this as a convenient example) is misguided. Whether an action, or a kind of activity, or a form of deprivation, really does atone for an offence is, obviously, judged on completely different criteria. It is, if anything, an ethical form of evaluation rather than a technical one. It may, for these reasons, leave room for disagreement; but the disagreement cannot be any greater than the disputes over the 'effectiveness' of various (so-called) techniques.

Does not this analysis leave something out? Are we not at all concerned about the offender's future behaviour? Is there not a rather large gap in the theory of atonement in that it does not make allowance for this concern? Well, of course something is missing, and of course we are concerned. But – a crucial point – what we are trying to do is separate atonement from prevention. Something is missing from the theory of atonement if, and only if, we assume that penalties (whatever else they do) should be designed to prevent further offences. It is this assumption which we believe to be mistaken. Prevention may be necessary, but it should not be, so to speak, built into atonement. It should be a quite separate policy issue. What is needed is a concept of prevention, and a way of preventing, that does not depend on the administration of penalties. At which point we come full circle and return to the discussion of prevention theory *v.* diversion and the pro-active approach.

DIVERSION

We have argued that the adoption of 'prevention theory' (the individuated concept) following the implementation of the 1969 CYPA helped to bring about results that were the opposite of those intended. The vertical integration of the two systems of juvenile justice has, ironically, brought more children before the courts and created an increasing demand for secure and custodial places.

This kind of irony is by no means unusual in the operation of any system. In the case of juvenile justice, making the courts less 'harsh' – putting a greater emphasis on treatment, welfare and supervision – encourages everybody, police as well as social workers, to use them more. Moreover, arguments for the introduction of a number of other improvements, although superficially cogent, can easily be reversed. For example, 'intermediate' measures between supervision and removal from home may 'slow down' the development of a delinquent career; interposing options that fall short of the final, drastic decision may, in some cases, make that decision unnecessary. On the other hand, it may instead make each consecutive decision easier to take, with the result that delinquent careers are promoted, even accelerated. To vary the metaphor: putting more rungs in the middle of the ladder makes it that much easier to climb.

Similarly, it is possible to question other aspects of received wisdom. Is the appointment of specialists so obviously a good thing? Will not specialist officers and specialist units simply generate more new clients? Experience suggests that this does often happen (for example, in the case of drug squads and juvenile bureaux). Again, is increased co-operation between different agencies so undeniably worthwhile? Granted, it may serve to oil bureaucratic wheels and thereby make it easier to deliver the appropriate services; but on the other hand it may make the client more vulnerable by making him 'known' to more departments and organisations, and by dispersing and substantially increasing the amount of information about him – information on which any agency may draw in order to confirm its own version, or the generally agreed version, of his 'case'.

It is questions of this kind that the diversion strategy must consider. Again, we must emphasise that there is no one 'solution', no 'right' way of going about diversion. This is because there is no one juvenile criminal justice system, only an aggregate of local systems, local practices and local procedures – and, as an earlier chapter has already made clear, local situations differ widely. Hence, diversionary intervention also calls for research skills on the part of the practitioner. Local data must be collected and analysed, and appropriately local strategies suggested and discussed.

In addition to questions of practice, therefore, the social worker must also ask himself questions of 'process' – questions about the structures of policy and procedure in various local agencies. 'How is information used and organised by these agencies?' 'What procedures are characteristic of each agency?' 'How do they interact with the procedures of other agencies?' 'To what effect?', and so on.

Here is one very crude example of the kind of question that might signal a switch to the diversionary strategy: If we wish to reduce the number of offenders coming into care, is it more effective to upgrade preventive work, or to provide non-residential alternatives, or simply to reduce the number of places the authority is prepared to provide? In this question, the first two options are framed in terms of 'practice', the third in terms of 'process' (though perhaps in an oversimplified way). There are clearly many other strategies that could be suggested. For example, making care order recommendations in criminal proceedings a managerial responsibility; introducing strict criteria for admission to care; placing a ban on first-time care orders (unless the circumstances are exceptional); pre-empting criminal proceedings by instituting care proceedings (so that the care or control test would have to be applied).

However, the scope of 'system management' would extend well beyond the making of care orders. A good case would be made for a general 'gate-keeping' mechanism designed to oversee, as far as possible, the entire network of policy and procedure. The function of this mechanism could be both to influence and to monitor, terms of reference that would involve a considerable research effort.

A number of interesting ideas suggest themselves, one being, in effect, the informal implementation of dormant sections of the 1969 CYPA. An obvious example is Section 5 which requires that it be demonstrated, prior to prosecution, that all possible alternatives have been tried and found wanting. A strategy of this kind implies effective liaison with the police and a certain amount of horse-trading – earlier intervention (or a degree of reparation – the informal mode of atonement) in return for a prosecution dropped. If such intervention counts as 'preventive work', it is at least prevention designed to influence decisions – a form of diversion – rather than prevention designed to assess the child's needs or change his behaviour.

The development of the Scottish system (and the English experience of cautioning) indicates that when diversionary mechanisms are introduced there is a tendency for the number of referrals to rise by way of compensation, with the result that the system as a whole simply expands. Co-operation with the police or access to police decision-making is therefore essential. In this connection, it is worth noting that a circular due to be issued jointly by the Home Office, DES and DHSS specifically recommends, among other things, secondments from one service to another. Why not, then, social worker secondments to the juvenile bureaux – a sort of 'juvenile liaison liaison'? A scheme of this kind, the Police–Social Work Bureaux, has actually started in Exeter. In the short term, this might be the

most effective way of gaining access; and in the longer term it might be a
way of acquiring some influence over decision-making, once appropriate
criteria for prosecutions, cautions and 'no further actions' have been
worked out. The inflation of police referrals might then be avoided by
agreeing some kind of quota system, the idea of which would be to increase
the percentage of cautions and 'no further actions' (in return for social work
intervention) without increasing overall numbers.

The crux of the matter is that this kind of active negotiation can go on
independently of the actual face-to-face work. At least one intermediate
project has discovered that its success in reducing the numbers of court
appearances among its clients is thanks mainly to effective police liaison
(rather than the substance of its social work 'input'). This has led,
interestingly, to a 'bandwagon' effect: the very fact that the number of court
appearances or reconvictions has been reduced (by using this strategy) can
be used as a persuasive statistical argument in subsequent negotiation. The
project is obviously successful, so children who might otherwise be
prosecuted can reasonably be diverted towards it. This amounts to an
enterprising use of what is known as the 'policy effect' (positive
discrimination in favour of clients known to be receiving experimental
treatment), which, ironically, is something researchers normally try to
control for.

There is, of course, another risk associated with individuated 'preventive
work' — the information risk, discussed earlier. But the whole point of
active diversion, 'process' intervention as opposed to 'practice' intervention,
is to avoid putting the child in a situation (primarily the court) in which
information generated by preventive work is likely to make him more
vulnerable. Besides, there is no reason why diversionary tactics should not
make full use of volunteers and voluntary organisations, reserving the
imponderable weight of social work intervention for cases in which, despite
everything, a delinquent career has begun.

Even here, though, the kind of information that is made available to the
courts and assessment centres, and the way in which it is used, should be
such as to delay entry to care or custody for as long as possible. This may
involve suppressing casework details and urging discharges and fines rather
than care or supervision orders. By all means let casework and supervision
continue where necessary, but not as the ambiguous consequence of a court
appearance — even if, at a later stage, 'enforced problem-solving' in the form
of a supervision order is regarded as an unavoidable step.

Ultimately, no doubt, the sanction of removal from home will be
necessary for a minority. Where possible, such decisions should be made on
the basis of the seriousness of the offence, the length of time spent in an
institution being determined by the same criterion. This would involve
short-term use of CHEs on a par with detention centres, the choice between
regimes being left, ideally, to the individual concerned. This would at least

avoid the moral absurdity of children being detained for excessive periods of time in cases which, were the offender an adult, would hardly merit a prison sentence. For a rather different minority, those who 'pass' the care or control test (and where this has been proved), longer-term care would be available.

We have not attempted to put these suggestions together in a systematic way (though it should be noted that several of the strategies we recommend have actually been put into effect). As yet we have had no opportunity to develop a comprehensive diversion strategy and, in any case, we are still very wary of the possible 'backfire' effects which may accompany premature innovation. But the integration of 'practice' intervention and 'process' intervention, giving the main emphasis, perhaps, to the latter, still seems to us to have a better chance of success than a 'practice' strategy alone. Indeed, as we have already argued, there is reason to think that it is the only way of overcoming the proliferation of unintended consequences, with 'process' counteracting 'practice', that has been so obvious and unwelcome a feature of the partial implementation of the 1969 CYPA.

THE PRO-ACTIVE APPROACH

As we have already explained, the term 'pro-active' is taken from the work of John Alderson, Chief Constable of Devon and Cornwall, who has probably done more thinking about crime prevention in this sense than anyone else. Devon and Cornwall has also been the scene of some experiments in 'community policing', although the idea is now spreading to a number of other forces. It is as well to note, however, that in many areas the concept of 'community policing' is identified simply with the policy of putting police officers back on foot-patrol, in selected neighbourhoods – whereas for Alderson it means rather more than this.

Alderson's slogan might well be 'Back to 1829' since he has urged a return to the basic principles of policing and the ideals of the Metropolitan Police Act. Certainly, he is concerned to reverse the accelerating trend towards a complete alienation of police from public and public from police. Ultimately, he wishes to say that the community polices itself, or ought to police itself, and that police officers, being of, as well as in, the community, are the public's servants (rather than mere public servants). It is this reidentification of the main agent of police work – the public itself – which is the key to his thought.

The pro-active approach, then, goes well beyond the return of bobbies to the beat. In one sense, it involves an application of the 'village bobby' idea to urban and inner-city areas – resident constables, as opposed to non-resident officers on patrol, but it also involves the recognition, crucially, that the role of the police officer is not simply law enforcement. This is a point to notice because it has been suggested that the return of the foot-patrol might coincide with a greater effort of surveillance and control. This might, indeed, be the case if the point of the new policy were merely to improve sources of information and increase clear-up rates – as Alderson himself notes. But it is not. Enforcement is emphatically not the key issue. As servants of the community, as residents themselves, police officers should see their function as the protection of that community – from crime and the fear of crime – and the creation of conditions in which the community will no longer need to inflict criminal activity on itself.

Where does social work come into all this? We are coming to that. The pro-active police role – as Alderson again observes – inevitably involves a social work component. Indeed, it has been calculated that 70–80 per cent of police time is already taken up with social work and other non-criminal problems (domestic disputes, and the like), although this is something that many police officers are loath to admit. The pro-active function would mean not only admitting it, but recognising and welcoming it. And not simply because it improves relations with the public (who might then be more inclined to pass on useful enforcement information), but because it is precisely social work-type functions that help to create the conditions for a crime-free community. As with diversion, this is obviously an area in which police/social work co-operation, supposing it to be possible at all, is highly desirable.

The pro-active approach is encouraged to the degree to which the community itself can be brought to accept the concept of self-policing. Aside from more specifically social work functions, then, there is an additional task – exhibiting the community to itself as crime-producing and crime-suffering. One of the earliest Exeter projects provides an example of this.[7] In this particular case, the police took the initiative and carried out a research project in which the nature, incidence and frequency of various offences were plotted on to a street map of the city. In this way, a number of highly delinquent neighbourhoods were identified. Rather than simply step up patrols and surveillance in these neighbourhoods, however, an attempt was made to present the results of the research to the communities concerned, at public meetings, in schools, and so on; and the invitation was issued: What are we, as a community, going to do about this? Once persuaded that this image of itself was true, at least one of these communities proved to be both imaginative and resourceful in its efforts to improve the situation.

This seems to us a useful model which could be elaborated in a number of different ways. One particularly attractive option is to enlist the help of the community at an earlier stage, inviting local people, and especially children, to take part in the survey work. There are a number of reasons for this. In the first place, the more people know what is going on, the better; second, local people know what are the relevant questions to ask; third, the results will be experienced more directly and immediately; fourth, in the collection of data, ideas which imply possible solutions are almost bound to emerge. And it is a natural consequence that having produced findings, the community should be allowed to set its own objectives and monitor its own outcomes. It will be said, no doubt, that this is only an ideal, and an optimistic one at that. Possibly; but it is a blueprint from which to work and without some idea of what we are aiming towards it is impossible to choose from what is feasible. Some of these issues are taken up again in the final chapter.

Another possible outcome is one which is implicit in any successful community work; the establishment of informal sanctions and informal controls. A community which does not know and is afraid of itself is on a downward spiral. It is fear of the unknown – unknown people, unknown children, unknown dangers and risks – which inhibits informal controls and prevents people from recognising the community's own policing function. The more it knows itself, the more people can put names to faces, and faces to names, the more they will feel able to take initiatives of their own. 'Experts' have created conditions in which communities can slowly destroy themselves; ultimately, it is up to the community itself to get those conditions changed and find the means of resurrection.

Of course there are problems, and unanswered questions. There always are with new and barely tried ideas. What, for example, is a 'community'? How do we identify it, and how do we persuade it to identify itself? How are 'pro-active' ventures evaluated and justified? How do we solve the political problems, such as persuading recalcitrant chief constables that the concept is a respectable one, or such as finding resources? We do not pretend to have ready answers to these questions. But we are convinced of the value – and logic – of the pro-active approach. What it desperately needs, of course, is more acceptance, more experiment and more evaluation. Hopefully, these will eventually be forthcoming.

CONCLUSION

In these two chapters, we have outlined and argued for a new framework for thinking about work with, and on behalf of, the juvenile offender. As we observed at the beginning, it has not simply been a matter of listing ideas and techniques, though a more detailed description of some possibilities will follow. What matters is not so much what is done as the reason for which it is done, and the conceptual context in which it takes place. Also its relation to other things that are being done or which might be done. As for Cézanne, what is significant is not the shape of things, but the shapes between things. So that if the social worker cannot do everything, what he can do will be determined by its position within the whole theoretical structure.

This structure breaks down into main halves: the non-individuated preventive tasks of diversion and pro-action, and the new approaches to offence-related social work and socialisation. The concept of atonement, which we have suggested should take an increasingly central role in the penal system, stands slightly behind, while overlooking, these two. Certainly, the informal modes of atonement provide links between both diversion and pro-action, on the one hand, and socialisation on the other – although our remarks under the latter heading hardly amount to an endorsement of that concept. In this sense, the concept which is most easily considered independently of the others (although in this framework it is still closely related to them) is the one which most closely resembles conventional social work approaches to the offender: what we have referred to as offence-related social work. We would be surprised if most readers did not feel better equipped to start here than anywhere else – and it is the area in which we ourselves have most experience. It is, accordingly, the subject of the next chapter.

REFERENCES: CHAPTER 6

1 Bottoms, A. E. and McWilliams, W., 'A non-treatment paradigm for probation practice', *British Journal of Social Work*, vol. 9, no. 2, June 1979, pp. 159–202.
2 Matza, D., *Becoming Deviant* (Englewood Cliffs, NJ: Prentice-Hall, 1969).
3 See Gouldner, A., *The Future of Intellectuals and the Rise of the New Class* (London: Macmillan, 1979); Sennett, R., *The Fall of Public Man* (Cambridge: Cambridge University Press, 1977); and Peter Wilby's article 'Habermas and the language of the modern state', *New Society*, 22 March 1979.
4 See expressions above from Sennett, op. cit.
5 Honderich, T., *Punishment: The Supposed Justifications* (Harmondsworth: Penguin, 1976).
6 See Rawls, J., *A Theory of Justice* (Oxford: Oxford University Press, 1971).
7 For an evaluation of the Exeter scheme, see Moore, C., 'From crime statistics to social policy: an evaluation of the work of the Devon and Cornwall Crime Prevention Unit' (unpublished M. Sc. thesis, Cranfield Institute of Technology, 1979).

7
Working with Adolescent Offenders

One of the two policy objectives of a reformed juvenile criminal justice system is the provision of services for individual juvenile offenders in the community. The assumptions lying behind such provision are based on the evidence that juvenile offenders are drawn from the most deprived and disadvantaged sector of the adolescent population and that in order to reduce the likelihood of further offending it is necessary, as far as possible, to compensate for these deprivations. Clearly, however, the concept of deprivation can be interpreted very widely and the broader the interpretation, the more likely it is that whatever measures are adopted will lose sight of the individual delinquent. The links between inadequate educational and leisure facilities, low social class, poor and overcrowded housing, unemployment, poverty and delinquency have been well established. One of the major contradictions lying at the core of social work theory and practice is the seeming inadequacy of micro-intervention (at the level of individuals and families) in situations where material stress and status-frustration appear to make a major contribution to social dysfunction. Most if not all of the factors listed under the heading of 'broad' social deprivation appear to imply that very fundamental changes in the social and economic structure of society would be needed to bring about change. Decisions about changes in social and economic structure can only be made, by and large, at the highest political levels. In contrast, the social worker is usually responsible to a relatively local group of elected representatives, and his operations are confined to much smaller geographical areas in fairly well-defined communities. The social worker's professional responsibility is primarily to deal with these very local issues, and a more detailed description of the development of broad programmes designed to deal with local determinants of delinquency will be contained in the final chapter. Suffice it to say at this stage that there are many specifically local factors which generate delinquency, and that these can be fairly systematically identified by the social worker.

This chapter, however, is addressed to the 'face-to-face' issues of social work with juvenile offenders and is about intervention focused on individually labelled juvenile offenders. In that respect, in this chapter, when the word 'delinquent' is used, it refers specifically to a child who has been arrested, charged and been found guilty of, or been cautioned for, a criminal offence. Similarly, the expression 'delinquent group' refers to a group of labelled offenders.

Crudely speaking, this work takes two complementary directions. The first is connected with the actual provision of rewarding social experiences, leisure pastimes and even employment opportunities. The second is connected with the control and modification of infractious behaviour. The two together form the basic services on which any correctional programme must be built.

If delinquency is so clearly linked to social and emotional deprivation then measures have to be applied which will compensate for at least some of the more easily identifiable and rectifiable deprivations. It must be emphasised at this stage that such compensation has to be effected in the individual delinquent's fairly immediate social and material environment. The major disadvantage of many current correctional programmes is that some services – those of remedial education, vocational training and leisure activities – are provided in a custodial setting. The result of this is that when a juvenile offender is discharged from an institution into the community, the services generally cease to be available to him. This may in part explain the high post-release recidivism rates of the old approved schools and the present CHEs. Hirschi[1] claims that the extent to which an adolescent is likely to commit delinquent acts may largely be a function of the degree to which that young person is bound to the conventional moral order. To put it another way, those who are least likely to be delinquent are those who have most to lose by it. Adolescents who have relatively low stakes in society, for example in terms of limited employment possibilities or difficulties at home and school, do not derive much benefit from conforming to a society which has little interest in them and offers few opportunities in return. In many respects, this theory of delinquency causation adequately fits the well-established links between crime and deprivation. Rather than viewing the delinquent as a person who is compelled to commit offences by powerful internal psychological stresses, it suggests that anti-social drives as such do not exist but neither, as such, do drives to conform. In view of the very limited or non-existent rewards available to them for conforming behaviour, it is clear that a substantial number of deprived adolescents are likely to be more prone to delinquency that their better-off counterparts. Deprivation creates delinquency not so much by generating psychological abnormality as by loosening attachment to society. Those with bright futures derive much from the system and are at least prepared to play along with it because of what it promises. Those whom the system fails are inevitably more ready to abandon any attempt to live up to its demands. It is the task of the social worker to strengthen the delinquent's commitment to society by means of positive discrimination. Plant[2] sees social work as being involved in mediating the demands society makes of conforming individuals, and conversely the demands conforming individuals make of society, for it is clear in this 'exchange' model of social obligation that he who receives little is likely to give little. Control is exercised not by the stick but by offering the carrot. The model of delinquency implicit in this chapter is that offered by 'control' theories which see constraints on behaviour as a function of 'exchange' and not as a function of subcultural opposition to social norms or emotional disorder. Perhaps the best known of 'control' theorists is Matza[3] whose concept of 'soft determinism' explains the processes leading up to a delinquent act in terms of 'a drift occasioned by the gradual and undramatic loosing of restraints on behaviour as a result of a range of experiences'. To put it crudely, Matza identified these experiences as the withdrawal of authority from the law and the adult world – presumably because they demand much for little return – and responses to suggestions made by peers once the authority of the conventional moral order is neutralised. Hirschi, whose 'control' theory is mentioned above, carried out a survey of over 4,000 American junior and senior high school students.[4] The survey compared police records on delinquent behaviour with responses to questions about attachment to parents, attachment to school, attachment to peers, belief in, and commitment to, conventional lines of action, involvement in conventional activities and personal values. The study represented a very ambitious attempt to test a number of theories of delinquency and its results predictably tended to confirm many of those which offer explanations in terms of lack of interest and concern by parents, poor scholastic attainment and indifference to school, the selection of delinquent peers and the acquisition, ultimately, of a set of values quite different from those reflected in the criminal law. Hirschi was also able to chart the relative strengths and weaknesses of these factors in forming combinations which led to delinquency. Perhaps one of the most interesting findings was related to the influence of peers. Hitherto, 'control' theories had assumed that adolescents whose parents showed them little interest would be less affected by parental disapproval of their behaviour and hence more likely to be delinquent, and that this was often combined with a lack of commitment to conventional activities. However, Hirschi's study revealed that association with other delinquents appeared to be a very powerful and crucial factor. He says that while control

> theory underestimated the importance of delinquent friends, it overestimated the significance of involvement in conventional activities. Both of these miscalculations appear to stem from the same source, the assumption of 'natural motivation' to delinquency. If such natural

motivation could legitimately be assumed, *delinquent friends would be unnecessary* [our emphasis] and involvement in conventional activities would curtail the commission of delinquent acts.

In other words, failure to incorporate some notions of what delinquency does for the adolescent probably accounts for the failure of the theory in these areas. Notions about the contribution delinquent activities make to the person's self-concept or self-esteem would also seem to be necessary in accounting for much of the potency of the adult-status items, such as smoking, drinking, dating and driving a car.[5]

By interpreting his findings in this way, Hirschi appears to have discovered an anomalous factor in the emotional and material deprivation themes of delinquency. If it were simply a matter of disrupted and inconsistent parenting, or a domestically learnt 'conduct disorder', or poverty, or even all of these in combination, then one would expect the delinquent to commit his offences in isolation. The fact is that the majority of delinquents actively seek out and maintain the company of other delinquents. A cursory glance at any study on juvenile offenders will confirm this. One of the most recent is a study of the juvenile justice system in a northern town which gives the results shown in Table 7.1.

Table 7·1. *Juvenile offending and peers, first offence Northtown M.D.C. September 1977 to March 1979*

	Frequency	Percentage
Jointly charged	654	73
Singly charged	240	26·8
	894	100

Offending in the company of peers seems, at least in the early stages of a delinquent career, to be a significant factor in learning delinquent behaviour. Even a very cursory glance at a juvenile court list confirms that many young people who are prosecuted are jointly charged and both social enquiry reports as well as comments by magistrates frequently express the opinion that juvenile delinquents are 'easily led'. By any standards, such comments betray a fundamental misunderstanding of the 'situation of company', as Matza calls it, and inevitably beg the question: Why is the child in question easily led in an anti-social direction rather than in the direction of conformity to social norms? To put the question more clearly, one would ask what are the rewards derived by the individual delinquent from his associates, and what reward is there in delinquent activity? The logic of the situation suggests that if these questions can be answered, then change targets can be identified in both the area of self-image and that of behaviour. Of necessity, these imply highly individualised answers and solutions.

At this stage, the theory suggests a separation of three interconnected factors:

(1) material and emotional deprivation;
(2) the selection of delinquent peers;
(3) the rewards of delinquent behaviour.

What appears to happen is that the original deprivation precipitating the selection of delinquent peers gets lost somewhere, and the peer group and delinquency completely take over and obscure the original causes from the child himself. This appears to explain why, when a juvenile offender is brought into a programme which offers a lot of material and emotional compensation, the delinquent behaviour does not stop. Although Hirschi's chain of causation is expressed thus:[6]

Attitudes toward conventional persons or institutions	→	Delinquent companions	→	Delinquent acts

it is clear that the delinquent behaviour assumes a life of its own, as Ryall says:

> The delinquent adopts distinct techniques for viewing and assessing the actions of authorities. In the first place, he is *selective* about those actions of authority which he takes cognisance of. He is quick to notice and mentally record any actions which support a negative view of authority, but will ignore actions which show authority in a good light. In the second place, where possible he will *interpret* actions so that they support these hostile views. For example, as noted above, he will interpret attempts of magistrates to *individualise* justice as demonstrating the *absence* of justice. These techniques of selective perception and biased interpretation will be reinforced by his contact with other delinquents, and they will become automatic and unconscious determinants of his response to the actions of authority.
>
> To sum up the characteristics outlined here of the behaviour of the persistent delinquent: it is a learned, self-reinforcing behaviour pattern which is central to the delinquent's self-image, and which is supported by a self-consistent set of attitudes hostile to conventional social values and authority figures. These attitudes themselves are strengthened by the delinquent's techniques of viewing and interpreting events in his social environment. His delinquent behaviour may originally have been caused by one or a number of many possible determining factors, but it is likely

that the significance of this initial causation will diminish as the learned behaviour pattern becomes well established.[7]

What Ryall is suggesting here is that once delinquent behaviour occurs in the peer group, it becomes autonomous and independent of the individual's low status in society. The self-reinforcing rewards of delinquent behaviour seem to be located in peer-group status, excitement (or freedom from boredom) and perhaps, in the later stages of a delinquent career, actual material gain. It cannot escape even the casual observer that delinquents frequently account for their behaviour in terms of 'having a laugh' or that they were usually 'bored' when the chain of events leading to an offence began. Moreover, even if the bonds with delinquent peers are of only a very tenuous nature (an issue which will be explored later), delinquent associations and attitudes become even more strongly reinforced by contact with penal agents.

A modification, therefore, to Hirschi's diagram would set out the social and psychological systems of delinquent behaviour as shown in Figure 7.1.

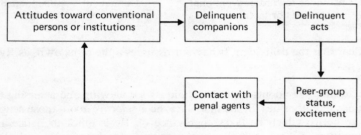

Figure 7.1

Policemen, magistrates, social workers and probation officers take a dim view of delinquent acts. Since these very acts are designed to increase the delinquent's status and since it is precisely that status which is denied by those who administer the juvenile criminal justice system, then inevitably their disapproval leads the delinquent to withdraw even more credibility from such adults and instead return to those who reinforce a positive self-image. Thus by their very interventions, juvenile criminal justice system officials are likely to add to the cycle of reinforcement.

While all of this can appear very depressing to those whose task it is to control delinquent behaviour, there are several possibilities for intervention which may break the cycle. If the delinquent peer group is a central and mediating factor in the social system of delinquency, then a study of its social dynamics and the meanings which an individual attaches to his associations in that system could potentially reveal opportunities for altering either the dynamics of such a group or the behaviour of the individual in it. At this stage, then, the social worker has three questions:

(1) Why did the child select delinquent friends?
(2) What are the essential dynamics of the delinquent group?
(3) What kinds of rewards does the child gain from delinquent activities in that group?

The correctional agent very rarely has access to the delinquent group and even if he did have access, it is likely that his presence would merely serve to submerge the specific interactions which lead to infraction. It may be more fruitful, therefore, to examine the social processes of the group from the point of view of the individuals in it.

It is popularly assumed that the delinquent group is a happy, comfortable and safe place for the individuals in it. In fact, nothing could be further from the truth. Hirschi comments:

> Attachment to peers does not foster alienation from conventional persons and institutions; it if anything fosters commitment to them. There is no foundation for the belief that the delinquent gang is an intensely solidary group comprising 'the most fit and able youngsters in their community'. On the contrary, those committing delinquent acts are not likely to think much of each other; distrust and suspicion, not intense solidarity, are the foundations of the delinquent gang.[8]

Moreover, Hirschi maintains that 'the less cohesive the gang, the greater its involvement in delinquency'. In other words, it is the very tensions within the group itself which generate the behaviour. Paradoxically, the less a youngster likes and respects his delinquent associates, the more likely it is that that association will promote delinquent behaviour. The group dynamics become self-reinforcing and appear once more to assume a life of their own. Why is it then that a child becomes heavily influenced by friends for whom he has little respect? The answer is at least in part supplied by Matza's concept of 'sounding', or as it may frequently be described on this side of the Atlantic, 'testing out'. Matza analyses the processes involved in this:

> Sounding is a key term in the vocabulary of delinquents, referring to perhaps the most frequent class of events in day-to-day mundane behaviour of delinquents. Used properly, an analysis of sounding may be a choice instrument in an understanding of delinquent values. Like most terms in the delinquent part of the world, it has a double meaning, one conventional, the other esoteric. The conventional meaning refers to the plumbing of depth — a probing of how deep the facade of personal appearance goes — and by gradual adaptation a testing of one's status.

The esoteric meaning of sounding is of more immediate relevance. It refers to the primary means through which status is probed – insults. What is insult? Insult is an imputation of *negative* characteristics. Offense is taken only if the recipient at least partially concurs with the perpetrator on the negative evaluation of the substance of the remark. We may not insult people for the possession of qualities they wholly celebrate. Boys who live in the subculture of delinquency may be sounded because their brothers are in jail. Moreover, they may be, and are, sounded on the grounds of being bad or mean. 'Man, you are a pretty bad (or mean) character, ain't you?' is the method of sounding a peer who claims to have attained an advanced stage of delinquency. Being bad is simultaneously honorific and grounds for insult.

Delinquents take offense if they are falsely accused. Partially this is because they wish to prevent the punitive action which ordinarily follows accusation, but also because they concur in the conventional assessment of delinquency. The imputation of delinquency is not only denied, which would happen in any event merely for truth's sake, it is also resented. If the subculture of delinquency were committed to delinquency, if it were oppositional, then imputations of delinquency might be true or false but in any case complimentary and hardly capable of eliciting resentment.[9]

Testing out, then, appears to be a crucial process in the dynamic of the delinquent group. On the one hand, it serves to maintain a sense of insecurity in the recipient of such actions and, on the other, it clearly stimulates and maintains a delinquent response. Such behaviour is very much 'social' behaviour, since the phenomenon of 'testing out' can be observed in all social situations where a person's facade is checked out. The implication here, therefore, for the correctional practitioner is to teach a child a range of responses to such a situation, rather than permit him to maintain a stereotyped delinquent one. If 'sounding' has a double meaning, if it is ambiguous, then it is open to a range of responses, some of which can involve neither loss of face to an implied insult nor a delinquent act to save face. This is very much a matter of social learning, not one of simply compensating for deprivation. We are talking here of social learning in a very specific kind of social situation, not the kind of social learning generally used in correctional programmes which broadly attempts to 'improve attitudes and relationships' with peers, adults and authority figures. We are referring to responses to suggestions in what Matza calls 'the situation of company'. Perhaps even more importantly, the social work profession has in recent years begun to develop techniques for social learning which are focused on very specific social situations. Such techniques have a number of advantages, namely that objectives can be relatively easily set, in so far as dysfunctional behaviour can be broken down with the client into its component parts, and alternative behaviours in response to specific stimuli can be rehearsed, reinforced and gradually applied in real-life situations.

To sum up the position so far:

(1) Social and emotional deprivation causes children to have few stakes in society, and relatively little to gain from conforming to social norms.

(2) One of the possible responses to this is to become associated with others in a similar position (selection of delinquent peers).

(3) The company of delinquent peers can potentially offer status denied by the adult world, even though delinquents may not have a lot of respect for each other.

(4) The central dynamic of the delinquent peer group is a testing-out process which leads to delinquent acts in order to maintain status.

(5) Delinquent acts give status, excitement and sometimes material gain.

(6) The attitudes and actions of juvenile criminal justice system officials reinforce dependence on delinquent peers and the rejection of conventional values.

The implications of the above for social work practice are self-evident. They suggest a programme which provides a wide range of activities offering non-delinquent opportunities for status-building, and a very tightly structured social-skills training programme which is tailored to modify specific behaviours in specific settings. Such a programme can be carried out within the framework of Section 12 of the 1969 CYPA – the intermediate treatment conditions attached to a supervision order which empower the supervisor to compel a child to attend a facility or facilities for up to ninety days. It is clear that for high-risk persistent juvenile offenders a fairly intensive programme is needed, focused around the child's home and fairly immediate social environment. A more detailed explanation of the full range of community-based facilities for intermediate treatment is given in the next chapter. The present chapter deals primarily with the kind of programme which would be appropriate to medium- and high-intensity facilities.

In the past seven years, social workers have discovered something which most school teachers already knew – that children enjoy activities they are good at and tend not to like doing things which they may not be able to do very well. Many intermediate treatment practitioners claim that certain activities – outdoor pursuits are an obvious example – are beneficial to delinquents. However, no one has as yet provided any evidence that any particular activity is any more beneficial than any other. It stands to reason that children who are physically unfit, have low stress thresholds and do not like being out of doors, will not benefit from mountain walking or rock climbing. Nevertheless, it is important to remember that a child is potentially good at at least one activity: the implication is that a correctional programme should systematically offer as great a variety of activities as is possible within budgetary and geographical limits. Even more important, these activities need to continue to be realistically available to the child after the completion of the intermediate treatment requirements, for they can form the basis of a developing commitment to conventional as opposed to delinquent activity and are also sources of status and self-esteem. The social worker in the intermediate treatment group should draw up a list of locally available facilities and volunteers willing to give personal or group instruction in particular activities. These could be listed under a series of headings:

(1) *Leisure activities* — the standard pastimes of adolescents, including hobbies, handicrafts, spectator and participatory sports, etc. Volunteers willing to help with fishing, craftwork, music-making, etc. would come under this list.

(2) *Educational activities* — interesting places such as museums, places of historical interest, places of importance in the community such as hospitals, etc.

(3) *Challenge activities* — usually outdoor pursuits.

(4) *Expressive activities* — modelling, drama, painting, etc., and a list of volunteers willing to teach children.

(5) *Life-skills* — cooking, sewing, decorating, etc.

(6) *Local youth facilities* — a list of all clubs, cadet corps, etc. in the locality willing to include delinquent children amongst their members after the termination of the correctional programme.

None of these activities have a special correctional merit in themselves. Their value to the delinquent lies in the opportunities they present for a non-delinquent means of acquiring status. Even very small successes, if pointedly reinforced, can generate a cycle of positive feedback from both non-delinquent peers and adults. It is this feedback which gives a child a stake in society, a reason not to get into trouble again because of the threatened loss of interesting activities and the disapproval of valued people. It can reverse the cycle of alienation and disapproval which is often an important precondition to the development of delinquent expressions of the need for status and the learning of delinquent behaviour in a peer group.

Parallel to the provision of 'activity' services by social workers and volunteers is the service which we shall call the 'correctional curriculum'. This expression refers to the social skills/behaviour modification curriculum which is designed to help the individual child in trouble to develop non-delinquent responses to suggestion and testing out by peers. There are two important factors to be taken into account here. First, the child has to be taught a conceptual framework with which he can comprehend the group processes in which he is involved – partly by reference to his own experience and partly by direct reference to the social events within the intermediate treatment group itself. Secondly, non-delinquent responses to suggestion need to be rehearsed – not only in respect of the natural peer group but also in the treatment setting, so that they can be monitored and tested out in real-life situations.

A paradigm for learning both at conceptual and behavioural levels already exists in educational theory. This paradigm has the ability to convey sophisticated concepts as well as the possibilities of developing self-awareness and as a result changing one's behaviour. The method here is not that of standard behaviour modifications, it is more a matter of supplying a child with the tools to modify his own behaviour where and when it is appropriate. This curriculum has four distinct phases:

(1) contrast;
(2) hypothesis-making;
(3) participation;
(4) self-awareness.

The first phase, 'contrast', consists of a process in which the taken-for-grantedness of phenomena is stripped away by the presentation of conflicting explanations. It involves offering a different interpretation of the meaning of a particular event. Everyone tends to assume that his own experience of an event, and the meaning he attaches to it, are true – the only possible way of seeing things. A contrasting account brings in the possibility that there are other, equally valid interpretations and this forces the individual to look again at what he had assumed to be an unchangeable datum of his experience. Most learning in any field involves contrast; we only know what a door is because we have seen a window, and what a delinquent act is because we know that other acts are not delinquent. Thus the experience of the delinquent peer group should be presented in a different light and given a different meaning. Once the taken-for-grantedness has been taken away, the child is inevitably forced to find new explanations – the hypothesis-making phase. Usually, the social worker will at this stage offer a range of explanations, although in the end the child will accept one which makes sense of his experience. The third phase, participation, involves the child in performing certain actions which test out the new hypothesis, while the fourth phase, self-awareness, leads to the internalisation and acceptance of new social meanings of the self.

The correctional curriculum, then, is firmly based on a theory of social education which demands sequential programming. For delinquents, 'the situation of company' is used as the subject of learning, and the treatment group and its interactions as a medium in which such learning can occur and, initially at least, be tested. 'The situation of company' and the social

events surrounding delinquent acts can be articulated and explored in some
depth by asking each child to produce a comic strip or cartoon of the most
recent delinquent episode in which he was involved. This exercise is used to
enable the child to explore the meanings attached to the event and to
understand them at a depth for which simple verbal descriptions are likely to
be inadequate. Each frame on the cartoon strip is discussed, with particular
attention being given to cues and responses, especially 'sounding' cues and
acts in response to them. As Matza has commented, delinquents in fact
rarely articulate to each other the actions in which they are about to
participate, or consider the consequences: 'The company is in a state of
acute mutual dependence since there is no coherent ideology which may be
consulted. There are only specific and concrete slogans. But there is no
general theory.'[10] Thus, Matza suggests, a kind of pluralistic ignorance
develops in the delinquent group. Each member supposes that the others
are truly committed to delinquency, that this is a delinquent subculture. But
each member also knows that he himself has no such commitment; he
knows that in a whole range of situations he behaves in a conventional
way. Perhaps each believes himself to be the one uncommitted delinquent
in the group. But there is no way in which this can be tested. A discussion
of the attitudes each member has to delinquent acts would clear everything
up, but a public discussion is simply not possible in such situations because
of 'status anxiety', fears of being thought of as inadequate which are
constantly present in the delinquent peer group as a result of 'sounding' and
'testing out'. Much of the sounding and testing out probes that very self-
esteem and ensures the cohesiveness of the group by means of maintaining
high anxiety levels. It is the anxiety which causes the individual delinquent
not to consider either the immediate effects (in terms of victim suffering) or
the longer-term consequences (police apprehension and prosecution) of his
actions. Far from being the mutually supportive, comradely band imagined
by the theorists of 'oppositional' subcultures, the delinquent gang is, then,
characterised by the absence of trust and openness and a high level of
anxiety and suspicion.

The point of the in-depth exploration of the delinquent episode by means
of drawing comic strips and frames is to enable the absence of public
discussion in the social events surrounding delinquent acts to come to the
fore. All the social worker needs to ask at the crucial time is: 'What did you
actually say to each other, can you remember the conversations you were
having just before you did it?' Once a fairly clear picture has emerged of the
social interactions and activities immediately prior to the offence being
committed, the cartoon strip, with its attendant notes made during
discussion of the events, can be used as the script for a video-televised role-
play. Sometimes, in order to clarify the confusion surrounding the events
and the vital 'who said what to whom and when' questions, it is useful to
draw up a list of the characters involved before proceeding with drawing

the cartoon. This operation may, however, be performed after the drawings, but in either case it is an important aid to directing the role-play. The individual child who developed the script by means of a cartoon does not act in the role-play, but directs it. The characters in the cartoon are played by other children and the social workers in the intermediate treatment group. Once the episode has been role-played and taped, it is then played back for discussion.

In many respects, the playback (and the skill with which it is handled) is a key point of the curriculum programme, for it is during this process that the children are asked to look for the cues or suggestions of peers on the tape and consider alternative ways of responding which do not involve the development of a delinquent act or the loss of face normally associated with backing down. The alternative models of behaviour are then scripted by means of drawing several more cartoons. They can then be role-played and video-taped again. These alternatives must be the children's own suggestions, in their language and capable of being rehearsed. The major point of the exercise is to elaborate, by use of the children's own experience of the delinquent peer group, on the social events within it, hence the scripting and role-play, followed by the development of viable alternative responses to 'sounding' and suggestion. Face-saving alternatives to delinquent acts are necessary to keep down the anxiety levels which, Matza suggests, are an important feature of delinquent peer groups and are a consequence of a child's status being threatened by sounding. The ideal sequence to be followed in the correctional curriculum would therefore be as follows:

(1) List of characters in the delinquent episode.
(2) Articulate the episode by drawing it as a cartoon strip.
(3) Discuss the cartoon and elaborate on the social interactions with particular reference to comments from peers which created status anxiety, leading to undiscussed delinquent activity. Notes are taken on the script.
(4) Role-play the cartoon which is used as a script. The child who took part in and cartooned the episode directs the role-play.
(5) Play back the video-tape and discuss possible and realistic alternative verbal and non-verbal responses to the cues which preceded delinquent activity.
(6) Cartoon these responses, and use the cartoon as a script for further role-play and video-taping.

As with all social-skills training, the problem of application to real-life situations requires a lot of attention. The problem is how to generalise from the artificial group to the real world. In the case of learning new responses to 'sounding' cues, it is helpful to produce as great a range of such cues as possible. Clearly, this is done in the intermediate treatment group when the clients portray a wide variety of social situations antecedent to delinquency, and by means of role-play and discussion learn to discriminate between different anxiety-provoking stimuli. If it is the anxiety which produces the delinquent response (the outcome behaviour of particular stimuli), then face-saving formulae must be designed not so much to get the child out of the peer group, as to reduce anxiety. In that sense very simple responses such as the production of cigarettes after being 'sounded' (an action which, for juveniles, is an immediate distraction and status-conferrer) can be considered.

However, another method of discovering anxiety-reducing responses exists, and that is derived from direct observation by the social workers of the cueing and responding which actually occurs in the 'treatment' situation itself – in other words learning by means of exploiting the processes occurring in the intermediate treatment group. All intermediate treatment practitioners are aware of 'sounding' and testing out as a persistent feature of the adolescent groups with which they work. Such interactions are, of course, a direct reflection of behaviour the children have learnt in their natural delinquent peer groups. The video television recorder (VTR) provides an ideal tool for producing very accurate records of these events and, moreover, such recording can actually take place while the children in the group are performing the primary task of cartooning and scripting – tasks which normally take a long time and are subject to constant interruptions, when the children sound each other out. These records can then be used to look not only at situations where disruptive responses did emerge as a result of 'sounding', but also where such stimuli produced non-disruptive, anxiety-reducing responses. This allows both the workers and children to make important connections between past and present events, by examining delinquent episodes which occurred in the past and comparing them with similar events in the here and now. Of special value are the here-and-now responses which are not disruptive and which reduce anxiety, since these can be selected from the process tapes and added to the repertoire of non-delinquent, anxiety-reducing behaviours being developed and rehearsed around the role-played delinquent episodes. In this respect, process tapes offer very important clues about the ways in which the children individually have already developed adaptive responses to 'sounding' and its consequent anxieties. Again, such appropriate responses, like the inappropriate ones, can be cartooned from stills from the video-tape, stopped at significant points during the playback and if necessary even by role-playing them from the cartoon scripts. These are, of course, very small pieces of behaviour which never last longer than three to five minutes. Moreover, process tapes do not lie; unlike the delinquent-episode cartoon which has to be recalled from memory, the television camera sees all and records all – and it can be played back in an 'action replay' manner which allows a highly detailed analysis of very brief verbal exchanges and activities.

By this means, process events are used to explain, illustrate and illuminate the task of looking at 'the situation of company' and the learning of new social behaviours, as well as the internalisation of a new and more realistic self-image.

The correctional curriculum can therefore be conceptualised in the following manner:

TASK LEVEL
(1)   Cartoon delinquent episode.
(2)   Discuss 'sounding' in the episode.
(3)   Role-play and video-tape (TAPE DECK 2).
(4)   Playback and discuss alternative responses.
(5)   Cartoon alternative responses.
(6)   Role-play and video-tape alternative responses (rehearsed) (TAPE DECK 2).

PROCESS LEVEL
(1)   Video-tape the cartooning and discussions listed above (TAPE DECK 1).
(2)   Select cues which represent sounding behaviour and disruptive and non-disruptive responses.
(3)   Playback cue and disruptive responses.
(4)   Cartoon off the monitor and link it to the 'sounding' on the delinquent-episode cartoon.
(5)   Playback cue and non-disruptive, anxiety-reducing response.
(6)   Cartoon off the monitor and link it to alternative repertoire of responses.

An important procedure to follow before commencing the curriculum is to explain it in some detail and allow the children to get used to handling the camera and video television equipment − it will be discovered that after initially producing funny faces, making obscene comments and talking about being 'spied on', they rapidly settle to the task and ignore the presence of the camera. Two video television recording decks are a very useful asset in the procedure (these appear in the above summary as TAPE DECKS 1 and 2). One tape and deck is reserved for recording the role-played delinquent episodes, while the other is used for recording the group processes and cartooning. Both the camera and television monitor are switched between the two tape decks depending on whether task or process events are being recorded or played back.

Essentially, then, the correctional curriculum is undertaken in a work-shop. The workshop should have adequate lighting and sound-proofing and be wired to record sound. Chairs and a large table (for drawing) should be provided as well as the materials for writing and drawing (felt-tipped pens and paper). Sufficient space should be planned for the role-plays. While the two video-tape decks can be placed on a side bench, the camera should be mounted on a sturdy, wheeled tripod so that it can be moved around the workshop.

In 1977, the authors of this book conducted an experimental thirty-day, high-intensity intermediate treatment project at the New Planet Trust, a charitable community-based sports/arts venture in Lancaster. One of the authors is a member of the trust, and after receiving permission from the trust a programme was planned with the Director of the New Planet which utilised Planet staff (on a job creation scheme) and the full range of facilities available in the building. With the assistance and co-operation of Lancashire County Council Social Services Department, which financed the scheme, and the probation service in Lancaster, six high-risk clients were selected for the group on the basis that each one had committed several offences and would be likely to receive a custodial sentence if further delinquency occurred. All six clients were males aged 12–15 years and subject to supervision orders to either the local authority or probation service, with attached thirty-day conditions for intermediate treatment.

The project had three objectives. These were:

(1)   to stop further delinquent behaviour;
(2)   to introduce the boys to a range of non-delinquent activities which they could continue after their period of treatment ended; and
(3)   to explore and alleviate, where possible, other delinquency-generating factors including distorted family relationships and poor self-image.

These objectives were to be met by:

(1)   the use of the correctional curriculum to reduce the possibility of future offending;
(2)   the use of all the New Planet's considerable competitive and non-competitive sports facilities, an outdoor pursuits programme and an arts/theatre programme; and
(3)   regular meetings between project staff and the boys' parents designed to include them, as far as possible, in the programme.

Regular meetings and frequent contact with the supervising probation officers and social workers to discuss particular issues relating to environmental factors which appeared to link with the boys' delinquency were also an essential part of the programme.

Since this was a high-intensity programme, the boys were compelled to attend for at least eight hours every day except during the residential periods when attendance was required for twenty-four hours per day. The thirty days were organised as follows:

Day 1:
: Orientation day. Meeting the project staff, participating in the centre's activities – table tennis, pool, trampoline, darts, badminton, etc. A meeting also took place with the supervising social workers and probation officers and with the parents separately in the evening to explain the programme in detail.

Days 2 and 3:
: Residential weekend – camping and fishing.

Days 4 to 8:
: The correctional curriculum in the workshop at the centre. Two-hour 'work' periods were interspersed with one- or two-hour breaks. Parental group meeting at the end.

Day 9:
: The centre had a stall in a local park during a festival. The boys erected and manned the stall. Meeting with supervisors.

Days 10 and 11:
: Residential weekend – camping and fishing.

Days 12 to 15:
: Development of a musical drama at the centre for a street theatre production in the town. Making and using instruments. Making up songs, costumes, etc. Meeting with parents and supervisors.

Day 16:
: Presentation of the street theatre production with other children from the centre in the town's market square.

Days 17 and 18:
: Ice-skating, cinema, short walk, general leisure activities.

Days 19 and 20:
: Centre activities – indoor games, etc.

Days 21 and 22:
: Re-examination of the correctional curriculum.

Days 23 to 30:
: Outdoor pursuits. Climbing the highest mountains in England, Scotland and Wales.

The intention was to expose the boys to as broad a range of activities as was feasible, but to build the programme round the correctional curriculum, the music and drama production and outdoor pursuits at the end. Most activities were to take place at the centre itself, so that once the boys had met and mixed with other children (particularly on the street theatre production) and familiarised themselves with the centre's facilities and staff, they could continue to attend after the compulsory period was over. Overall the project contained a combination of techniques from the social work, educational and youth-work fields which included socio-drama (role-play), curriculum-adapted group work, expressive drama and outdoor pursuits.

Initially, a contract was made with each boy. The contract offered a broad range of activities, including some which they themselves added to the list, in return for attendance at the centre and four hours of 'work' per day during the first phase of the programme. The correctional curriculum was explained in detail. It was emphasised that failure to comply with the attendance requirements of the programme was a matter for the supervising social worker or probation officer. The objectives of the programme were stated unequivocally: 'You have been in trouble. If you want to stay out of trouble in future then we think we can help. If you don't want to stay out of trouble then don't come – take your chances with your supervisor and the juvenile court.' This might appear, on the surface at least, to be a rather brutal opening statement. It does, however, tell the simple truth about these children's predicament. One of the more disturbing aspects of the juvenile criminal justice system is undoubtedly the way in which the rationale for custodial programmes is presented by CHE staff to delinquents – and the way in which delinquents understand the reasons for their incarcerations. If a visitor to a CHE was to ask a member of staff why a particular child was there, two main reasons would be given. In descending order of importance, they might be expressed thus:

(1) The child has many problems at home, so he cannot live there.
(2) These problems at home caused the child to commit offences.

In contrast to that, if the child were asked he would be likely to say:

(1) I was sent here by the juvenile court.
(2) The court sent me because I did something wrong.

The rationales for custody presented by staff and inmates are fundamentally at variance with each other. If pressed further, the staff might embark on an in-depth discussion of treatment programmes, while the child would talk about the difficulties of avoiding detection and being 'shopped' by friends. Unfortunately, however, in the custodial setting it is the staff definition of reality which holds sway and determines release dates. In community-based programmes it is important that the commitment required of individual juvenile offenders is spelt out in terms of 'trouble' and how to stay out of it, and that a programme's objectives are declared to be very specifically correctional as opposed to vaguely therapeutic. Moreover, the time limit is legally and clearly defined. It is the absence of such clarity which makes a nonsense of the semi-indeterminate Section 7(7) care order and the sucking in of 'at risk' children into intermediate treatment groups. The absence of clearly defined goals, specific learning objectives and time-limited involvement in the bulk of rehabilitation programmes for juvenile offenders is the cause of much discredit of social workers amongst delinquents.

Having made the contracts and met the parents and supervisors, the project got under way. The residential weekend was used to develop informal communication between staff and clients and to give operational meaning to the rules – offending was not permitted, domestic chores such as cooking and cleaning were to be shared. 'Ice-breaking' exercises were used for people to get to know each other. Very early on, one boy, Alan, emerged as an unhappy, isolated scapegoat. In this capacity he proved himself enormously useful to the other five boys who happily continued to set him up and then blame him for everything that went wrong. On the second day he attempted to leave, unable to bear the pressure, threatening to call his father to take him home (a characteristic response in this boy to all stress, particularly at school). The next day, the boys began scripting their delinquent episodes. The exercise went well, with only spasmodic interruptions – mostly from Alan. On such occasions, work stopped and the leaders discussed the interruptions with the boys, who made it quite clear that they thought it was Alan's fault. Particularly vociferous in this respect was Roger – physically much bigger than the others and a popular member of several of the town's delinquent peer groups. Roger stated that Alan was a 'nutter' and described in detail his eating habits, his nervous destructiveness and his whining anxiousness. Roger also ridiculed Alan's delinquencies as being only very minor infractions. Towards the end of one of these discussions, Alan appeared to provoke a small disruption which stopped the conversation. The incident was played back from the VTR which had been recording the group processes. It clearly showed Alan being set up by Roger. The actions were very discreet and would have gone unnoticed without the VTR. Roger began by non-verbally taunting Alan while the conversation around the table centred elsewhere. The taunts consisted of mouthed 'soundings' and facial expressions of insult and disdain. Alan reacted by reaching across the table to touch Harry who was sitting next to Roger. At that point, Roger rose up and quite pointedly grabbed Alan's arm and flung it away, exclaiming that he was being a nuisance again. One of the group leaders observed the last few seconds of the interaction and called for an 'action replay' of it. By that time, of course, the boys had become very familiar with the VTR and calmly sat through the replay in which the tape was frozen every few seconds. The incident was drawn as a cartoon off the video stills. There was no dispute among the participants about what had happened over the five frames which represented the incident. There was, however, a lot of discussion about the motives of the two principal actors – Alan and Roger. The cartoons clearly depicted Roger setting Alan up as the scapegoat and blaming him at the end for disrupting the discussion. The group leaders began to make the point about the 'set up' drawing out the parallels between the cues and responses on the video-tape with similar incidents in the delinquent episodes in which the boys had been involved and which they were cartooning. The process of setting someone up for 'a laugh', which in the context of the group was a relatively trivial and innocuous activity, was seen to have fairly serious consequences in the natural peer group. The video-recorded and cartooned incident between Alan and Roger was role-played – it was a very small sequence of events of which the cartoon provided a precise script for the actions of individuals and it only lasted five minutes. The role-play was successfully completed. One of the group leaders then talked about the possible alternative behaviours Alan and Roger could have performed so that they could both have got out of the situation without losing face and thus reduced their anxiety levels. The leaders hoped that the experience of cartooning a series of events, role-playing them, discussing them and then role-playing alternatives would become a central feature of that first phase of the programme. The first alternative to be role-played – in which one of the leaders, playing Roger, calmly defused the issue by moving Alan's arm gently out of the way instead of grabbing it forcefully – produced an explosive reaction from Roger. There was little doubt that he considered *that* way of responding to a cue as an unacceptable one. That type of feedback was very important for the leaders, for they had to help Roger develop a repertoire of responses which were acceptable to him.

As the week went by and each boy developed and then directed a script, a very wide range of 'sounding' cues were displayed and an even greater range of alternative responses developed, each one tailored to the peculiarities of the status-anxieties articulated. Indeed, so great was the pressure of work that the breaks between working periods grew shorter as the boys became more involved in the task. It was clear that some important behavioural and self-image changes were taking place, for while the work was going on at the centre with its concentration on delinquency, interactions in peer and intermediate treatment groups and role-play, a separate scenario was being enacted in the boys' homes.

The original intention had been to hold very few meetings with the boys' parents, one at the start of the programme, one in the middle and one at the end. However, on the second day of the first phase, Alan failed to attend the centre and when his parents were contacted the group workers were told that he had complained about being bullied by the other boys, so they had withdrawn him. The social worker responsible for the family visited and succeeded in persuading Alan's father to attend a parents' group meeting that evening. At the meeting he explained his position to the other boys' parents and the group workers stated they had seen no signs of such bullying as Alan was alleging. After a heated exchange, during which Alan's social worker said that if he did not complete the thirty days at New Planet then other arrangements would have to be made, Alan's father agreed to bring him again and wait and see what happened. He did this primarily to appease other parents who were very angry about the allegations. Other anxieties were voiced by parents – Nick's mother was worried about his sudden refusal to work, change his clothes and behave in a generally co-operative way. She described her son as 'my little chicken'.

WORKING WITH ADOLESCENT OFFENDERS   155

Normally clean and polite at home, he appeared to have begun to behave like the 14-year-old he was. In contrast, Roger's mother was worried by his withdrawal and depression – very different from his normal boisterous and vociferous behaviour at home. Both Roger and Nick were supervised by probation officers who agreed to provide extra visits in support.

It transpired that Alan's normally disruptive and delinquent behaviour had always been dealt with by his father going down to the police station, school or social services department to 'sort out' whoever was complaining. These actions did not, however, stem from a desire to protect his son, but were primarily a result of pressure from his wife who threatened to leave him every time Alan was in trouble. She proved to be quite exceptionally overprotective, while her husband was aggressive and demanding, severely chastising Alan at home for his misdemeanors. Had Alan not been referred to the high-intensity intermediate treatment scheme but entered a CHE instead, then the inconsistency of control to which he was subject, as a result of a very stressful and unhappy relationship between his parents, would never have emerged. Similar marital and family stresses in the other boys' backgrounds suddenly became the focus of work for the supervisors. The high-intensity programme had effectively forced them out in the open. Ironically, the group workers were well aware that a residential programme in a CHE would normally have the opposite effect since it seems to be the usual pattern that when a juvenile delinquent is removed from the community, work with the family actually becomes less intensive, and the family, far from airing its difficulties, will frequently close ranks against those who have taken their child away or, in angry rejection, against the child himself.

The second phase of the programme entailed involving the boys in a dramatic production along with other children who attended the New Planet in a voluntary capacity. Initially, two of the boys, Harry and Roger, refused to have anything to do with it. One factor of significance at that stage was that phase 2 was being supervised by New Planet staff who had not been present during the curriculum development phase, and who were primarily experts in teaching music, drama and the development of street theatre. The group workers from the first phase had to be recalled to undertake twice-daily group meetings in order that the programme could continue. The street theatre was held in the town's market place on a Saturday afternoon and although Roger stood on the sidelines initially, after the play had ended he was seen to go to the head of the costumed procession, seize the drum and then lead the procession out of the town centre.

The week after the public performance of the street theatre, school holidays ended, so the day-care part of the programme also ceased as the boys returned to school. Alan departed for a residential maladjusted school since his own school considered him uncontainable in certain respects.

Alan had been the only solo offender in the group. His problems were clearly linked more with his family circumstances than with a peer group and the experimental intermediate treatment project could not continue to give him the day care he required. Had the social services department decided to provide an on-going day-care programme then Alan would not have left his home since despite the problems in his parents' marriage, they were containable given adequate community support of Alan.

A series of weekend meetings were held with the group in order to orient them towards the outdoor-pursuits week planned for their half-term holiday. These activities included ice-skating, rock climbing, fell and country walking as well as visits to the theatre, cinema and a mixture of sporting events. Some of these activities were programmed into New Planet's weekend schemes so that the group met on its own, as well as with the general population of adolescents which used New Planet.

The ascents of Snowdon, Scafell and Ben Nevis during the final few days, at half-term, had originally been intended as a final confidence-booster for the boys. At the time the project was planned, the authors had only just begun to undertake a larger-scale study of intermediate treatment in another local authority and were therefore by and large unaware of the irrelevance of outdoor pursuits to intermediate treatment. Subsequent investigation has suggested to the authors that to delinquents, Blackpool funfair is more entertaining that the Lake District. As far as the experimental group in Lancaster was concerned, it was a matter of relearning what the teachers already knew — that children enjoy things they are good at. Bad weather forced the abandonment of Ben Nevis, but ascents were made by all the boys of Snowdon, Scafell and other mountains in north Wales and the Lake District. Some of the boys enjoyed it, some did not.

Whatever views one might take in general of the value of outdoor pursuits to juvenile offenders, when the boys were interviewed by someone not involved in the programme they appeared to express the opinion that it was the curriculum-development phase, the cartooning, VTR and role-play which they remembered most and valued most. The experimental programme included a very large range of techniques, exercises and activities to meet a variety of objectives. The extent to which the objectives were met could be measured (subject to interpretive discussion) by changes in attitudes to self, attitudes to peers, attitudes to adults and changes in specific areas of social behaviour. Within limits the attitudes can be assessed by means of the repertory grid derived from personal construct theory and, in the case of the experimental scheme, there was some indication that the objectives were met. As far as social skills were concerned, while there appeared to be a (subjective) change within the treatment context, it is not possible to know whether or not these changes were generalised to other contexts. The results of the experiment could not be compared with the effectiveness of other juvenile correctional programmes, because no comparable study has been conducted in the United Kingdom either of intermediate treatment or of custodial programmes.

We cannot be certain which parts of the programme created these changes, but our experiences have suggested several modifications which might help to refine the programme. Such modifications could include a greater degree of built-in evaluation, particularly with regard to estimating the relative degree of enjoyment derived from particular exercises or activities, and a rephasing or even abandonment of the outdoor-pursuits exercise which may be of limited value.

One of the issues highlighted by the experiment was the need for effective liaison with social workers and probation officers. The limited success achieved with some of the children was undoubtedly due to strenuous efforts by some agency staff to keep parents coming to meetings. Similarly, problems of co-ordination and liaison existed within the New Planet itself, responsibility for the programme being divided at different times between eight different full-time, voluntary workers. This type of high-intensity intermediate treatment may function more effectively if fewer people are involved.

The project was evaluated by attempting an assessment of attitude change by the boys before and after the programme began and ended. A report was produced for the probation officers and social workers responsible for the boys' supervision. This evaluation report ran as follows:

RESEARCH FINDINGS

This report (in which all names have been changed) should be read only after the following points have been noted.

(1)   The Research Team agreed to evaluate the project only on the understanding that they regarded it as an opportunity to experiment with various techniques being considered for a larger study. The New Planet staff accepted this.

(2)   The techniques that were used have not been 'validated'; they are not recognised instruments, and they are not measures that have been standardised, or used in comparable projects.

(3)   Although the tests were administered both at the beginning of the project and towards the end, and any differences in results can therefore be interpreted as 'change', it would be rash to assume that such an interpretation is correct.

(4)   Even if the differences do indicate changes in attitude, or anything else, it cannot be shown, in the absence of a control procedure, that the project itself is responsible.

(5) It cannot be assumed that the use of such tests is inherently more 'objective' than other forms of assessment or evaluation.

INSTRUMENT

The technique employed was a substantially modified version of the repertory grid, designed to explore some of the ideas a respondent has about himself, and some of the thoughts that he imagines other people might have about him.

From the data which the test provides, two scores can be derived: one which may be interpreted as a measure of self-esteem, and another which can be taken to indicate how far the informant's understanding of himself agrees with what he regards as the opinions of others, in this case significant adults.

The first of these will be referred to as the 'self-esteem' score; the second as the 'adult convergence' score, since it indicates the degree of convergence between what the informant thinks of himself and what he thinks various adults think of him.

SUBJECTS AND SCALES

Only five of the boys who participated in the project completed the test on both occasions.

The scales used − in repertory grid language 'constructs' − are supplied by the subject. This means that they varied from boy to boy, and cannot be discussed in a general way. More will be said about them when each boy is discussed individually. In no case, however, were there fewer than eight or more than ten.

Each boy rated his own perceptions of himself, and what he saw as adults' perceptions of himself, on each of the scales supplied. Scores derived from both occasions on which the test was administered were treated statistically and compared. Because of the nature of the test, it is not possible to use 'raw scores' as a measure of comparison between subjects: each boy could, therefore, only be assessed by comparing his first set of results with his second, and any change expressed as a percentage variation on his original score. These percentage changes are indicated in Table 1.

At this stage, it may be assumed that 'plus' scores represent improvement − increased self-esteem, or a greater convergence with adults. It will be argued later that this may not always be the case.

Roughly, then, it can be said that while only three of the boys ended the project with enhanced self-esteem, all five exhibited a greater degree of convergence with adults (although Roger's score in the second category is so small as to be virtually equivalent to 'no change').

Table 1.

	Overall variation as a percentage of original scores	
	Self-esteem	Adult-convergence
	%	%
Philip	+8	+13
John	+15	+20
Nick	+38	+60
Harry	−8	+18
Roger	−14	+3

SCALE VARIANCE

Table 1 represents overall scores; but there were variations on individual scales in the case of each boy. These variations are indicated on Table 2.

Table 2.

	Number of scales showing improvement, no change, or deterioration					
	Self-esteem			Adult-convergence		
	+	0	−	+	0	−
Philip	5	2	1	3	2	3
John	4	2	3	4	2	4
Nick	3	5	1	7	0	2
Harry	4	1	4	8	1	0
Roger	2	4	4	4	2	4

INDIVIDUAL BOYS

Harry
Harry's results are the most interesting. The most remarkable feature is the 8 + score under 'adult-convergence', especially in view of the very undramatic self-esteem score. What is going on here?

It is very interesting to compare the scales on which self-esteem shows improvement with the ones on which it does not. These are set out below:

Plus	*Minus*
Good worker	Idle
Gets on with people	A cadger
Helpful	A right villain
Doesn't act clever	Destructive

On the positive qualities, then, Harry's self-esteem seems to have improved, while on the negative ones it has decreased – in other words, he sees himself more as idle, destructive, and so on. This suggests that he is more ready to acknowledge his faults or weaknesses, while deriving more satisfaction from his good points. The 'adult-convergence' score underlines this, suggesting that he is now more willing to accept some of the negative things that the adults he knows might say about him.

Further analysis also indicates that the adult with whom he has converged most is his father. When the test was first administered, the father emerged as being very negative about his son; on the second occasion it appeared that there had been considerable improvement; and with Harry taking a somewhat more realistic view of himself, the two have converged quite dramatically.

The example of Harry indicates that 'improved self-esteem' (as equated here with a plus score) does not necessarily count as improvement. If aspirations become more realistic, or if, as in this case, there is greater readiness to acknowledge one's faults, it can be argued that progress has been made, even if, as here, the self-esteem score shows as a minus.

John

In one minor aspect, there is an interesting similarity between John's self-esteem score and Harry's. Of John's nine constructs, only two are negative – 'Destructive' and 'Does wrong sometimes'. Both of them score minus. As in Harry's case, this may indicate greater willingness to recognise negative tendencies or faults.

Another feature of John's data, within the overall convergence with adults, is a remarkable improvement in his relationship with his social worker and (to only a slightly lesser extent) his mother. The overall improvement here was, perhaps, to be expected: when the test was first administered, the distance between John's perceptions of himself, and what he took to be adults' perceptions, was greater than for any of the other boys.

Nick

At first sight, Nick's results look too good to be true – and it is tempting to suspect some degree of 'calculation' in his responses on the second test. However, Table 2 indicates that his self-esteem scales show less dramatic improvement than some of the other boys, and it is, in fact, just one scale that accounts for the bulk of the variance. Normalising this scale – bringing it into line with the others – reduces the overall self-esteem score to $+15$ per cent, which may be more reasonable.

As in John's case, the dramatic increase in adult-convergence is partly accounted for by the fact that Nick's first test showed a considerable distance between his self-perceptions and his account of adult-perceptions (he came second only to John in this respect). If only for statistical reasons, one would expect a swing back. Again, three of the nine scales account for the biggest part of the variation, although there appears to be no special connection between these three.

One possible interpretation of the greater degree of convergence with adults exhibited by both Nick and John is as follows. Neither boy appears to be seriously delinquent, and it may be that they both overestimated the degree to which an offence would mean alienation from significant adults. With time, one would expect a more balanced view to emerge – which is apparently the case now. Whether or not the intermediate treatment project had anything to do with this is, of course, another matter.

Philip

There is not a great deal to add here. Variation between scales appears to conform to no particular pattern, and this feature, added to the fact that there is a strong tendency, in both tests, to group figures at one end of the scale, suggests that Philip may be a boy of fairly low discriminating ability – between adults at least – and the scale variation under 'adult-convergence' tends to confirm this. That, or he is giving nothing away. Only one of his scales was negatively defined – which, if it indicates nothing else, suggests that he does try to conform to what he sees as adults' expectations of him.

Roger

Roger's exaggerative and 'all-or-nothing' tendencies make the analysis of his tests a hazardous business: his predeliction for putting everyone in the same category, on a yes-or-no basis, is revealing, but does not make the test much of a guide. The key construct, in his case, is probably 'straight with people' as a description of himself. It would imply, if it were true, that everybody knows where they are with him, so that they would all say the same things about him, with equal strength. Roger, it would appear, is not one for subtleties. The fact that he had far more negatively defined constructs than any of the others says a lot about his self-image and his awareness of a 'reputation'.

An interesting feature is that there is a reversal of the effect noted with Harry and John: whereas their self-esteem improved on positive qualities and fell on negative ones, with Roger the opposite is true. Of the four positive constructs, three end up with minus scores under 'self-esteem'; two of the negative ones end up with a plus score. He apparently does not find it as easy to see himself as helpful, honest with people, and as getting on with them. And the same three constructs also score minus on the 'adult-convergence' score, as if Roger's realisation that other people do not always see him in quite such a good light had affected his self-esteem accordingly. There is certainly an indication here that the opinions of (some) adults might mean more to Roger than he would care to admit.

This project has been described in detail because it gives some indication of the sort of programme implied by a determination to work in a highly focused way with a group of persistent juvenile offenders. It suggests one possible way of evaluating such a programme, a way that is at least as valid as the customary reference to reconviction rates. The description is offered not as a blueprint or a 'painting by numbers' kit, but as a spur to further thought and development. If the community support of juvenile offenders develops as it should, the description will no doubt look crude and primitive in a very few years. We are conscious of being in the position of mediaeval map-makers: our instruments are crude, and unknown territory surrounds us. But it is at least a start.

REFERENCES: CHAPTER 7

1   Hirschi, T., *Causes of Delinquency* (Berkeley, Cal.: University of California Press, 1971).
2   Plant, R., *Social and Moral Theory in Casework* (London: Routledge & Kegan Paul, 1970).
3   Matza, D., *Delinquency and Drift* (New York: John Wiley, 1964).
4   Hirschi, op. cit.
5   ibid., pp. 230–1.
6   ibid., p. 155.
7   Ryall, R., 'Delinquency: the problem for treatment', *Social Work Today*, vol. 5., no. 4. (16 May 1974), p. 99.
8   Hirschi, op. cit., p. 154.
9   Matza, op. cit., p. 43.
10 ibid., p. 52.

The Organisation and Development of Community Support

In this final chapter we offer conclusions of two kinds, both drawn from the theoretical perspective, the research findings and the recommendations for social work practice presented in earlier chapters. The first set of conclusions is fairly detailed and specific; it refers to policies which, in principle, could be implemented now, in the world we know. The second may, by contrast, appear far-fetched, unrealistic or frankly utopian; but the long term has to start somewhere and our final, admittedly more speculative, proposals are implied by the positions adopted throughout the book on juvenile offending and official responses to it.

It may be convenient first of all to present our specific proposals in a summarised, schematic form. They refer, in the present context, primarily to social services departments, but are also relevant to the probation service where it deals with juvenile offenders. The brief points made below will be developed and clarified in a moment.

1   Clear policy decisions should be taken, and directions established, by social work agencies dealing with juvenile offenders. Their initial aim should be the decarceration of children from expensive and largely ineffective CHEs and the redeployment of finance and resources to community-based facilities.
2   These facilities should consist of high-, medium- and low-intensity programmes designed to provide services for clearly defined categories of juvenile offenders. The high- and medium-intensity programmes should rigidly exclude all non-offenders.
3   The high-intensity facilities should be run from specialised centres providing day- and evening-care programmes. The other facilities should be based on social work area teams. Area-based workers should monitor as closely as possible the workings of the local juvenile criminal justice system. Their work should be co-ordinated by an intermediate treatment officer responsible to the agency's central management.
4   Both at management and area levels the agency should develop closer

links with the police, the education department and the youth services. The aim should be to increase the cautioning rate and, in co-operation with these agencies and other interested parties such as local retailers, to develop crime prevention programmes based not on pre-emptive work with supposedly 'at risk' individuals or groups but on a reduction of opportunities for petty property offences.

5   As far as possible the agency should aim to manage juvenile delinquency in the community. Through negotiation with the courts, police and other agencies, and the establishment of alternative facilities, juvenile offenders should be diverted from prosecution and from custody.

6   The implementation of policy changes should be very closely monitored, researched and evaluated. The changes required for a decarceration strategy have implications for the training of social workers, in using research, in group work practice, and in negotiation with other agencies.

These brief recommendations may now be expanded. Clearly they are inter-related and the clarifications which follow do not always refer to a single point. The first makes an immediate and obvious appeal to local authorities which have no CHEs of their own and therefore have constantly to pay other authorities for children placed there. At the present cost of about £150 per child per week, CHEs are not cheap; we need not labour their ineffectiveness. The use of economic arguments as a tactic is most clearly applicable here. Authorities which do have their own CHEs, and for whom a decarceration programme would therefore involve the redeployment of more than money, present rather more problems. The staff of these institutions are naturally not inclined readily to admit that they have been wasting their time and energies and would be better employed elsewhere. Some of them, of course, could be, in the facilities developed in the community; it was argued in the first chapter that one of the problems with institutions is the sudden breaking of valued relationships at the end of a child's stay. The more general point is that for any policy change to be possible some positive management decisions must be taken, and almost any conceivable change is going to involve conflict with someone. In fact, it would be a major step forward for many agencies to have a policy – almost any policy – towards juvenile delinquency, instead of reacting to it in the *ad hoc* opportunistic way which characterises them at the moment. And it has results. In two areas which have implemented this most fundamental of policy decisions – the transfer of resources from residential or custodial facilities to services in the community – the number of children made subject to Section 7(7) care orders and the number placed in CHEs have been reduced to about a quarter of their former level within two years.[1]

The kinds of programme envisaged by the second recommendation, and the kinds of children for whom each is intended, are set out in Table 8.1.[2]

Table 8·1. *The organisation of community support for juvenile offenders*

Facility	Programme	Staffing	Client	Disposal
High intensity day care (some weekend work).	Correctional curriculum. Vocational training. Remedial education. Leisure activities.	Intermediate treatment centre social workers. Remedial teachers. Trade instructors. Volunteers.	High-risk persistent offender (decarcerated or diverted from custody). Unable to attend school or work.	To evening care or weekly group.
High-intensity evening care (some week-end work).	Correctional curriculum. Vocational training and remedial education if necessary. Leisure activities.	Intermediate treatment centre social workers. Remedial teachers and trade instructors, if necessary. Volunteers.	High-risk persistent offender (decarcerated or diverted from custody). Attending school or working.	To weekly group or youth club.
Medium-intensity weekly group (perhaps some weekend work).	Modified correctional curriculum. Leisure activities.	Area intermediate treatment social worker. Other social workers/ youth workers. Volunteers.	Persistent petty offender, at risk of further offending.	To youth club or other positive leisure activity.
Low-intensity (youth club or other structured leisure activity).	Leisure activities.	Youth workers. Volunteers.	Occasional offender.	Continuing attendance without official direction.

This is a development of the 'continuum of care' model of intermediate treatment, first suggested by two of the present authors over five years ago.[3] It will be noted that most of what currently passes for intermediate treatment belongs to the low-intensity or at best the medium-intensity levels. The point of the high-intensity programmes is that if we are serious about decarceration and diversion from custody we must offer a serious alternative – one which is very clearly and specifically focused on the reason the children are there in the first place: that they commit offences. While it may seen harsh, and certainly runs counter to much current practice, to exclude all but the most persistent offenders from the high- and medium-intensity programmes, this rigorous gate-keeping is essential if intermediate treatment programmes are not to suck in more and more children suddenly discovered to be 'at risk' before they have committed any offences. In any case, a group work curriculum which is based on the definition of persistent offending as a problem can only make sense to children who are in the early stages of an officially sponsored delinquent career.

The area intermediate treatment social worker is a crucial figure if our third recommendation is to be implemented. This is the key position in the local monitoring of the juvenile criminal justice system. At least six tasks can be identified as elements of the necessary job description for this post:

1 Monitoring the system's operation by liaising with the police over referrals, with a view to increasing the cautioning rate.
2 Checking all social enquiry reports and applying to each the 'care or control' test.
3 Organising the local medium-intensity operation in which, if they wish, social workers in the area team can participate.
4 Organising the low-intensity facilities, simply by maintaining a list of appropriate youth clubs and other facilities to which children can be referred.
5 Organising and directing a crime-prevention programme in the area with representatives of the police, local schools and local retailers, with a view to identifying which schools seem to produce high rates of delinquency and truancy,[4] and which shops most need to tighten up their internal control.
6 Acting as the source of referrals to all conventional youth facilities. In addition it might well be appropriate for this worker to carry a small caseload of children receiving intermediate treatment services.

The high-intensity programmes cannot, however, be managed within the resources available to an area team. They require their own buildings, their own facilities (VTR equipment and workshops, for example) and their own specialised social work and educational staff. Social services departments are not generally short of buildings which could be adapted for this purpose, nor are the skills involved in planning and running a correctional curriculum particularly difficult or arcane. One must assume that if special training in them were thought necessary it could be paid for with money transferred from the CHE budget, and the same applies to the equipment the centre would require. What is equally essential, and perhaps more problematic, is that the centre should be used. This is primarily a management responsibility, although the centre staff may have to undertake some educative or propagandist work on their own account. It is important that when a shift in policy towards decarceration is being implemented all levels of agency staff should be fully consulted and informed. An intermediate treatment centre can only survive if it gets referrals from the field, and this means that it must be firmly part of the professional consciousness of field social workers: no area intermediate treatment worker can be expected to put up indefinitely with the indifference or hostility of his colleagues to his application of the 'care or control' test to their court reports.

The fourth point, implied by the third, is that there needs to be a commitment to the policy at all levels. The 'hierarchy of credibility' is important here: chief constables, for example, may listen to the director when they would not even speak to an area officer. It is part of the folklore of social work agencies (and of the police) that the arrival of a chief inspector with a particular interest in a particular kind of criminality is likely very quickly to alter the pattern of official crime in that neighbourhood. At a more exalted level, the professional ideologies of the present chief constables of Greater Manchester and of Devon and Cornwall seem to be having a marked effect on the volume of recorded crime in their domains. It was argued earlier that social workers are in a good position to take the initiative in changing policy towards juvenile offending, and this applies equally to social work managers. They ultimately have to take responsibility for implementing and justifying the policies of the agency, and once again it is vital that these policies should be clear, specific and capable of being explained to non-social workers. Social work has been damaged both by lacking clear policy aims and by claiming that there is a policy but that its essential nature is fundamentally incommunicable to all but fellow-initiates of the social work community.

The fifth recommendation refers to those children who enter the prison system directly, without being touched by the child care services of the local authority. At the moment they are the responsibility of the probation service and are, perhaps, a group who risk being neglected, since local authorities do not pay directly for the services offered in detention centres and borstals. The involvement of two social work agencies with juvenile offenders, contrary to the provisions of the 1969 CYPA, undoubtedly complicates the process of changing policy and, given the not always easy relationship between the two services, may, unless both are involved in an explicit strategy of diversion from custody at the outset, positively hinder it. The probation service has, however, traditionally enjoyed or endured a relationship with the courts and specifically, through case committees, with the magistracy, from which local authority social workers may be able to benefit. This is not to claim that, on the whole, probation officers have successfully overcome their natural deference to magistrates to the point of achieving radical changes in sentencing practice; but with all its limitations, its archaic overtones and its occasional ludicrousness, the case committee, as a regular forum in which social workers operating in the courts can meet with sentencers, may have something to offer as a model. Certainly the lack of such a forum is frequently bemoaned by social workers. But, as we have seen, it is not magistrates' punitiveness but the preoccupation of social workers with considerations of 'treatment' which is the primary cause of so many unnecessary and unfair incarcerations. While it is clearly essential for social workers to have a relationship with magistrates which gives them some credibility and respect, they cannot go on for much longer claiming that all would be well if only the courts were as enlightened as they are themselves.

Finally, the need for research and the implications for training. The two are intimately related, for it was suggested above that the social work skills involved in a correctional curriculum are not especially difficult (although it would be a help if more basic training courses included some specific teaching on the topic). What is crucial is that social workers should be able to understand and employ some straightforward research methods of information gathering and analysis. Arguably the general failure of social work practitioners to make much use of research findings stems from the fact that these have usually come from outside – from academics who can easily be described, sometimes justly, as unsympathetic to social work and unaware of the difficulties it entails. In the areas in which progress has been made towards decarceration, the initial research was undertaken by a panel which included representatives of all levels within the social work agency as well as academic researchers who acted as the initiators of the research and subsequently as consultants. Thus from the outset agency staff were committed to the research, understood the principles behind it, and were able to own the results even when these were, by implication, highly critical of existing policy and practice. Social work training courses invariably contain a large element of teaching on social policy and social workers constantly claim a right to be listened to when new policy is being framed. They have not, however, been particularly successful and very specific, localised research projects (for example, an analysis of all the Section 7(7) cases in an authority at any given time) are likely to be the most productive means of giving some reality to what has tended to remain a slogan or a pious hope.

With this in mind the short post-qualifying course run at Lancaster University by the present authors over the past two years has contained as much theoretical and practice work on research methods as on group work practice with adolescents. The two were seen as indissolubly linked and equally important parts of the students' work during a seven-week placement, in which they ran a high-intensity group for persistent juvenile offenders as well as beginning an analysis of the operation of the juvenile criminal justice system in their placement areas. As any former students of the course who read this will want to protest, this represents the course's ideal rather than what actually happened: there were problems about getting appropriate groups of decarcerated or diverted children and access to the research data was not always easy. However, the course was very much an experimental venture, containing new and unfamiliar assumptions about the relationship of social work training to agency policy; we are confident that we could do better next time. The irony is that there is no certainty that there will be a next time, as it proved extremely difficult to recruit enough students to make the course viable. The problem was not lack of interest – we received many appropriate applications – but lack of opportunities for finance. This is, of course, a universal complaint in these times and the kind of specialised training we envisaged may understandably be thought to deserve less priority within agencies' hard-pressed training budgets than basic qualifying courses. Nevertheless, and not simply out of self-interest, we would argue that the potential return – of qualified staff capable of initiating and running juvenile decarceration and diversion programmes – would amply repay the fairly modest initial expenditure entailed by such a course. Alternatively, the staff of basic training courses could begin to take more seriously their own protestations about the links between social work and social policy and begin to teach highly specific and practical research methods, to some students at least, as just as important a component of a social work education as the teaching of conventional skills and methods.

Research is important in a further sense, one which bridges the immediate and practical concerns of this section with the apparently more remote proposals which follow. This is its capacity to demystify reality. To discover that on the whole the offences of juveniles are not particularly heinous or dangerous; that it is not true that the intentions of the 1969 CYPA have been fulfilled and that they are now treated more leniently; that this is largely the responsibility of social workers and not of sentencers: these are discoveries which, after the initial surprise, can be liberating, and not simply to those agencies which they set free to develop new, more creative and imaginative policies. They are also potentially liberating for the communities which the agencies are meant to serve. Made widely know, they could free the public from needless fears and anxieties and begin the necessary process of moving away from stereotypical images of the offender as an alien, not quite human being who haunts the dark horizons of respectable society, towards a more rational acceptance of his humanity, his social reality and his full complexity. This movement is necessary if the full potential of the decriminalisation and decarceration strategies is to be realised. It will not be easy to start the process, particularly at the moment, when the rumbling of the law-and-order bandwagon threatens to drown out all dissenting voices. And there will always be genuine victims of juvenile crime who are doubly victimised by the insistent, and disingenuous, attention of the media on the effects of an offence on their private lives. What needs to be asked is in what sense such victims – and the victims of more mundane petty thefts and burglaries – benefit from the present policy of prosecution (in the name of the state, not the victim) and incarceration. It is here, perhaps, that a start can be made in opening out the question of the nature of the criminal law and the purposes it serves, and in beginning to suggest an alternative way of managing delinquency – a way that takes more authentic account of the actual experience of an offence from the standpoint of both offender and victim.

It has been suggested at various points in this book that the criminal justice system is an inappropriate means of dealing with juvenile deviance. This is only partly a matter of the bad effects which have resulted from the failure fully to implement the 1969 CYPA, though the uneasy co-existence of justice and welfare principles in the present system has added a new dimension of confusion and new possibilities of stigmatisation and injustice. Nor is it simply that any strengthening of the criminal justice element in the administrative apparatus could, in the present context, lead only to more punitive and damaging sentencing. It is rather that of its very nature any criminal justice system renders the events it deals with unintelligible – to the offender, to the victim, and to the public as a whole. It achieves this by removing the offence from its local human context and by turning a real offence against a real individual into an abstract offence against the state. Both victim and offender lose their actual human identity, the one coming to stand for all respectable society, the other for all that threatens it. For a complex social event the criminal justice system substitutes a dramatically staged vision of 'society' and the offender locked in combat, and for the drama to reach its proper conclusion it is essential that might as well as right should clearly be seen to be on society's side. This partly explains the appeal that criminal cases have for the media. They do not have to be restructured in a dramatic, newsworthy form; they have already been given that structure by the criminal justice system itself.

It is important to be clear at this point that our argument is about different kinds of legal system, not about the rule of law itself. Fundamental legal principles remain obviously and vitally important in the finding of guilt or innocence, for example; indeed, they need to be defended against the encroachment of principles of administrative convenience. There are also principles associated specifically with the criminal law which require some proportionality between the seriousness of the offence and the sentence imposed, and are crucial if the courts are to retain any semblance of fairness or, in the case of juvenile courts, to regain it. But, in general, the principles of law are not only applicable to criminal justice systems. They derive largely from the eighteenth century, in which a major component of our present system – a bureaucratic state apparatus which decides whether or not an offender should be prosecuted – simply did not exist. They apply equally to civil law, and it is by comparing the legal processes involved in cases of civil wrongs – or torts – with those in criminal cases that a possible way forward towards a more rational and honest system of justice begins to appear.

The crucial distinction between crimes and 'tortious' acts lies not in the nature of the acts themselves but in the nature of the legal processes which are brought to bear on them:

> From a sociological point of view, there are ingredients in many tortious acts – such as assaults, or trespass against goods – which make them sometimes difficult to distinguish from acts which are regarded as criminal, but from a strictly legal point of view the important distinction lies in the manner in which the legal action is initiated and the sanctions which are applied.[5]

Thus it is not the amount of harm done by a particular act nor, always, the general moral disapproval it arouses which determines its categorisation as a crime or a civil wrong. Some criminal acts have no victims, for example drug abuse or public drunkenness, or incur little general condemnation, such as smuggling an extra bottle of whisky. Nor is every harmful act subject to legal sanctions. Nevertheless, often for complex historical reasons, certain acts fall within the scope of the criminal law and as such are regarded as offences against the law, and by extension the state, rather than against a particular individual, even when there is a very obvious victim. This means that responsibility for initiating proceedings lies with the police, or, in complicated or sensitive cases, the Director of Public Prosecutions, rather than with the aggrieved party. In fact, prosecution may go ahead even against the express wishes of the victim, as often in the case of domestic disputes, or where the victim has been fully compensated, as in a case of fraud. In civil cases, by contrast, the decision lies solely with the 'victim', who cannot be forced to sue for damages. The second important distinction between criminal and civil proceedings lies in the nature of the legal sanctions available. While an award for damages may amount to a large sum it does not, in general, carry with it any lasting stigma; involvement in civil proceedings is readily compatible with respectability. A criminal conviction, however, automatically turns one into an ex-offender at best, a criminal at worst. The Rehabilitation of Offenders Act did not have to include in its provisions persons against whom civil judgements had been made.

On the one hand, then, there are civil courts in which aggrieved parties initiate the proceedings and confront their antagonists in a legally mediated argument in which the aim is to discover what compensation, if any, is appropriate. The alleged victim and the alleged perpetrator of the tortious act have relatively direct access to the workings of the legal system and can, to a degree, control them in what they conceive to be their interests: many libel actions, for example, are settled out of court. Criminal courts, on the other hand, adjudicate on matters brought at the instigation of the police. The victim generally participates only as a witness for the state. Reparation is rarely the primary aim of the sentence; it is only since 1972 that it has been possible to order financial compensation and priority is still given to the payment of a fine, which cannot benefit the victim at all. Instead of the relatively open, rational and straightforward processes of civil courts, the criminal court offers a lurid stereotypical drama, in which good confronts evil in a deliberately awesome ritual. The lay public have no direct access to the reality of law-breaking and law enforcement; the criminal justice system acts as a screen through which only shadows can be seen.

It may be argued that this drama serves an important function in maintaining social cohesion: that people require dramatic assertions – the descendants of public executions – of the power and goodness of the state, and of the conquest of evil. Perhaps our society cannot bear to own its deviants as fellow-citizens rather than mythical monsters? To which one answer might be that we have 'learned after several centuries to do without the concept of witchcraft'[6] and that we can learn also to do without the handy mystifications and opportunities for denial which a criminal justice system provides. It seems likely that our present 'folk devils' – juvenile offenders well to the fore – do serve the same kind of function as witches, heretics, Protestants, Catholics, Jews, and so on did at various times for our ancestors; but this should not be accepted as the foundation of a penal policy. A self-fulfilling prophecy is maintained by the present system, founded as it is on prosecution and incarceration, as Morris has noted:

> A great deal must depend upon public tolerance of the lawbreakers in its midst and this in turn must depend upon the extent to which public beliefs about offenders accord with reality. While the penal system *removes* offenders from society, they being remote from it, become the victims of mythologies; when individuals in the community become involved in face to face contacts with those who have offended they not infrequently discover their humanity.[7]

This has been the traditional plea of those whose involvement in the criminal justice system has had, however ambiguously, a humanitarian motivation – of the probation service, for example. The problem with translating it into reality is not so much that there is a fundamental need in the collective psyche to turn offenders into creatures of myth, as that the present criminal justice system excludes the great majority of people from any participation in it. The root of this may well be a need to disown and deny any responsibility for offenders, but any proposals for reforming the system would be so much wasted breath if this need were not thought susceptible to modification at least. It is inconceivable that a rational penal policy should be founded upon it. There are, however, serious practical problems about starting the process of demythologising, let alone transforming the criminal justice system as a whole. We have noted that the suggestions of the Marxist heirs of the labelling perspective have not generally been helpful: the merest gestures towards 'socialist justice', perhaps organised through neighbourhood courts or tribunals. Historical experience, whether of the Provisional IRA's reprisals against 'traitors', or of summary executions in the name of the people in more overtly revolutionary contexts, should make us wary. As Cohen has pointed out, some of the more specific proposals that have been advanced are hardly more attractive, for instance those of Oscar Newman, the theoretician of 'defensible space', 'which, under the banner of neighbourhood control, provide blueprints for paranoid fortress communities patrolled by local vigilante squads'.[8] This kind of vision should remind us that an important function of the criminal law and of custodial institutions is, and will continue to be, the prevention of lynching.

Some of the suggested means of reforming the correctional system in the directions envisaged in this book – towards greater tolerance, community involvement, honesty and undistorted relationships – look, then, even less appealing than what we have now. Indeed, there is a good deal of ambiguity about the ultimate intentions of the recent radical critiques. Arguments which start with the indisputable fact that the criminal law is not equally enforced against all harmful acts and does not cover some at all, while effectively turning a blind eye to others and redefining still others as more akin to civil wrongs, often seem to lead to the conclusion that more people should be prosecuted and criminalised in the interests of even-handedness. Thus Frank Pearce and Jock Young sought to expose 'the crimes of the powerful', and demonstrated the existence of a large, new and potentially captive population hitherto neglected by the criminal justice system. The implicit point was, of course, that they were more guilty than many of those incarcerated at present and a reconstitution rather than an enlargement of the prison population was what was envisaged. Such critiques have been vital in documenting the inequities of the law which have, in any case, always been part of the popular conception of it. But while it is possible to extract a certain vengeful anarchic glee from the idea of negligent factory-owners and wealthy tax-dodgers serving long prison sentences, this hardly advances the project of decriminalisation and humanising our approach to offending which forms the other part of the radical critique.

Young, Quinney and others have thus also argued for decentralisation of

174 OUT OF CARE

the control apparatus and the inauguration of local, community-based forms of control. The anti-urbanism and anti-industrialism implicit in such calls for a return to simplified neighbourhood institutions is reminiscent of the Arcadianism of the 'child savers'. The political ambiguity of that pioneering movement was noted in Chapter 2, and it remains ambiguous. Magistrates and at least some tradition-conscious policemen are as likely as any radical criminologist to long for the image of social control epitomised by the village bobby who, because of his membership of a somewhat idealised community, can deal with all but the most serious deviance without recourse to the bureaucratic machinery. There is no reason to reject an idea because, by different routes, both conservatives and radicals can come to hold it, but it is worth pointing to the coincidence of interest; one ought to know who one's bedfellows are. In practice it does matter by what route one gets there; community service orders, for example, were viewed by some magistrates as the modern equivalent of the stocks, and welcomed as such, while their most enthusiastic advocates in the probation service were claiming them as a truly humanist means towards satisfying 'new careers' and full social integration for offenders. No doubt the statement would be as true with the personnel reversed. We should make it clear, therefore, that in arguing for the community support of juvenile offenders, for the involvement of volunteers, for the constructive use of local youth organisations and for a decentralised and demystified system of control for juvenile deviants we do not in any way support the presently fashionable attacks on social work and the whole of the welfare state and the advocacy which accompanies them of de-professionalised care by, rather than in, the community. We are emphatically not arguing that juvenile offenders, along with everyone else, should receive third-rate services on the cheap.

What, then, do we advocate in place of the punitive, unjust, confused and abstract juvenile justice system we have at present? Our proposals are intended to refer specifically to juveniles, though with some qualifications they could also apply to adult offending. Our basic position, from the correctional standpoint, is that juveniles should be squarely confronted with their responsibility for their actions and the reality of their consequences. This is just what bureaucratic prosecution and incarceration make impossible. It implies confrontation between the offender and the victim. It implies a humanly intelligible debate, conducted within a procedural framework derived from civil law, about such matters as degree of culpability, the amount of damage done and the appropriate penalty – conceived as reparation, not as punishment. It implies a much tougher ethical and moral dilemma for the offender than he ever has to confront now, when his own guilt is so often removed by the court's evident injustice and the institution, with its waiting armoury of neutralisation techniques, completes the process of denial. It implies that fundamental issues of playground fairness, for example the ability of the victim to defend himself, or his economic status, will become part of a negotiation conducted in terms familiar to both parties, and with reference to everyday rather than legal conceptions of guilt, blame and damage. The offender will no longer be able to claim that a burglary represents no more than a material loss (rather than a lasting sense of invasion and threat), nor that smashing a telephone box is no more than an act of playfulness (rather than one which can endanger life).

This last example raises a difficulty. The feasibility of confrontation and negotiation between victim and offender is fairly clear in cases where a specific victim or victims can be indentified. Particularly where some relationship existed between them before the offence, there is an opportunity to use the court for the arbitration and management of conflict instead of the *ex cathedra* imposition of punishment. Where there was no pre-existing relationship a relationship can be established, in the particular context of a wrong done and harm suffered. But what about cases where there is no victim? The example of vandalism, in particular, raises the spectre of the lynch mob: an irate community (or perhaps the tenants' association committee as its alleged representative) demanding vengeance. One might argue that this is pretty much what happens now. It is, however, possible to envisage a more constructive response, in which local people would be invited to testify to their personal experience of inconvenience or danger as a result of acts of vandalism and the court could take on an educative function, rendering the victims no longer anonymous and the harm done real and specific.

From the perspective of increasing tolerance in the community of juvenile offending, this kind of model would at least strip away the defensive armour of professionalism and bureaucracy which at present denies ordinary citizens access to the legal system. Decentralisation may in itself be no guarantee of greater tolerance, but it seems probable that a judicial process which enabled the offender to be seen as a human being, and to give some account (however prevaricating) of his view of the offence and of his own motivation, would make it harder to sustain stereotypical images of offenders as being so drastically unlike ourselves as to be responsive only to the crudest kinds of punishment. It would also facilitate a more rational and exact calculation of the extent of harm done by an offence. Whereas now sentences are often determined by the stereotypical images, derived from the media, which are all the judiciary know of the damage done by particular kinds of offence, this model would encourage a focus on the actual, local harm done to real people by the specific offence under consideration.

This kind of speculation may seem far removed from the central concern of this book which is to argue for a shift of emphasis and resources in our dealings with juvenile offenders away from custodial institutions and on to support in the community, and to suggest strategies and a model of planning and practice for social workers which would make this feasible. But another important theme which has been implicit throughout concerns the unity of theory and practice. Theorising is traditionally the business of the academics; social workers are supposed to be mere consumers of theory. Academic research, too, has been 'consumed' by social workers, but often in a defensive way so that the response is that the research is interesting but irrelevant, or relevant but not new, merely a ponderous scholastic way of saying what social workers have known all the time. In either case, there is no need for the research to affect one's practice; the research that does have an effect is often that which comes from within the agencies themselves, which recently has meant that it has been designed to justify the saving of money. A further split is observable within criminology itself, in which the 'new' criminologies have tended to disdain all empirical research and to concentrate on ever greater theoretical sophistication in an ever dwindling conceptual space, while the positivist tradition (represented, say, by West's longitudinal study of delinquency) has continued along its old lines. For all their theorising and in-fighting, the radical criminologists have come up with little which need seriously disturb a positivist's prejudices, at least since the early work, which was firmly rooted in the field, of Cohen on mods and rockers and Young on drugtakers in Notting Hill. We have tried in this book to overcome some of the difficulties these splits have caused by writing from a standpoint which, we hope, is fairly close to that of field-level practitioners, but also to combine with this perspective data derived from research which is academically defensible even if not sophisticated, a firm commitment to the value of policy change within the present agency structure, and a certain level of theoretical awareness. The book is meant to be difficult to pigeon-hole as either academic criminology or a practice guide for social workers. It seems consistent, then, to theorise a little about the future as well as the past and present, and to offer the preceding brief sketch of a humanised, locally responsive justice system as the sort of long-term project implied by our interest in immediate changes in policy and practice. Further, while characteristically such fundamental changes seem to happen somewhere else — Cuba, China, Tanzania — and can therefore be dismissed as intellectually intriguing but irrelevant to ourselves, the present dissatisfaction on all sides with the juvenile justice system means that an opportunity does exist for those prepared to argue for change and capable of achieving some credibility with practitioners, policy makers and academics. It is the readiness to change, not the conservation and rigidity, of social work agencies at all levels which has been striking in our research enterprises, carried out, as noted above, in the closest possible collaboration with agency workers. Indeed, there has been an encouraging sign recently, in the initiative taken in at least one authority to research its Section 7(7) care orders and apply the care or control test, that an independent academic presence in such exercises may soon become redundant. It may be that the heyday of custody as the preferred method of treatment for juvenile offenders is over.

The harder task remains: of moving beyond the agency and into the community, so that research findings like those reported here can begin to undo the public distortions of crime perpetrated by the courts and the media, with a view to reducing fear and anxiety and increasing tolerance and the chances of a creative response by the community to its deviants. There is clearly a risk here of sounding like a grotesque caricature of a sentimental social worker, endlessly claiming that juvenile offenders are all lovable really and only need a little understanding. As should by now be clear, juvenile offenders, at least while offending, are not all that lovable and the alternatives to custody which we have outlined – even the short-term correctional curriculum – actually represent a much tougher confrontation with the realities of offending behaviour than is provided by the present arrangements. A worse risk may be that of sounding like bland inhabitants of an ivory tower who in their relative affluence and insulation from the world can afford cheerily to dismiss the real anxieties experienced, with reason, by many people about increases in crimes of violence or vandalism. We have no wish to deny that in some areas these anxieties are well founded, but it remains important both to re-establish a sense of proportion by clearly articulating the facts, as far as we can know them, of juvenile offending, and secondly to begin to combat the politically convenient exploitation of such anxieties by sections of the media and the ideologues of law and order.

The means exist for the policy changes advocated in this book. The research and analysis which underpin the changes is not particularly elaborate; the techniques and styles which effective group work with juvenile offenders requires are not especially esoteric. The techniques can be learnt, the styles acquired in practice, at least by workers who have some root affinity with the experience of delinquency. It is the ethical commitment to decarceration and diversion, and the political will to carry them through, which are lacking at present. But there are grounds for hope. The juvenile justice system is not the monolithic structure social workers sometimes suppose. True, it often has that aspect in court; but there are magistrates who are aware of the lack of proportion in the sentences they are compelled to impose, and who know that custodial institutions have failed dismally. There are lawyers who know that basic principles of equity and due process have been abandoned in the juvenile court. There are policemen who have other criteria of excellence than the number of arrests made and prosecutions successfully concluded, and who know that most juvenile offences are trivial and could be dealt with more creatively than by the bureaucratic machinery of law enforcement. There are social services managers who know that their residential establishments for offenders are a useless waste of money and staff talent and energy, and that their staff are demoralised and incapacitated by the lack of more constructive alternatives. There are civil servants who, behind the scenes, are working to influence national policy towards more rational ends. There are even some politicians, both locally and nationally, who are prepared to shout back at the strident ranks of the law-and-order brigades and to stand up for values once associated with the British left – compassion, commitment to the underdog, help and understanding rather than coercion and punishment. For their part, there are social workers who are not the naïve pragmatists of social control conjured up by their radical academic critics, who are capable of sustained research and committed, honest and intelligent practice, who are aware, but not cripplingly so, of the ambiguities of their social function, and whose capacity for disciplined helping has not been eroded by bureaucratic constraints or careerist aspirations.

The system, then, is full of contradictions and thus of possibilities. But this has been more clearly true before: as recently as 1971, perhaps, when the social services departments came into being. We have suggested that one of the major reasons for the failure of the intentions of the 1969 CYPA to be realised has been the preoccupation in these departments with 'prevention', so that intermediate treatment, designed as a provision for offenders, has in many areas been used for everyone except offenders. This vagueness, this lack of specificity about the goals, the techniques or the duration of social work intervention has, in its self-deluding grandiosity, a certain kinship with the other major reason for the Act's failure: the preoccupation with residential or custodial institutions as the proper location of 'treatment'. This preoccupation is founded on a refusal to call things by their right names, a long-standing failing in social work with children, as was shown in Chapter 2. The kind of preventive work in which no one is clear what they are meant to be preventing, how they should prevent it, how long they should go on trying and how they will know whether they have failed or succeeded might be better named interference. The kind of treatment meted out in CHEs, detention centres and borstals would undoubtedly be better named punishment. If intermediate treatment is to be the means of an authentic decarceration and the basis for a more just, rational and humane approach to juvenile offending it must work with very clear aims, with a specific and rigidly defined client group, with a legal background and time limit set by the court, and with a set of techniques, skills and methods designed for, and focused upon, a specified problem about which both parties are clear: that of offending. Otherwise we shall find that the well-intentioned, enlightened Frankenstein of social work has created yet another monster. The renewed emphasis on honesty, openness and clarity about the reasons for being there at all is perhaps the most significant achievement of recent social work writing. The application of these principles is as urgent in the field of juvenile offending as in any other;

the consequences of dishonesty and confusion we know from the bitter experience of the last decade.

Preventing delinquency is not a matter of singling out hapless children at random from disorderly families and setting up what amount to adolescent playgroups. Social workers who indulge in the habit of 'preventive intermediate treatment' have most certainly not read the literature on the effectiveness of social work with juvenile delinquents and are also clearly turning a blind eye to the factors which create adolescent recidivism in the juvenile criminal justice system as well as in their local communities. Delinquency prevention programmes must of necessity look at where the opportunities for delinquent acts lie, in neighbourhoods, at the schools which by their curricula and internal structures generate truancy and delinquency, at local policing practices and the general availability of youth facilities and opportunities for non-delinquent outlets. We would ask them to inquire about the kinds of appropriate and practical steps which can be taken in collaboration with local retailers, policemen, headteachers and councillors to reduce delinquency. Again, the indication here is for careful research into local patterns of delinquency, the frequency and location of offending, attendance records and differing rates of delinquency in schools serving the same locality. In the case of the identified delinquent, practical steps must be taken to put wrongs right in ways which do least damage to both victim and wrongdoer. Such measures should be designed to integrate the delinquent and not alienate him, as criminal prosecution does in a symbolic sense and incarceration in a literal and physical sense, for alienation is, of course, in the end the worst possible way to develop commitment to the conventional moral order.

Good social work practice with juvenile offenders does not mean meeting children's needs in a loose, unstructured and undisciplined way. It means taking delinquency itself seriously and developing carefully researched strategies with both communities and individuals, with very specific objectives and practical actions.

REFERENCES: CHAPTER 8

1   Information from research and monitoring in Wakefield and Basildon undertaken by David Thorpe and Chris Green.
2   Adapted from Thorpe, D., 'Intermediate treatment', in Tutt, N. (ed.), *Alternative Strategies for Coping with Crime* (Oxford and London: Blackwell and Martin Robertson, 1978).
3   Paley, J. and Thorpe, D., *Children: Handle with Care* (Leicester: National Youth Bureau, 1974), pp. 84–93.
4   See, for example, Power, M. J., Benn, R.T. and Morris, J. N., 'Neighbourhood, school and juveniles before the courts', *British Journal of Criminology*, vol. 12, no. 2, April 1972, pp. 111–32.
5   Morris, T., *Deviance and Control – the Secular Heresy* (London: Hutchinson, 1976), p. 41.

6 Hulsman, L. H. G., 'The Causes and Manifestations of Recent Trends in Juvenile Delinquency – Their Impact on Policies of Prevention, Treatment and Rehabilitation of Offenders' (mimeographed paper given to UN Seminar on 'New Approaches to the Treatment of Young Offenders', Lillehammer, 1977), p. 20.

7 Morris, op. cit., p. 139.

8 Cohen, S., 'Guilt, justice and tolerance', in Downes, D. and Rock, P. (eds), *Deviant Interpretations* (London: Martin Robertson, 1979), p. 46.

Index